William Jay

William Jay
Abolitionist and Anticolonialist

Stephen P. Budney

Westport, Connecticut
London

Library of Congress Cataloging-in-Publication Data

Budney, Stephen P., 1950–
    William Jay : abolitionist and anticolonialist / Stephen P. Budney.
       p. cm.
    Includes bibliographical references and index.
    ISBN 0–275–98555–5 (alk. paper)
       1. Jay, William, 1789–1858. 2. Abolitionists—United States—
Biography. 3. Social reformers—United States—Biography. 4. Antislavery
movements—New York (State)—History—19th century. 5. New York State Anti-
Slavery Society. 6. Antislavery movements—United States—History—19th
century. 7. Anti-imperialist movements—United States—History—19th
century. I. Title.
E449.J4254   2005
326′.8′092—dc22   2004022484

British Library Cataloguing in Publication Data is available.

Library of Congress Catalog Card Number: 2004022484
ISBN: 0–275–98555–5

First published in 2005

Praeger Publishers, 88 Post Road West, Westport, CT 06881
An imprint of Greenwood Publishing Group, Inc.
www.praeger.com

Printed in the United States of America

Contents

Preface   vii

Introduction   1

1   Influences   7

2   "A Wonderful Apathy Prevails"   27

3   "I Am an Abolitionist, and I Thank God I Am"   55

4   "On the Altar of Moloch"   85

5   "The Time Has Come for Christians and   113
    Churches to Act"

Notes   135

Bibliography   157

Index   167

Preface

Regardless of their discipline, I believe that everyone in academe lives in two different worlds. There is the real world that we must confront every day, and there is the relatively safe and insulated world of ideas where we practice our craft. We could do well in one world or the other, but our existence in both requires adaptability because the world of air conditioning and automotive repairs is quite different from the world of students and research. With this dichotomy in mind, I should first like to thank those who have helped and supported me in the real world.

I have been fortunate enough to receive support from my family and my wife, Heidi. My family encouraged me and always provided a base from which I could do my research when visiting New York City or Philadelphia. My mother infused me with the desire to read, but it has been my wife who has put up with my dogs and my motorcycles for many years. She has endured my distance with patience and been capable enough to handle some of the more mundane problems of life, thus shielding me from distractions in graduate school and beyond.

My obeisance to the other world is somewhat easier. At the University of Mississippi I owe a tremendous debt to the two people who supported me enthusiastically; Winthrop Jordan and Sheila Skemp. They both had a confidence in me that I did not have in myself. The germ of the idea for this book was born at the University of Maine. There I owe my thanks to Bill Baker, Marli Weiner, Stuart Bruchey, and Andrea Hawkes. There are also those people you meet are various functions and bend their ear in order to get their opinions on the direction of your research. Let me thank them for their endurance, patience, and insights. James Brewer Stewart reviewed my work and was incredibly generous with his time. Stephanie McCurry and Ronald G. Walters were also kind enough to listen and contribute ideas. There are also the numerous people at institutions of higher learning who aided my efforts. Thanks to the staffs at Columbia's Rare Books and Manuscripts Collection, the American Peace Society Collection at Swarthmore, and the people at Bangor Theological who allowed me access to their fine collection of American Tract Society pamphlets and other reform literature. I would also be ungrateful if I failed to thank our division secretary at Pikeville College, Cathy Maynard. Cathy has given unselfishly of her time and helped with the word-processing on the original manuscript. Thank you all. You may take the credit for whatever strengths this book might exhibit, I will take responsibility for its weaknesses.

Introduction

Early in 1835, William Jay's *Inquiry into the Character and Tendency of the American Colonization and American Anti-Slavery Societies* was published. Already active in social reform efforts, Jay was well acquainted with many abolitionists and sympathized with their efforts. But sympathies aside, Jay remained circumspect, restraining himself from direct involvement in their organization. That self-imposed distancing changed after a wave of antiabolitionist and antiblack violence shook New York in July of 1834. Earlier that year, noted abolitionist Arthur Tappan had invited black clergyman Samuel Cornish to worship with him, and even sit in the same pew at the Laight Street Church. Tappan's innocent action soon prompted speculation that the abolitionists were promoting amalgamation, or mixing of the races. Rumors even began to circulate that Arthur Tappan had divorced his wife to marry a Negress.[1]

In response to the calumny, mobs of antiabolitionist demonstrators soon took to the streets. Targeting the churches and homes of abolitionists, they smashed windows and committed other outrageous acts of vandalism. The crowds were urged on by officials of the American Colonization Society, whose expressed mission was to send all free blacks back to Africa. The violence directed at African Americans was especially virulent in New York's notorious Five Points District, and at least 500 people were forced to flee their homes.[2] Shaken and disgusted by the mob rule of that summer, Jay wrote *Inquiry* to defend the abolitionists against the charges leveled at them, and to discredit the motives of colonization's supporters.

When she examined the New York City race riots of 1834, historian Linda Kerber recognized William Jay's role, and noted that he had been "undeservedly ignored by most histories of the (antislavery) movement." Likewise, Bertram Wyatt-Brown, in his biography of Jay's fellow antislavery crusader Lewis Tappan (brother of Arthur), observed that Jay was a "much neglected figure."[3] The neglect of Jay by historians of the abolitionist movement is made more curious by William Wiecek's later contention that Jay was "one of the most fascinating of the abolitionists."[4] With such strong recommendations from reputable and respected sources, the question becomes: "Why have historians overlooked William Jay?" Part of the problem resides in Jay's perceived conservatism.

A large body of the research focusing on the abolitionists was created in the 1960s and 1970s. In a time of social protest and upheaval promoted by the civil rights movement and American involvement in Vietnam, many emerging historians found the abolitionists compelling. The American social reform movement of the early nineteenth century attracted many of these twentieth-century examiners because they were able to liken it to their own experience with domestic unrest in the United States. Howard Zinn, no stranger to activism, likened the actions of antislavery agitators to those of the Freedom Riders of the civil rights movement. Although no longer as popular as an object of historical inquiry, the abolitionist movement continues to appeal to those who matured in the 1960s. Henry Mayer, author of the latest biography on William Lloyd Garrison, readily admits: "As a man whose political consciousness was shaped in the civil rights and antiwar movements of the 1960s, I was readily intrigued by this agitator who abhorred party politics and called out the transformative energies of the beloved community."[5]

Garrison, then, exuded a magnetism that is still palpable. The Garrisonian movement has been justly credited with serving as birthplace of American feminism.[6] Garrison was imbued with a powerful sense of symbolism, and once burned a copy of the U.S. Constitution to protest that document's complicity in allowing slavery to continue. Yet Garrison's colorful sense of demonstrative drama was far too overt for many abolitionists, not to mention scores of average Americans. His actions frequently served to exacerbate the frangibility of the movement. Many contemporaries admired the ardor and rectitude of the Garrisonians, but his true believers remained largely constrained to a New England minority.[7] Simply put, the majority of U.S. citizens in the first half of the nineteenth century were indifferent to the plight of American slaves. And even if they opposed the institution, the recommendations of the Garrisonians were too radical for them to adopt.

William Jay and Garrison were opposites. Jay was not colorful, and while he could be incited to anger, he never spewed forth the searing rhetoric of a Garrison. If Jay exuded any charismatic aura, it was only visible to followers of the antislavery doctrine. Garrison was the child of a man who had worked alternately as a farmer, lumberjack, and sailor.[8] Jay was a child of privilege, scion of a New York family possessed of rank and wealth. William Jay attended Yale, later studied law, and rose to a judgeship in New York State. Garrison began his career as a printer's devil and worked his way up to newspaper editor.[9] Garrison represents that portion of nineteenth century Americans who were constantly striving to make their way upward from the lower rungs of the social ladder. Garrison knew what it was like to be an outsider. He looked upon the American institutions of government and church with mistrust. Clearly, Jay was born an insider. He was imbued with an unassailable belief that America's institutions were essential to the nation's vitality, and that Americans could work within those structures to effect change. Garrison was raw emotion; Jay was reserved. Two men so different, yet they shared the conviction that slavery was a chancre upon the American republic, a lesion that foretold of future corruption and rot.

When categorizing the abolitionists, historians once conjoined them as "Jacobins" or "radicals." More recently the classifications of moderate and conservative have been appended. The roots of William Jay's conservatism had their basis in Federalism and religious piety. Thus, like many other abolitionists, William Jay was heir to Federalist orthodoxy. Federalism blended political ideology and social expectations with attitudes about citizenship and American identity that developed in late-eighteenth-century America. Federalists, like their counterparts in Jefferson's Republican Party, held a firm belief in republicanism.[10] A republic is a state where the supreme power of government lies in the body of citizens entitled to vote, not in a monarch or dictator. The two most attractive examples of the republican system of government, and those most often cited by American political philosophers, were the ancient city-states of Greece and Rome. But those models also held a lesson for those who would attempt to emulate them. Republics depended upon a virtuous citizenry that would subsume its own interests for the good of the body politic. The alternative was disintegration and tyranny.

William Jay imbibed this ideology from his patriot father, John Jay. Federalism, with its accompanying belief system, was part of William Jay's inheritance, and one that he looked upon as a great responsibility. David Lowenthal had summed up the power of inheritance in a manner that applies directly to Jay: "The family legacy betokens faith in the national heritage, its worthiness a mythic affirmation of American History."[11] William Jay understood that an integral part of his "legacy" was the republic that his father had helped to create. He revealed his sense of responsibility, and his concern for the American republic, in a letter to his friend James Fenimore Cooper:

> There is I presume no city in which all the arts that minister to sensual gratification are carried to greater perfection than in Paris; nor is there I suspect any city in which there is less real substantial happiness enjoyed. Vice and luxury lead to universal selfishness, and selfishness, by sacrificing the interests and happiness of others to individual gratification mars and interrupts the general welfare. . . . May our republican simplicity and religious habits never be exchanged for the magnificence, heartlessness, and wretchedness of France.[12]

Few writings could encapsulate so succinctly the spirit of republicanism.

William Jay inherited something else from his father and the Federalists: a tradition of antislavery sentiment. Jay's father, while a slave owner himself, had joined with Alexander Hamilton to form the New York Manumission Society. Indeed, most Federalists believed slavery was incompatible with the language of the American Revolution and the republic it had given birth to. But the Federalists had been gradualists, believing that slavery could be eliminated with the passage of time. For many individuals concerned with the plight of slaves in America, gradualism evolved into immediatism; the belief that slavery must be ended without hesitation. Thanks to the influence of the Quakers, much of this change in attitude came from the conviction that slavery was a sin against God. William Jay agreed that slavery was a sin, and invoked religion in his antislavery arguments. But Jay also believed that slavery, as a threat to the morality of the nation, was also an increasing danger to the virtue of the republic.[13]

Jay and many other adherents to the antislavery cause subscribed to the idea of a federal consensus. They believed that the framers of the Constitution had compromised on the issue of slavery and left the matter of its continuance or demise to the individual states. There was therefore no constitutional basis for legal interference by the federal government in controlling slavery within those sovereign states.[14] But if the federal government had no power to interfere with slavery, neither did it have the right to act as an advocate for its expansion and continue vitality. After the Missouri Compromise of 1820, there was an increasing suspicion among antislavery activists that this was exactly what was happening. The federal government was actively involved in promoting slavery, at the behest of the slaveholding interests. If slavery was a sin, then the stain of that sin was now imparted to the government and, by their participation, to the citizens who composed the body politic. For anyone concerned with the health of the American Republic, the increasing influence of slavery in politics was clear evidence of corruption, and corruption spelled death to a republic.

If slavery posed a clear danger to the American nation, how were antislavery forces supposed to awaken complacent American citizens to the threat? As one of the most prolific American antislavery writers, William Jay attempted to alert Americans through an appeal joining republican concerns with religious fervor. Like his father, Jay was an Episcopalian. But Jay brought an activism to his Episcopalian beliefs. He represented an "evangelical" element within the staid New York Episcopalian Church. He frequently clashed with the intractable church hierarchy over reform issues, particularly slavery, but never succumbed to the "come-outerism" that infected many other reformers. Jay believed that the church could be part of the solution on the question of slavery. But he also believed that the church, like the nation, could be corrupted by any association with slavery.[15]

The Second Great Awakening began in the 1790s, and peaked in the 1830s. The new religious revival stressed individual agency, that man was a sinner by his own choosing, not by the Calvinistic tenet of predestination. If man could choose sinfulness, man could also choose salvation. The Second Great Awakening spawned an upsurge of reformist activity in the Northeast because, even if the movement taught individual salvation, the Christian community was still responsible for those who remained sinful. William Jay possessed a powerful belief in God. Because of his piety, he easily extended community responsibility for sin to the morality of the nation. He thus bound the collective concerns of republicanism with the mutual accountability of religion. The laws of a nation reflected the morality of its citizens. Those laws should be instituted to protect more than property; they should extend to shield the lowest of its inhabitants (and therefore not necessarily citizens) from abuse and degradation. Jay feared the day that an angry God would apply the same principles of "moral government" to the United States that the deity enforced against individuals. When that day came, God would invoke the maxim "Whatsoever a man soweth [*sic*], that shall he also reap."[16]

By the time William Jay became active in antislavery efforts, Federalism was no longer a political force. The tenets of Federalism and its value system were not dead, however; they were kept alive by men like William Jay. Historians recognize the Federalist factor in abolitionism, but seldom examine it satisfactorily. Jay's value here is his prolificacy as an antislavery writer. From the Missouri Compromise until his death in 1857, we can see Jay evolve, retaining the old Federalist principles even as he modifies them by applying new concepts. In Jay's writings the old Federalism meets the new religion, and constitutional antislavery confronts political antislavery. The views of Jay the antislavery author remain grounded in his most firmly held beliefs, and yet they change. His works reveal his personal evolution. They also provide evidence of the ideological baggage he carried, as events drew him in from the periphery of organized antislavery to the full involvement of a true believer.

1

Influences

Believe me my dear father, that altho' so far removed from you,
I think of you . . . and remain your very affectionate son.
                                    —William Jay to John Jay, 1817

Wwilliam Jay was born in New York City on June 16, 1789, the
second son of John Jay and Sarah Van Brugh Livingston Jay. Of
Huguenot descent, the Jay family lineage traced its origins in North
America back to the arrival of Augustus Jay in Charleston, South
Carolina, from La Rochelle, France, after the Edict of Nantes forced
many Protestants to flee that country in 1685. Details are vague, but
within a year Augustus had journeyed up the eastern seaboard
from Charleston and arrived in New York City. There he established
what would spread into tendrils of extended familial influence
when he married Anna Maria Bayard in 1687. Anna was the daughter of Balthzar Bayard, a fellow descendant of French Protestants
and a nephew of the former Dutch colonial governor Peter
Stuyvesant. On her mother's side, Anna Maria could claim kinship
ties to some of the most influential Dutch families in New York,
among them the Van Cortlandts, Van Renssaleers, and Schuylers.
Each of these families possessed extensive landholdings in Manhattan, and was engaged in acquiring thousands of acres along the

Hudson River. These Dutch connections gave Augustus social position and—although he already possessed solid mercantile credentials—a pathway to greater financial success.[1]

William was from the third generation of Jays born in New York. He was most likely born in the Broadway house that this father had begun construction on in 1785. That same year a young John Quincy Adams, freshly returned from Europe, visited John Jay while the "stone house" was under construction. The son of future president John Adams, John Quincy's correspondence revealed that now well-populated sections of New York were then thinly inhabited, for Jay was able to erect his home "a quarter of a mile from any other dwelling."[2] Jay undoubtedly built his home on the Trinity Church lands that adjoined Broadway on the Hudson River side. Here he would have been able to obtain a favorable, long-term lease. Trinity Church was one of the six largest landholders in New York City, and was in the practice of leasing land at favorable terms to well-placed church members and other wealthy luminaries.[3] Jay himself held an honored pew in Trinity Church, and Great-Grandfather Augustus had been a vestryman.[4]

At the time of Adams's visit, New York City was the capital of the United States under the Articles of Confederation. The city was still recovering from the effects of the Revolutionary War. As Adams entered New York harbor, he noticed numerous abandoned British forts on Staten Island. The war had also had a savage effect on the surrounding countryside, as British regulars, patriots, and unallied freebooters had roamed, fought, and pillaged there. New York could only claim a population of 13,000 in 1783. But that number swelled to 25,000 by 1785, as survivors of the war in the countryside moved to the city attempting to rebuild their disrupted lives. The city would be a Federalist stronghold for many years. When Thomas Jefferson arrived to begin his duties as secretary of state in the spring of 1790, he noted—with some humorous exaggeration—that he was the only republican in town.[5]

At the time of William's birth, John Jay was serving as secretary for foreign affairs, an office created in 1781 under the Articles of Confederation. Jay had been appointed to the position in May of 1784, but withheld his acceptance of the assignment until the peripatetic Congress decided to move from Trenton, New Jersey, to New York.[6] With the eventual creation of the federal government in 1789, John Jay was appointed the first chief justice of the U.S. Supreme Court in 1790, a post that he held until 1795. In that year, while serving as a special envoy to Great Britain, he was elected in absentia as governor of the state of New York.

William Jay would later note that his father had politically "attached himself to the Federalists, and adhered to their principles throughout his life."[7] John Jay had been an English Loyalist up until the very outset of the American Revolution. As a member of the Continental Congress, he had drafted a petition to George III seeking reconciliation with the crown in spite of the "unhappy Dissentions [sic]" of the colonials.[8] Nevertheless, once committed to the revolution, Jay served the cause in every capacity thrust upon him.[9] But merely because John Jay had worked to liberate the colonies from English influence did not mean that he was averse to an English presence in North America, or that he was incapable of viewing English policies objectively.

By 1794, many Americans were increasingly infatuated with revolutionary France and antagonistic toward Great Britain. This was largely the result of Britain's continued maintenance of western outposts along the borders of the fledgling American republic, and by its seizure of American merchant vessels transporting cargo to French ports.[10] The Federalists realized that there was a distinct need to send a special envoy to parley with the British, gain some concessions, and assuage the growing war fever at home. The first man many Federalists suggested for the mission was Alexander Hamilton. "Who but Hamilton would perfectly satisfy all our wishes?" asked Massachusetts representative Fisher Ames. But Hamilton's selection was ultimately rejected by the Federalist faithful, based upon the realization that his candidacy would have never survived the onslaught of the anti-Federalist opposition. Their second choice was Chief Justice John Jay.[11]

Other than the pro-English Hamilton, there may well have been no other New Yorker more despised by the Jeffersonian opposition than John Jay. Like Hamilton, Jay had penned Federalist papers promoting ratification of the Constitution. He echoed Hamilton's sentiments that those who opposed ratification often did so because they feared to lose their powers to behave in the manner of "little kings" at home.[12] This was clearly a slap at the process of self-interested politics, and one that served as an indictment of all who opposed ratification whatever their reasons. But much more damning than his personal philosophy was the fact that Jay, while acting in his previous capacity as secretary for foreign affairs, had submitted a report to Congress stating that England was justified in maintaining its western outposts.[13] Regardless, based upon his performance as minister to Spain during the days of the revolution, the Federalist-controlled Senate approved Jay's appointment as envoy after a short, sharp, political battle.

The mission was thankless and fraught with difficulties. Reluctant to see northeastern merchants emerge as the primary beneficiaries of Jay's negotiations, Southern political leaders clamored for compensation or the return of property in slaves taken by the British during the revolution. Indeed, Virginia and South Carolina may have lost some 50,000 runaway slaves to the British who had promised the fugitives freedom. Jay was therefore under constant pressure from Secretary of State Edmund Randolph, himself a Southerner, to gain some restitution for this loss of property. Jay understood the justice of monetary compensation to slave owners, but he was unable to gain reparations from the British and refused to wreck the treaty process over the issue. Thus he earned the enmity of men such as Thomas Jefferson and James Madison.[14]

Jay did obtain some concessions: an opening of the West Indian trade and compensation at a future date for British depredations against American shipping. Also included was removal of the British from their western outposts, but not to begin until well over a year after the treaty was signed. On the other hand, the treaty was quite favorable to British interests. England obtained navigation and trade rights on the Mississippi, an agreement to obtain payment for all debts owed British creditors by America citizens, and access to American ports for British vessels.[15] The Republicans greeted news of the terms with a firestorm of vituperation directed against every member of the administration, including the venerable George Washington. Political enemies singled out Jay for special attention; effigies of him were hanged and he was otherwise publicly humiliated in cities throughout the nation.

In later years William Jay reflected upon his father's actions in his own biography of the patriarch. William contended that much of the opposition to Jay's treaty was—in spite of protestations to the contrary—as much a matter of Republican political opportunism as it was indicative of any genuine reflection of affection for France. Indeed, a great deal of the opposition appeared in print before the terms of the treaty were even made public. William asserted that the Jay Treaty not only preserved the peace, but also resulted in compensation for American merchants valued at over $10 million.[16]

When William later experienced public censure for his antislavery stance, he looked to his father's composure in the wake of the

Jay Treaty as an example of how to weather undeserved contempt. John Jay's willingness to serve what he considered the public well-being, in spite of the vilification he received at the hands of his political enemies, revealed fortitude and self-confidence. But beyond his sense of public duty, John Jay held other beliefs that would be revealed, sometimes subtly, within the very fabric of William's work. In the Federalist view, the commercial well-being of the nation rested upon the "goodwill" of men of property. Too much "democratic spirit" was a danger because it led to violence against property.[17] John Jay too prized the needs of the nation's commercial interests and mistrusted the democratic designs of the masses. It was not so much the ability of the people to act and choose politically that concerned John Jay and other Federalists, but rather their capability to decide intelligently. Initially an enthusiast of the French Revolution, Jay came to view it with loathing. If many observers felt that the lower strata of French society behaved abominably during the revolution, Jay wrote to a friend that that "portion" of the people did not even mean well.[18]

To summarily dismiss John Jay or Alexander Hamilton as mere plutocrats is simplistic and ignores the significance of their influence. Certainly their sense of obligation to serve national interests indicated an impulse to defend more than commerce and property. Far more than that was at stake in the Federalist view. There was the very real possibility that the flames of popular passions, fanned by opportunistic politicians and their sycophants, could literally vitiate the essence of intelligent discourse at every level of American society. Men of letters such as John Sylvester, John Gardner, and Joseph Stevens Buckminster attempted to alert American society to this possibility. If an individual possessed genius, it was no protection against intellectual corruption. Even an intellect such as John Milton had bent his knee to the "odious usurper" Cromwell.[19] Jay's politics and worldview exerted their influence upon his youngest son. Later, William claimed that politically he, too, was of the "old Washington [Federalist] school."[20]

By the time he returned to New York from his mission in England, John Jay and wife, Sarah, could count five children. Peter Augustus, the eldest, had been born in 1776. Then came William and three sisters: Anna, William's senior by six years, Maria, and Sarah Louisa. An infant, Susan, had died in Spain and been interred in Madrid in 1780. Jay's term as governor required moving the family to Albany when the state legislature began to meet there in 1797, and the Jays took their youngest children with them.[21] In Albany young William began his education under the tutelage of Reverend Thomas Ellison. Ellison, the rector of St. Peter's Church in Albany, was a graduate of Oxford and an unabashed Anglophile. While studying with Ellison, Jay was joined by a fellow student and child-hood friend who would remain a lifelong companion, fellow New Yorker James Cooper. Cooper would later distinguish himself as an author, and have his name legally changed to James Fenimore Cooper.[22] Through the later correspondence of the two boys as adults comes Cooper's unflattering portrait of their mentor:

> Thirty-six years ago, you and I were school fellows and classmates at the house of a clergyman of the true English school. The man was an epitome of the national prejudices and in some respects of the national character. Ellison . . . graduated at Oxford and admitted to orders; entertained a most profound reverence for the king and no-bility; was not backward in expressing his contempt for all classes of dissenters and ungentlemanly sects; . . . detested a democrat as he did the devil; cracked his jokes daily about Mr. Jefferson and Black Sal, never failing to place his libertinism in strong relief against the approved morals of George III, of several passages in whose history it is charitable to assume he was ignorant.[23]

Although recent scholarship has shown that James Fenimore Cooper's father, William, carefully cultivated the friendship of es-tablished families such as the Jays in order to gain social and po-litical prestige, the friendship of James and William remained unsoiled by such ambitions.[24] Young Cooper was a frequent guest of the Jays. The literary character Harvey Birch, who appeared in Cooper's first successful novel, *The Spy* (1821), was based upon sto-ries that John Jay had entertained his son and young Cooper with at his country home in Bedford. In fact, Cooper read a large part of his manuscript to the Jays prior to its publication.[25] A few years later, Cooper dedicated a far less successful novel, *Lionel Lincoln* (1825), to William Jay in hopes that "an unbroken intimacy of four and twenty years might justify the present use of your name." In a nostalgic letter to a contemporary, Cooper recalled that "with Jay I have ever been united in close and sincere friendship—We were nearer of an age . . . slept together, played together, and sometimes quarreled for each other."[26]

In 1804, at the age of fifteen, William Jay entered Yale College in New Haven, Connecticut. Yale seems an odd choice when both William's father and brother Peter had attended Columbia. The de-cision might well have been grounded in the fact that the president of Yale, Timothy Dwight, was a dedicated Federalist. Such leadership would seem to indicate a commitment to discipline, yet Yale of the early nineteenth century had a boisterous reputation. Evidence of any boyhood pranks or levity, however, are absent from William's remembrance, which depicted university life as drudgery.[27] "The freshmen, like the sizars in an English university, were obliged to wait on the seniors. The wretched infants rose at five-thirty, built fires, lugged water from the college well for their 'sire,' often wading through the snow."[28]

The viands provided at the institution did nothing to diminish the apparent tedium, consisting primarily of salt beef and dried cod, with stewed oysters on Sundays.[29] While attending Yale, Jay was at least reunited with his friend James Fenimore Cooper; but Cooper's term lasted only two years before he and another boy engaged in a fistfight and were expelled. Cooper did not return. Another of Jay's classmates was a young man whose opinions would diametrically oppose those of Jay in the future, South Carolinian John C. Calhoun.[30]

Jay graduated Yale in 1807, having damaged his eyesight while studying in insufficient lighting; it would prove to be a disability that would discomfit him for the rest of his life. He returned to Albany and studied law in the office of John B. Henry. Like many others with whom William Jay associated in his early years, Henry had been active in Federalist politics for a number of years and had even received an appointment as comptroller of New York State in 1800.[31] William was joined in Albany by his sister Maria and her daughter Sally. Maria had married Goldsborough Banyer in 1801, but he had died in 1806, and their infant son died a couple of months after his father.

Jay's letters home during this period reveal that neither he nor Maria were in the best of health. William wrote that his sister's health was "delicate," and that she suffered from an excess of salivation. Maria was attended by at least two physicians, both of whom seemed to be at a loss to diagnose her condition. Dr. Pomeroy recommended the administration, in small doses, of salt of tartar mixed with vinegar, while Dr. Stringer opined that Maria's condition was a result of some sympathetic reaction to a glandular condition. After a period of almost a year, the best that William could report home was that Maria was "not worse."[32] As Maria clung to her tenuous health, William's eyesight was cause for increasing concern, and again doctors provided conflicting counsel. One physician recommended that William wear green-tinted glasses, while another advised that such eyewear would "prove predjudicial [sic]." One doctor told William to apply "stimulants" to his eyes, but another cautioned that such applications "debilitate" rather than strengthen the patient's eyes. So despairing was Jay of improving his condition that he considered traveling to England to see an ocular specialist.[33]

Finally, in the late summer of 1809, William wrote his father: "It is not lately that I have begun to regard the prospect of being here-after able to pursue the profession I have adopted as extremely doubtful." He continued that he had been considering taking up agriculture since his last visit home, and he had been trying to learn more about "husbandry." The primary impediment to Jay return-ing home was Maria, who seems to have still been suffering from the loss of her husband and son and was only just beginning to lose "her aversion to enter any house but her own." William believed his presence to be important to his sister, that he could "offer con-solation in her moments of dejection" and "might tend in some measure to heal the wounds which, sunk deep at the time they were inflicted; and threatened to imbitter and make loathsome the re-mainder of her life."[34]

William could consider taking up agriculture because his fam-ily had once again moved, and this time to the more pastoral set-ting of Bedford in Westchester County, some forty miles from New York City. There were multiple reasons for the Jay family's rural retreat. John Jay had retired from politics in 1801, finding the frac-tious arena of New York politics increasingly upsetting as his popu-larity declined and Republican fortunes rose. Federalists wanted to keep him involved in public life, but Jay declined, even refusing President John Adams's offer to return to the U.S. Supreme Court as chief justice. With the patriarch determined to withdraw from public life, there was little reason for the family to remain in the political hub of Albany. New York City, with its ever increasing bustle and periodic yellow fever epidemics, would also have proved a poor choice for retirement.[35] The family thus decided to build upon land that the former governor had inherited from his mother. The land had been purchased from the Indians in 1703 by her father, Jacobus Van Cortlandt.[36]

Estimates vary as to the amount of land the Jays held in Westchester, but they owned at least 400 acres, and the house was situated so as to command "a splendid view of the Kisco and Croton Valleys and the hills bordering on the Hudson River." The frame of the house had been erected by the summer of 1801 and the

Jays occupied it by 1802. Travel to the Jay's country residence was difficult. The journey between Bedford and New York City took two days, and the mail was delivered but once a week. Any luxuries or manufactured goods that the family required were usually not available in the nearby village. These items had to be procured by his brother Peter in New York, then either shipped to the family by stage or up the Hudson on board the sloop *Volunteer*.[37]

Transportation difficulties did not deter visitors from coming to Bedford. Not only did friends stop by to partake of John Jay's hospitality, but the great patriot was called upon to play the part of the country squire. The reminiscence of one visitor reveals the protocol of a social structure that was slowly disappearing. The observer noted how some of the "yeomanry" came to the elder Jay on a "visit of respect." The former governor received each man cordially, as each approached Jay with the "reverence a great man only can inspire."[38] Yet all was not hat-in-hand deference. Supervising the building of his Bedford home, Jay had noticed that local workmen were quite aware of their own worth and required gentle handling to prevent them from simply moving on to another job.

William moved to Bedford in 1809, and although his brother Peter remained in New York City to practice law, William did not want for siblings upon his return. Sisters Ann and Sarah Louisa lived with their father at Bedford, and Maria, referred to as Mrs. Banyer in most correspondence, soon followed William to the family home. A. H. Stevens would later recall a family scene that he had witnessed in the Jay's parlor during a visit to Bedford in 1816. Seeing "the venerable Patriarch" and his family there united in "thanksgiving, confession, and prayer" was an experience Stevens considered "worth more than all the sermons I ever listened to." The recollection is undoubtedly laden with hyperbole, but is nevertheless suggestive of strong familial bonds. William's mother, Sarah, whom his father had affectionately called "Sally" in their correspondence, did not live long after the move to Bedford. She died in May of 1802 at the age of forty-five.[39]

In September of 1812, at the age of twenty-three, William married Augusta McVickar, the daughter of a New York City merchant.[40] William also revealed a gradually increasing inclination to involve himself in matters that not only promoted the well-being of the Jay family, but that he perceived as contributing to the spiritual and moral health of the surrounding Westchester County community. Some of these forays into community affairs were mundane, but

William would soon be involved in more important, and visible, matters.

Like their father, both William Jay and his elder brother, Peter Augustus, were committed to public life. William began his public career gradually, starting out on the local level in 1815 as the secretary of the Society for the Suppression of Vice in Bedford. This was a temperance society that sought to restrict the sale of alcoholic spirits on credit.[41] William also maintained an interest in the family's farming. John Jay became infatuated with horticulture and husbandry in his retirement. When his interests led him to become president of the Westchester County Agricultural Society, William served as the organization's secretary.[42] Of much greater import, however, were William's efforts in assisting the formation of the American Bible Society in 1816.

Numerous regional Bible societies existed prior to the organization of a national society, but their efforts to distribute inexpensive Bibles to the poor lacked cohesiveness. The primary reason for their lack of direction was their denominational affiliations, which invariably led to fragmentation of their efforts. One of the foremost proponents of a harmonious, interdenominational effort was Elias Boudinot.[43] Retired and living in New Jersey, Boudinot was writing what would be his final work, *A Star in the West,* which argued that the Native Americans of North America were in fact one of the lost tribes of Israel.[44] In 1816, Boudinot was president of the New Jersey Bible Society; he also possessed the financial resources to aid in the formation of a new enterprise. But resistance to the organizational effort initially appeared strong, and advanced age and illness had strained his ability to engage in protracted debate.[45] No doubt the prospect of an all-inclusive organization siphoning the funds of devout Christians away from their respective churches was behind the opposition to the proposal.

In spite of resistance, an organizational convention was scheduled for May 1816. In March of that same year, Boudinot had received a sixteen-page "memoir" submitted by William Jay of the Westchester Bible Society.[46] The primary importance of Jay's letter was that it included a proposed constitution for the new society based on the one used by the British and Foreign Bible Society, thus relieving the ailing Boudinot of much of the organizational burden. Boudinot received Jay's suggestions gratefully, replying that the young man's efforts had given him strength.[47]

The convention went off without the anticipated contentiousness. Although unable to attend, Elias Boudinot was elected president of the new society, an appointment that he accepted in an open letter to the gathering as "the greatest honor . . . this side of the grave."[48] Although the Westchester Bible Society had not formally met to choose delegates to the convention, William Jay attended and was seated as one of their representatives. He was also elected one of the society's thirty-six original lay managers, while his father, due at least in part to a $150 contribution, was appointed one of the three vice presidents.[49]

William remained active in the society for years; it was his introduction to philanthropy on the national level. It also brought him into conflict with Episcopal bishop John Henry Hobart. An obstreperous man, Hobart was a formidable opponent who relished the arena of ecclesiastical debate. In 1805 he had published *A Companion for the Altar,* which asserted, among other things, that those who willingly rebelled against the established power of the church were in rebellion against God. Hobart's work supported the High Church position that Episcopalians who joined with others to distribute the Bible, without the accompanying recommended prayer-book, were in rebellion against the wishes of the church.[50] The bishop's statements sparked a running debate in the pages of the *Albany Centinel* that year.[51]

Hobart was not unknown to Jay, who frequently traveled to New York City to visit his brother Peter and to procure those items that the family could not secure in Bedford. In February of 1811, William visited Peter and reported back to is father: "I find that there are bitter and violent dissentions among some of the Episcopal clergymen in this city." The clamor was the result of a movement by some members of the clergy to block Hobart's election as bishop.[52] The controversy and enmity did not soon fade. Almost a year later a church committee was organized to meet with Hobart and restore harmony, but Hobart refused to acknowledge the authority of the committee, and would not recognize them with a reply unless they first petitioned him with a formal letter. The general committee that had sanctioned the subcommittee had been incensed by Hobart's response, but Hobart defended himself in a pamphlet. William sent a copy of Hobart's defense to his father at Bedford, noting that the work was "generally considered a feeble production."[53]

Four years later, when William defended the purpose of the American Bible Society to distribute Bibles to all, he found himself in direct opposition to the church hierarchy, and that meant Bishop Hobart. The debate that ensued between Jay and Hobart was not merely an exchange of letters in a cordial private colloquy. These letters were a source of controversy and interest to both Episco-palians and supporters of the Bible society. Most of the debates were published as pamphlets.

Hobart began the controversy while speaking before a diocesan convention in October of 1822. He contended that Bible societies were in error because they attempted to separate the word of God from the church. Hobart continued to state his belief that such in-terdenominational societies tended to render or view sectarian dif-ferences as immaterial. Further, it was Hobart's belief that those who supported and provided leadership for such societies were misguided, even if they were acting out of a "sense of duty." One of those misguided individuals whom Hobart singled out was his own parishioner John Jay.[54]

In an eighty-page anonymous response, William Jay rejected Hobart's stance, noting that interdenominational bible societies en-joyed widespread church support in the United States and Ireland, and were even approved by the Church of England. Hobart had too little confidence in the lay people's ability to interpret scripture without the guidance of the Book of Common Prayer. In Jay's opin-ion—and many supported it—not only did Hobart risk creating animosity among the many religious sects, but his illiberal intrac-tability also threatened schism in his own Episcopal church.[55] A paper war between the two men ensued, setting off a flurry of pam-phlets. No sooner did Jay fire off a salvo than the bombastic Hobart would counterpoint, in one instance patronizingly signing his re-sponse to Jay as the "corrector." Nor did the debate come to a rapid denouement, continuing through most of 1823 before the final pam-phlet was issued by Jay.[56]

All was not philanthropy and debate. In 1818, Governor Tompkins had appointed William a Westchester County Judge. William fretted over his ability to perform his job fairly and objec-tively. At one point he wrote to brother Peter noting that Westchester County was awash in insolvency cases. He asked for advice on how to be consistent in his decisions so that the "rights and interests of others my not be sacrificed through my own in-experience."[57] Despite its difficulties, the appointment allowed him to remain at Bedford. Clearly the atmosphere there agreed with William and he was not straining to escape his father's influence, nor the attention which must have been a by-product of living with a legendary patriot. How much influence John Jay had over the formation of William's emerging interest in reform is a matter of conjecture, but it seems to have been considerable. Still, it was one thing to collaborate in an agricultural society with his father, or a society created to distribute Bibles. America was still an agricultural nation under self-imposed Protestant hegemony. But what happened when philanthropy became a platform for social reform that many feared would rend the fabric of American society? How much did John Jay influence the antislavery stance that would be adopted by both of his sons?

To more fully understand why William Jay adopted an antislavery position, his father's efforts in the cause must be examined. Slavery was not an institution foreign to the Jay family; the first census of 1790 reveals that John Jay owned five slaves. But slavery did not necessarily denote a permanent condition in the Jay household. While sailing to Madrid to take his post as minister to Spain in 1780, the vessel John Jay was aboard paused at Martinique. While ashore, Jay purchased Benoit, a lad of fifteen. Benoit served Jay during his stay in Madrid, and received from his master an order of manumission to be effective three years after its issue in 1784.[58]

There is also compelling evidence that John Jay worked constantly in the cause of emancipation. During the New York Convention of 1777, the elder Jay wanted to have an article inserted into the state constitution that would have eliminated slavery.[59] The measure failed, partly because the influential Jay was absent from the convention for three weeks because of the death of his mother.[60] In 1780—with America in the throes of revolution—Jay wrote from his diplomatic post in Spain that "Till America comes into this measure [abolition], her Prayers to Heaven for Liberty will be impious."[61] Later, during peace negotiations with England, Jay attempted to restrict the importation of slaves by British subjects. He was also active upon his return to the states, joining with friend Alexander Hamilton to sign a law providing for gradual emancipation of the state's blacks.[62]

During the late eighteenth and early nineteenth centuries, many people believed that if the slave trade were abolished, then the institution itself would wither away. John Jay used his position as a diplomat to forge friendships with those abroad who were also interested in seeing the slave trade outlawed. Nowhere is this more evident than in the friendship between Jay and English abolition advocate William Wilberforce. Formed while Jay was in England negotiating the Jay Treaty, their friendship is apparent in the genial letters that the two exchanged in the years following Jay's mission. While they discussed diplomatic matters, they also elaborated upon their mutual efforts to bring the United States and Britain to an agreement on how best to stop the "abomidable [sic] traffic" in slaves that continued in spite of abolition laws.[63]

John Jay used every office at his command to improve the lot of the slaves in the United States. His belief in gradualist methods was not a symptom of some latent ambivalence; it reflected the prevailing humanitarian ethos regarding the steps required eliminate slavery. The evidence that the Jay family retained slaves does not reveal an ineffable hypocrisy; it must be leavened by the knowledge that Jay actively manumitted his slaves and provided support for them afterward.[64] Through his efforts, John Jay bequeathed a humanitarian legacy to his sons that complemented their political inheritance.

Two events during this period of William's life shed greater insight into the development of his emerging concern over the injustice of slavery. The first was the battle over Missouri statehood. New York Federalists, led by DeWitt Clinton and Rufus King, felt increasingly threatened by the expansion of slave-state power through the three-fifths clause. To curb that expansion, New York congressman James Tallmadge Jr. had introduced amendments to the Missouri statehood bill mandating that no further slaves should be allowed into Missouri, and that those who resided there should be manumitted at the age of twenty-five.[65] The debates over Tallmadge's amendments signaled the beginning of new political divisions at a time during which the Democratic Republicans had supplanted the Federalists as a national political power.[66]

It is hardly surprising that William Jay had opinions on the subject of slavery during the time of the Missouri debates. His elder brother, Peter, was actively involved in New York politics as a Federalist through much of the 1820s. At the New York Constitutional Convention in 1821, Peter had successfully led to a proposed constitutional amendment that would have declared male suffrage exclusively white.[67] William Jay eschewed the arena of state politics, with its increasingly fractious and strident battles between the Clintonians and Van Buren's Bucktails. But he did have an opinion on the Missouri debates, and fired off a letter to his friend Elias Boudinot. The contents of that letter, dated 1819, convey sentiments that seem to indicate Jay's desire for immediate emancipation:

> If our country is ever to be redeemed from the curse of slavery the present Congress must stand between the living and the dead and stay the plague. Now is the accepted time, now is the day of salvation. If slavery once takes root on the other side of the Mississippi,

it can never afterwards be exterminated, but will extend with the future Western empire, poisoning the feelings of humanity, checking
the growth of those principles of virtue and religion which consti-
tute alike the security and happiness of civil society.[68]

It would be difficult to find a clearer declaration of William Jay's
early antislavery sentiments than those revealed in his letter to
Boudinot. Revealed in those lines is the horror with which Jay
viewed the spread of slavery into the westward regions of the expanding nation. Once established in the West, slavery could only
vitiate virtue and religion, which were the guardians of morality.
For Jay the soul of the nation is at stake; his letter imparts a sense
of immediate disaster. He would not attribute virtue to political
institutions nor to those who took up residence in the halls of government. But politicians did have the obligation to behave respon-
sibly, and shelve petty disputes for the well-being of the country
as a whole. When Jay, in his letter, appealed to Congress to stand
between the living and the dead, he clearly saw the extension of
slavery as moral and social death for the nation.

Syncretizing Jay's attitudes regarding slavery and westward expansion is not difficult, given the fact that they remained remarkably consistent over the years yet to come. Did Jay link his
abhorrence of slavery with his distaste for westward expansion as
a result of overt Federalism? In the debates over the Louisiana
Purchase, northeastern Federalists had opposed the purchase of territory from France for two primary reasons. Ostensibly their opposition was based upon constitutional grounds, as they questioned
the expansion of executive power under Jefferson. But underneath
that veneer of intellectual debate lay a sectional power struggle, a
sense that westward expansion would come at the expense of the
political influence of the Northeast. Moreover, rapid western expansion represented more than political imbalance; it represented a
trend toward individualism that threatened the Federalist ideals of
community and civic responsibility.[69]

If William Jay embraced Federalist dogma, than it is entirely plausible to conjecture that his view was merely an expansion of East-
erners' fears of the South and West advancing their power and
exacerbating eastern impotence. Yet Jay's letter suggests that—even
if the debates had stimulated a Federalist political reaction to expansion on his part—a moral element dominated his concern. In
any case, William Jay's insistence upon the intervention of Congress
to halt the westward tide of slavery, an institution protected by the

Constitution, revealed his not surprising adherence to the law as a lawyer and judge.

Jay had his faith in Congress tested a few years later, in 1826, when he called for the abolition of the slave trade in the District of Columbia. This came about when a notice in a Washington, D.C., newspaper was brought to Jay's attention by a neighbor. The notice described a black man who had been arrested on suspicion of being a runaway slave, and stated that, unless his owner arrived to claim him, he would be sold as a slave to pay his jail fees. From the newspaper's description, the concerned neighbor believed the man in question to be one Gilbert Horton, a free person of color who had lived with the Owen family in the Westchester County town of Somers.[70]

Jay organized a county meeting that drafted a series of strong resolutions asking New York governor DeWitt Clinton to intercede on Horton's behalf. Clinton complied, dispatching a letter to President John Quincy Adams requesting—and receiving—Horton's release as a free citizen of New York. Further, Representative Aaron Ward introduced these "Westchester Resolutions," as they came to be known, into the New York state legislature and later read them before the U.S. Congress. In essence, Ward argued that Horton's civil rights had been violated.[71]

The mind of Jay the jurist was evident in Ward's motion, a motion that attacked the practice of slavery in the District of Columbia. Using the Westchester Resolutions, Ward argued that Horton's incarceration, and subsequent danger of being sold as a slave, had been in accordance with an older law of the state of Maryland. The laws of the District of Columbia were hybridized, retaining elements of both Virginia and Maryland law. The legal presumption in those states was that black people, traveling without proof of being free, were slaves. They could be arrested on suspicion of being slaves and imprisoned for three months, after which time they were hired out to pay their jail fees. The accused had twelve months to prove that he, or she, was a free person of color. If under the provisions of Washington County, Maryland—a portion of which was ceded to the District of Columbia—free persons apprehended as runaways were still liable for all legal fees applicable, even if they were able to prove they were not fugitives. This included the payment of any rewards that would have been paid for their apprehension if they had been runaways! Laws such as these were common in the upper portion of the Old South, where free persons of color were considered a subversive influence upon the general slave population, and such discriminatory laws were intended to curb the growth of a free black presence.[72]

Ward echoed Jay when he claimed that Horton was a free person of the state of New York. Regardless of the color of Horton's skin, he should have been afforded the same protection provided any other citizen under the U.S. Constitution. Horton had been denied due process because he had been arbitrarily imprisoned without a grand jury indictment, and his right to a fair and speedy public trial had been denied. Ward went on to point out that, even though the Maryland law under which Horton had been arrested had been repealed by the state, the law remained in effect in the District of Columbia. To repeal such an unjust law, one that continued to operate in the very seat of the U.S. government, could only serve to "vindicate the rights of freemen."[73]

Debate over the resolutions continued in Congress for two days, the primary goal of Ward and his allies was to place the law before the Committee of the District of Columbia, which reviewed District laws, for repeal. Southern representatives opposed the move, claiming that debate upon such matters only served to engender "irritated feelings." One representative went so far as to speculate that nothing could truly be done about the law because it did not specifically punish a crime. In the end the House did the politic thing: it failed to act. When finally placed before the District Committee, the resolution was amended so that the committee was required to review all laws that might be construed as unjust within its jurisdiction, and submit a report to Congress for future action. If the purpose of the citizens of Westchester had been to merely have their resolutions reviewed, then the political system had worked. But no tangible results materialized.[74]

In a subsequent letter to Pennsylvania representative Charles Miner—an individual (and a Federalist) who had previously introduced measures in the House calling for the abolition of slavery in the District of Columbia—Jay was moderately optimistic about the effect that the resolutions might have. "I do entertain the slightest hope that our petition will be favorably received," wrote Jay, "nor the slightest apprehensions that the cause we espouse will not finally triumph." Perseverance was the key, he continued. Even in the face of great opposition it was necessary to keep the issue of slavery before the public.[75] The debate over slavery in the District of Columbia would become a cornerstone of Jay's early arguments for abolition.

The three short years between the Gilbert Horton affair and the election of Andrew Jackson to the presidency in 1828 saw the United States become increasingly agitated over the question of slavery. For many New Yorkers, the question seemed to have been resolved. The New York State Act of 1817 had provided for full manumission of New York's slave population by July 4, 1827. This edict aside, evidence suggests that a goodly portion of the resident slave population had been well on the way to manumission as early as 1812.[76] But solving one moral dilemma furnished New Yorkers with another: What to do with a visible population of free people of color? The question defied easy solution, and divided New Yorkers along class lines.

Conservative property holders, many of whom held Federalist sympathies, did not view the manumission of their former slaves as a threat. The institution was not profitable after the eighteenth century, and therefore the more practical among them undoubtedly thought themselves well shunt of it. Individual holdings in human chattel were relatively unimpressive in the state, so distress over the financial loss resulting from the removal of such personal property was minimal. The 1790 census, for example, showed that the largest slave owner among Federalist officeholders was state chancellor Robert Livingston, who held fifteen. Others, such as Rufus King and Robert Troup, owned five slaves or fewer and were actively involved in manumission. Alexander Hamilton held no slaves. Moreover, there is some evidence that Federalists benefited from the fact that former slaves who met property requirements could acquire the vote. While they might be few in number, those freedmen who did meet the criteria tended to vote Federalist with their former masters, much to the indignation of the political opposition. As historian Paul Finkleman has argued, the freedmen's support of Federalism was as more a matter of practicality than evidence of loyalty to their former masters. Federalists supported emancipation in the North, and also populated the ranks of manumission societies. Federalists had also continued the trade with Haiti after that island's successful slave rebellion.[77]

Those historians who have studied the machinations of Empire State politics in the antebellum years have offered numerous explanations attempting to explain why New Yorkers voted as they did. Earlier observers, such as Dixon Ryan Fox, described political affiliation as economically driven.[78] The later contentions of Alvin Kass and Lee Benson suggest that those who sought political influence did so for reasons that seem almost compulsively driven by the narcotic of power, or by socioeconomic and ethnocultural considerations.[79] The plain fact is that New Yorkers were dividing at a rapid pace throughout the decade of the 1820s. One group—Jay would belong here—came to see the problem of slavery as having national implications. The other group, driven more by the exigencies of local politics, adopted a more provincial concern and attempted to consolidate their own political power by curtailing that of free blacks.

After the Gilbert Horton affair, William Jay seems to have spent his time marshaling his energies in the cause of religious reform. Until 1829, his public writings were sparse and either proposed reforms in the Episcopal Church, or dealt with his espousal of Sabbatarian sentiments.[80] William retained his judgeship and remained at Bedford, leaving it to brother Peter to bloody his knuckles in the rough and tumble environs of New York politics. John Jay, undoubtedly smarting from his own past experiences, admonished his sons never to accept public office "except from conviction of duty."[81] There never seems to have been any question that both sons would become public figures.

William's life to this point had been something of an anomaly. Like most young men of his time, he had lived in a semi-independent state between school and home. Yet once he had completed school and embarked upon his own career, William returned to the family home, an option that many young men did not exercise in the early nineteenth century. Home was a place that young warriors were leaving to prove themselves in the outside would of business. In a nation obsessed with mobility, moving out and moving along was the manly thing to do. If the familial home was an elevated as an ideal, a repository of virtue and piety, it also represented dependence and even submission.[82] But if William ever chafed under his circumstances, he left no evidence to that effect.

A certain amount of awed deference by a son for his father is often understandable. But William Jay's attitude toward his father represented more than mere filial piety: twenty years of propinquity to his father had not only influenced but also inspired him. William had absorbed Federalist principles and more. The abolition of slavery had been of great importance to John Jay. Both William and his brother Peter were involved in the antislavery cause and labored wholeheartedly in it. Their father had helped plant the humanitarian seed within them. Later, William proved that even the much derided Jay Treaty might have been more than an expedient to save a weak young nation from war with mighty Britain; it might hold the kernel of a future plan for world peace.[83]

When John Quincy Adams died in 1848, his grandson Henry noted that "the eighteenth century, as an actual and living companion, vanished."[84] Henry Adams often bemoaned his fate, claiming that he was born in the wrong century, but he was still, assuredly, a child of the nineteenth. William Jay had his feet firmly planted in both centuries. While the companionship of his father would soon disappear, the eighteenth-century ideals that had been instilled in William would still burn. Those ideals were inextricably linked to the increasingly moribund political entity that was Federalism.

2

"A Wonderful Apathy Prevails"

That the antediluvian world was favored with a revelation of the will of God, might be inferred in the absence of other testimony, from the awful punishment with which its guilt was visited.
—William Jay, *On the Divine Authority of the Sabbath*, 1827

John Jay died in 1829, leaving his Bedford estate to William. All of the father's manuscript books and considerable collection of correspondence were left in the joint possession of William and his brother Peter. Now forty years old, William spent the better part of the next four years editing selected correspondence of his father and incorporating it into his first major work, *The Life of John Jay* (1833). In the introduction he candidly admitted that his relationship to his father might have influenced his perspective, but he insisted that his bias would not alter the facts.[1] In the text William defended the Jay Treaty and praised the elder Jay for his work in manumission and abolition. He also extolled the virtues of his father's modest, almost ascetic life, making the elder Jay appear to be a pillar of temperance and rectitude.[2]

The true value of this work is questionable, for the selection of correspondence was carefully edited. Further, the biographical sections William penned were purposefully—and not surprisingly—

hagiographical. Historian and president of Harvard Jared Sparks knew that the two Jay brothers owned their father's papers and controlled access to them. Sparks repeatedly requested permission to examine the documents and permission was repeatedly denied. The brothers knew that their father had been sensitive about allowing letters from other correspondents in his collection to be printed without their permission. As evidence of his sensitivity on this matter, John Jay's will had clearly stated that his papers had to be thoroughly sorted by the brothers before they were made public. William and Peter's determination to adhere to their father's wishes was never in doubt, and the fact that Sparks had previously been critical of John Jay made their commitment to the patriarch's desires that much easier.[3]

Upon learning of William Jay's intention to publish his father's biography, John Quincy Adams wrote him to convey congratulations and comment about the patriarch's forthrightness. "Of your father," wrote Adams, "I think it was never said that he had a language official and a language confidential."[4] Adams continued by apologizing for not having initiated a more cordial relationship with William in the past. Adam's letter ultimately culminated in an exchange of correspondence between the two men, and their letters were increasingly preoccupied with anti-slavery issues.

Adams bears mention as the 1830s began their ascent to the zenith of Jacksonian democracy. Long disparaged as an ineffective president who could not staunch the popular tide of the Jacksonians, Adams has often been depicted as a hypercritical, embittered man after his ouster from office in 1828.[5] Recently, however, more historians have given greater credibility to Adam's assertions that his replacement by Jackson was a triumph for the South and slaveholders.[6] The plain truth is that no other manifestation of American democracy could so arouse the fears of anyone who nurtured a glimmer of orderly Federalist principle in their breast as the apparition of Jacksonian democracy. Jackson's policies brutally confronted earlier Federalist objections to an expansionist land policy, and Jackson's minions not only accepted mob violence, but also manipulated it.

Meanwhile, William Jay's pastoral Bedford home insulated him from the stress of city life, while it permitted him to continue his appeals for social reform. In 1829, Jay entered an essay contest and submitted *An Essay on Duelling* [sic] to the Anti-Dueling Society of Savannah, Georgia. Using an essentially biblical argument, Jay contended that dueling was murder and could never be excused by societal customs or "prevalence of practice."[7] Dismissing the field of honor hallowed by duelists, Jay went on to reason that the "satisfaction" awarded the winner of such a contest could never be equated with "vindication." In the "abolition and execration of the slave trade," which had been constitutionally "protected," he saw "a triumph of education and religious influence." By employing a similar appeal, Jay reasoned that dueling could be rendered equally unacceptable. Public condemnation of the practice could not be arrived at through "angry declamation or personal invective," but rather "by calm and frequent appeals to the understanding and conscience."[8] In this essay and in the future, reason and religion provided the essence, the very foundation, of all of Jay's reformist appeals. *An Essay on Duelling* was argued cogently enough that it garnered him a medal from the Anti-Dueling Society of Savannah.[9]

Jay's work in other social reform efforts continued unabated. In the second annual report of the American Tract Society—a distributor of pamphlets on religion and reform—Jay was listed as a member for life.[10] Jay also continued to promote temperance. However, temperance apparently did not mean abstinence for Jay and other reformers. A letter to Peter Jay from James Fenimore Cooper reveals that Cooper purchased wines for the Jays while he was residing in Europe.[11] He promised to send some samples along to Peter and the "Judge" (William), so that they might try it and have Cooper procure more. A later letter also revealed that Cooper avidly recommended German wines to the Jays. Supplying the Jays with wines, Cooper teased, would ensure that he would have a toast to his "health drunk on all proper occasions."[12]

Despite his desire for social reform, neither the sentiments that Jay had expressed regarding slavery and westward expansion, nor his actions in the Gilbert Horton affair, translated into any eagerness to publicly embrace emerging immediatist antislavery sentiment. This did not mean that Jay was sanguine about the lot of the slave, or that he was serenely deluded about the potentially dangerous course that the nation was upon. In 1832, as the crisis over nullification loomed in South Carolina, Jay conveyed his fears in a letter to his old friend Cooper. "A wonderful apathy" prevailed among the American people, wrote Jay. "It is but too true that the union is not regarded with that fond admiration and affection it once was." The South did not care about the Union so long as they could find a good market for their cotton. The North, on the other hand, would sacrifice the Union to uphold the tariff.[13]

Americans were apathetic, unwilling to believe that the Carolinians were as "foolish and wicked" as they professed to be when they proposed nullification of federal law. In Jay's opinion, the apathy of Americans derived from their prosperity. The nation was rich, "and beginning to feel the influence of wealth." Jay further confided: "Perhaps no nation exists in which so large a portion of its population enjoys the comforts of luxury and wealth as our own." But here there was a cautionary note. Jay emphasized that his remarks on prosperity applied only to the free states, for the southern states were under the "curse of slavery." In the South slaves were multiplying more rapidly than their masters and the masters needed to fear the potential wrath of their human property. Jay asked: "What think you—are these slaves to be the only portion of the human race that are forever to be denied the rights of humanity? I think their emancipation approaches; and its consummation will follow, at no distant period, the dissolution of the union."[14]

The U.S. Constitution "fettered" the slave and protected his master. But if the South Carolinians rejected the Constitution through nullification, they would make enemies of their northern brethren. Who then would stand beside them when their slaves finally asserted their rights? And even if the nullifiers failed, the South could not compete economically for much longer. Jay believed: "The progress of Science [*sic*] and the arts" was daily enhancing the advantages of free as opposed to slave labor. Such a state of affairs could only promote the well being of the North, while "subjecting the South to embarrassment and discontent."[15]

Jay clearly feared for the state of the Union and used the language of republicanism to convey his anxieties. Americans, distracted by the dissipation of wealth and luxury, were unfazed by the precarious state of the Union. This might help explain Jay's circumspection about throwing himself wholeheartedly into the antislavery cause. Jay was not yet prepared for entry into the antislavery arena, because he believed that strident criticism of slaveholders was self-defeating and might serve to exacerbate an already disruptive national crisis.

Jay continued to work in various benevolent societies, and his efforts brought him into contact with the people who were the technicians of the New York effort to create a "Benevolent Empire." Their efforts were an important component of the larger antebellum reform effort that consumed the Northeast.[16] The most prominent of the circle of philanthropists surrounding Jay included New Yorkers Lewis and Arthur Tappan, Amos A. Phelps, Theodore

Dwight Weld, George Whipple, and Jay himself. Other men of note, such as George Burrell Cheever and David Leavitt, contributed to the good works. Although the participants differed in material wealth, all but Jay were Congregationalists and the sons of men with New England Federalist sympathies.[17] These were the men who promoted and lent support to the "Great Eight benevolent societies" that exerted their influence in numerous causes for reformation and salvation of humankind. These august bodies were in turn supported by multifarious smaller societies that contributed to their financial well being and battled moral corruption on the local level. The American Temperance Society, for example, was the parent organization of the New York State Temperance Society. The New York society embraced some two thousand locals including young men's societies, women's auxiliaries, and infant societies.[18]

For the Tappan circle of reformers, the inspiration behind their moral conatus was revivalist Charles Grandison Finney. His theology animated the works that these disciples performed in concert with other New York reforming societies. A lawyer turned evangelist, Finney preached that Christianity was not for the idle. God demanded the best from every Christian, and he did not reward passivity. Every Christian was a moral steward of his fellow human beings; the salvation of sinners was the utmost priority. To realize these goals, and to save souls from corruption, required unwavering zeal; to do less would jeopardize one's own chances for salvation. Lewis Tappan was so enamored of Finney's teachings that he purchased the Chatham Street Chapel in New York City for Finney to preach in. The chapel was located near the city's notoriously debauched Five Points District, so Tappan had plenty of bait to lure the revivalist away from his base in Cincinnati. Imagine Finney's attraction to promises of a vibrant congregation populated with fresh souls to rescue.[19]

In direct relation to his exertions in the cause of reform, Lewis Tappan was instrumental in laying the groundwork for the New York antislavery effort. Concerned with the status of both the enslaved and free black people in America, Tappan had earlier lent moral and financial support to the American Colonization Society and its efforts to transport free people of color back to Africa of their own volition. But the aims of the society proved both impractical and expensive in their execution, thereby creating continuous dissension in the ranks of its membership.[20] Tappan became even more disillusioned when he learned that the society was promoting the importation of New England rum to its African colony of Liberia.

As a temperance advocate concerned with the wasting effects of alcohol upon the underprivileged, Tappan withdrew his support from the organization by 1828. By 1831 Tappan was subsidizing William Lloyd Garrison and his Boston antislavery newspaper *The Liberator,* but he still sought a more direct manner for promoting the good work of emancipation in New York.[21]

In the summer of 1833, having already established the New York abolitionist journal *Emancipator,* Lewis's brother Arthur wrote a letter to William Jay and probed his thoughts about forming a national antislavery society. Jay replied that he disagreed with William Lloyd Garrison's concept of a national society, and maintained that efforts to secure the end of slavery should instead be directed through local organizations. Jay clearly believed that the seeds of antislavery sentiment would be sown more efficiently at the more personal, local level. But Jay also feared that a national society would become an engine of factionalism if it attempted to interfere with the institution of slavery in the South. Further, Jay did not feel that blacks should be allowed to participate in a national society if one were created, nor should any fledgling society promote black suffrage. Jay reasoned that the presence of blacks as active members would only inflame those who opposed the society's efforts, and that any push for emancipation would only deflect attention from the true goal of emancipation. Finally, in a clear reference to Garrison's recent denunciation of the American Colonization Society (ACS) and a reaffirmation of his own non-confrontational methods, Jay stated his belief that that society should be ignored rather than excoriated. Acknowledging the ACS and its existence only lent credibility to its efforts.[22]

Although Jay was not yet ready to join an antislavery society, he did serve as a figurehead and advisor to New York abolitionists. A letter he had written to the *Emancipator* outlining his antislavery stance was reprinted on at least three separate occasions. On June 22, 1833, the paper used the letter to answer charges of fanaticism that were being leveled against the abolitionists by the ACS and elements of the New York press. Jay's community standing and reputation were clearly on display for the benefit of detractors, and a truncated editorial header proclaimed: "What will be said by apologists for slavery to such language, from such a source? Would the enemies of emancipation dare attempt to outfit Judge Jay in a "fanatic's jacket?"[23]

While much of his appeal as a spokesman for the antislavery cause derived from Jay's conservatism and social activism, antislavery forces also prized his lineage. Ever sensitive to charges of radicalism or fanaticism, abolitionists constantly tried to deflect criticism of their efforts through their association with high profile, patriotic activists whom they felt no true American could blithely dismiss. As confrontations between antislavery forces and those who preferred to maintain the status quo accelerated, the pages of the *Emancipator* repeatedly paid homage to New Yorkers who had participated in the American Revolution. Prominent among these, and particularly useful because of their efforts in the cause of manumission, were Alexander Hamilton and John Jay. Both men were pioneers in that cause before the "moral sense of the community had been perverted by colonization." If the abolitionists were fanatics, then these men, "our fathers," had been fanatics too.[24] Association with patriots could only imbue the holy cause of emancipation with honor and respectability, and that a descendant of one of these revered figures should choose to lend his support to their cause afforded the abolitionists and their mission credibility.

William Jay's oft-invoked letter to the *Emancipator* was a clear statement of immediatist intent, and it attempted to convince doubters that immediate emancipation was practical. The letter also served to perfectly define the abolitionist tactic of "moral suasion." Under that rubric, the only way to convince skeptics of the logic of immediatist arguments was through the plain "exhibition of truth." The truth could best be served by constant reference to the "moral, social, and political evils of slavery." The moral suasion that Jay referred to was the only practical means to effect immediate emancipation, for "constitutional restrictions" forbade all others. The right of northern citizens, indeed, their moral imperative, was to exhort the slave states to do their moral duty and ignore southern "threats and denunciations." And what of the American Colonization Society? Jay stated that the organization was "neither a vile conspiracy on the one hand, nor a panacea for slavery on the other." "Many wise and good men" belonged to the society and believed in its "efficacy." However, Jay did not believe that their colonization plans would hasten the demise of the institution. Even if the society succeeded in manumitting and removing half the slaves in the United States to Africa, the value of the remaining half would only be enhanced.[25]

The New York City riots and antiabolitionist violence that began in July 1834 undoubtedly inspired Jay's greater participation in the antislavery cause.[26] Because of the increasing instability of their social position and financial well-being, many small master artisans and journeymen joined in well organized demonstrations against abolitionists. They were led by members of the upper-middle-class political and business community who had recently attained their higher social position.[27] These were much more like "revolutionary crowds" than mobs, and they chose their targets to ensure that their actions expressed their displeasure with the advocates of antislavery. Among the objects of their wrath were Charles Finney's Chatham Street Chapel, the domiciles of Lewis and Arthur Tappan, and the home and church of antislavery minister Samuel H. Cox. Jay's son John was in New York City attending Columbia that summer. The concerned father wrote and expressed his fears about the potentially unstable conditions in the city. He wrote about the excitement and attraction of mobs and admonished his son to "avoid being a spectator of them." Too often those who were "merely curious" about the excitement were "injured by a random shot or stone."[28]

In many ways the abolitionists reaped the whirlwind of their own heady expectations. They had long railed against the dissolution engendered by alcohol consumption; so too they had made sexuality a question of propriety by assaulting prostitution and masturbation.[29] They warned of the dangers of overrich foods and prescribed a bland diet to coincide with a less sybaritic lifestyle. Their purview embraced the breadth of American society and found the nation lacking in the somber asceticism required to realize their chiliastic goals. With a distinctly Puritanical atavism, the abstemious New Yorkers rejected what they saw as America's new individuality and promoted the good of society as a whole.[30] But if these middle-class reformers saw the body of society being diminished by its indulgence in numerous iniquities, the working class perceived society's diminution at a more personal level. For them the calls for emancipation held the potential for economic competition with blacks in an already unstable market. As a result, working-class men responded to the often imperious edicts of the Tappans and Finneys in a very personal, often violent, manner.[31]

The abolitionists endured a barrage of accusations directed toward their efforts during the course of the riots, and charges against them continued in the aftermath of the disturbances. Newspapers such as the *New York Commercial Advertiser* and *The Courier* and *Advertiser* exerted considerable efforts to denounce and distort the work of the abolitionists while escalating racial tensions.[32] Included among the insinuations were charges that the abolitionists had a predilection for fanaticism and violence. There was also the implication that the abolitionists were joined in a shadowy transatlantic plot "seeking to destroy" the happy union.[33] Andrew Jackson later threw his political weight behind this calumny, chastising the abolitionists in an address before Congress for their "misguided," "unconstitutional," and "wicked" actions.[34]

While there were certainly other abolitionists capable of crafting a response to these attacks, William Jay's social status made him a desirable spokesperson to answer the charges leveled against the New York chapter of the antislavery society. *Inquiry into the Character and Tendencies of the American Colonization and American Anti-Slavery Societies* marked a modification in Jay's thought and approach. Seeing that members of the ACS had been in the vanguard of directing false charges against the abolitionists, Jay abandoned his former policy of not confronting colonization and compared the aims of the two groups. More important, Jay now aligned himself entirely with the cause of immediate abolition. He ceased lending mere moral support to the movement and joined the American Anti-Slavery Society (AASS).

Jay's decision came at an important time in the abolition effort. In 1835 the abolitionists—who had already gained recognition out of proportion to their meager influence—were preparing to confront American society with the evils of slavery. They were poised to launch their national postal campaign. With the names of some 20,000 Southerners on their mailing lists, the abolitionists inundated the United States mail with antislavery literature. Indeed, the abolitionist's mailings caused considerable outrage and discomfort in the South, whose citizens responded with mail burnings, torchlight protest parades, and the muttering of dark oaths coupled with threats of disunion in order to stay the northern menace. The Tappans also launched a new antislavery paper, *The Slave's Friend*, which attempted to indoctrinate a more youthful audience about the horrors of slavery and enlist them to the cause.[35] Even the staid *Emancipator* benefited from a facelift. No issue appeared in July. In August, however, the paper resurfaced as a monthly, as opposed to weekly, gazette. The publication also sported a more attractive type set and header. And perhaps in an effort to make the paper appear less imposing, its name was also modified. Once adorned with the lofty appellation of *The Emancipator and Journal of Public Morals*, the paper simply became *The Emancipator*.

William Jay's *Inquiry* was first published in February 1835. Hardly an objective critic, *The Emancipator* was effusive in its praise of *Inquiry*, which the periodical deemed an "important publication."

The paper went on to laud Jay for his character, "industry and acumen."[36] Jay began his two part treatise by examining the goals of the ACS and its constitution, and he then examined the plight of free blacks in the United States. Jay drew liberally from the official journal of the colonizationists, *The African Repository*, and from the speeches of the society's supporters to illuminate the impracticality of colonization.[37] His sense of irony, when directed toward colonization society efforts to convince free blacks to depart for Liberia, was often acerbic. It was true enough that free blacks had been "rendered by prejudice and persecution an ignorant and degraded class," observed Jay. But was it not wonderful that they were still "competent to appreciate" how practical colonization would be for them?[38]

Jay's analysis on the merits of the humane works that the ACS claimed to perform was not trend-setting. Garrison had already published a harangue against the colonizers in his *Thoughts on African Colonization*. The difference was in approach. Garrison's work had been a stinging diatribe. Hurling as much invective as fact at his audience, Garrison pummeled the senses of those on both sides of the argument. Jay's method was a rational dissection of the facts. In his closing arguments against the society, Jay acknowledged that the organization was "unquestionably" composed of many committed Christians. Yet the society also had many members who used lurid rhetoric to misinform Americans about the goals of the abolitionists. They openly charged the antislavery forces with being "disturbers of the peace," and depicted an America "drenched in gore" should the abolitionists realize their goals and the slaves be freed. The fact that some "bad" men supported the colonization society did not render the organization evil, but "when mobs and infidels espouse a particular object, it is because that object is recommended to them by other than religious considerations."[39]

Having rebuked the colonizers, Jay outlined the aims of the AASS and answered the contumely that had been directed against its membership. He repeatedly denied charges of fanaticism, or that the abolitionists were inciting the slaves to rebel. No proof existed to support such accusations, he contended, nothing but "naked assertion."[40] Jay admitted that slavery was legal under the law of the United States, and insisted that the abolitionists would do nothing to interfere with the rights of the individual states to decide for themselves whether to retain the institution or not. The abolitionists would never exert any force other than moral suasion to achieve their goals.[41]

Two other aspects of Jay's defense of abolition warrant examination. The first was his almost Peterine denial of the charges of amalgamation. He flatly denied that the abolitionists promoted mixed-race marriages, and then tried to define the future of racial relations. He could have done better. He could have merely pointed to the third article of the Anti-Slavery Society's constitution and contented himself with that. That article stated that blacks of the proper "intellectual and moral" worth could share equality with whites.[42] This was consistent with socially conservative ideas regarding class, in that it could be applied to women and many whites who fell into the same category as the unworthy members of the black race.[43] Jay reinforced this point, stating that anti-abolitionists would be insane to contend that, "because a man has a dark skin . . . he is entitled to a place at our tables." Jay felt that abolitionists would also withhold a place at the table from whites who indulged in "disagreeable" habits and had "repulsive" manners.[44] No doubt many of those unrefined whites Jay referred to had recently joined in lobbing brickbats at the abolitionists.

Inquiry closed with an extended recounting of slave rebellions in Guadalupe and Haiti to reinforce the practicality of emancipation. Jay used this final section to stress the wisdom and safety of immediate emancipation. Using South Carolina as an example, Jay stated that industry—and therefore profit—would expand in that state should immediate emancipation be enacted there.[45] Underlying Jay's exposition is his very palpable sense of the dangers that personal property faced should servile insurrection erupt. The vulnerability of property is a recurring theme throughout the final section. Thus Jay attempted to use fear to convince southern slaveholders to surrender their property in order to avoid the destruction of their real estate and bodily harm to themselves.[46]

Examined as a measure of character, *Inquiry* was pure Jay. This followed not only from its invocation of themes Americans held in common regarding the sanctity of property, but also from the structure of its prose. The reader often gets the feeling of bearing witness to a criminal case being argued before the bar. Also abundantly evident was Jay's belief in the power of moral suasion and martyrdom. The "violence and persecution" the abolitionists endured could only lead to more widespread discussion of the issues. The ultimate result would be a great clamor from the people, North and South, for the elimination of slavery.[47] In some ways Jay's Panglossian outlook was rewarded: *Inquiry* was a huge success and honored by ten printings. It greatly expanded upon Garrison's earlier effort to wound the credibility of the colonizers.[48] In turn, the New York abolitionists had found their advocate. Always attempting to gain influential allies, Lewis Tappan made sure that a copy of Jay's work was forwarded to Henry Clay, whom he wanted to be apprised of the work because of Clay's own "eloquent exertions in behalf of the oppressed."[49] Lydia Maria Child, antislavery author and soon to be editor of the *National Anti-Slavery Standard*, remarked that *Inquiry* had been written in a "clear and candid manner."[50]

Naturally Jay's work did not meet with universal acclaim; the ACS had its defenders. Prominent among these was David M. Reese, a medical doctor who had earlier observed and recorded the effects of the 1819 yellow fever epidemic in Baltimore. In a series of open letters to Jay, Reese praised Jay's lineage even as he accused him of "unsophisticated fanaticism." Reese had read Jay's biography of his father, and he compared the goals of the ACS with John Jay's avowed gradualism and slave ownership. Reese also included extensive tracts taken from the *New York Commercial Advertiser* that had, of course, been highly critical of William Jay's work. While William never issued a formal rebuttal to Reese, he did write to his brother Peter that Reese had made unfair accusations against their father, and that Reese's work was a "dishonest fabrication." But if William did not defend his own work, he was not about to let Reese, or the newspapers, defame his father.[51]

In a letter to the *New York Commercial Advertiser*, Jay disputed that the newspaper's—and Reese's—assertions that his father, who had been a slaveholder, "did not regard slaveholding a heinous crime." He cited legal documents for manumission written by his father that claimed "the children of men are equally free, and cannot, without injustice . . . be held in slavery." He also quoted a petition the elder Jay had sent to the New York Legislature in 1826, claiming that blacks, "although free by the law of God, are held in slavery by the laws of the state." Jay claimed that his father's "practice in reference to slavery . . . was in perfect and beautiful consistency with his professions." Because John Jay had been unable to procure free servants, he had purchased slaves. When the labor of those slaves had repaid him for his investment, he manumitted them and sometimes retained their labor at wages. Yes, John Jay had been a gradualist, but his contemporaries, including Wilberforce, had been gradualists too. "The abolition he [John Jay] proposed was gradual, but it was definite, certain, and compulsory." William closed his letter

saying: "My own vindication, not being the object of this communication, I refrain from any further notice of the remarks in question."[52]

Predictably, colonizers showered Reese with accolades. The
board of managers of the New York branch of the organization
thanked the doctor formally. Meanwhile, and with measured reserve, colonization supporter Theodore Frelinghuysen pronounced
Reese's work "very acceptable."[53]

Taken as a barometer of abolitionist sentiment, *Inquiry* revealed
that Jay was not immune to the ambivalence toward blacks—free
and slave—that most abolitionists held. He vehemently denied a
desire for amalgamation but, as Lewis Tappan had discovered, mere
association with blacks was nevertheless problematic in many
circles. In the socially conservative, middle-class world that most
antislavery proponents inhabited, individuals had to prove their
worth before they could be considered eligible for social or political inclusion. Abolitionists repeatedly encouraged American blacks
to embrace the virtues that would help them earn social acceptance:
frugality, industry, and intelligence. According to Benjamin Wade,
if one possessed these virtues in abundance, then "the colored skin
is nothing." This criteria for social advancement was one that
William Jay clearly subscribed to, and one that his Federalist father
would have heartily endorsed.[54] Nor was this solely the opinion of
white abolitionists. Former slave and abolition advocate Frederick
Douglass reminded free blacks that "natural equality" with whites
was not enough; they had to prove their "practical equality, or in
other words, equal attainments." Blacks needed to learn trades, not
continue to be menial laborers. They needed to better their station
through "moral, social, religious, and intellectual elevation."[55] True,
a generous amount of cultural chauvinism influenced such appeals,
but it would not have occurred to many reformers that blacks
would want to reject their advice.

Many abolitionists voiced the opinion that the condition of
blacks—free or slave—was degraded, and that degradation was a
consequence of their being denied human and intellectual freedom.
Subsequent inequities were therefore an environmental problem.[56]
The rules for realizing equality with whites were implanted in the
tenets of middle-class virtue. Intelligence might be achieved
through education, wealth through a better job and frugal habits.
Yet how were blacks to attain these goals when they lived in an
America of social, economic, and legal inequality? Worse, how were

they expected to overcome prejudice when those who championed their cause often withheld the tools required to realize their goals? For all of their altruism, the merchants Tappan never employed a black in any position higher than porter.[57] Jay himself, as a member of the executive committee of the New York branch of the American Anti-Slavery Society, helped obstruct any attempts to place blacks in leadership positions within the organization.[58] Within a year of *Inquiry*'s release, Jay opposed Lewis Tappan's plan to have Theodore S. Wright, a black Presbyterian minister, address the AASS. Threatening to resign if Wright spoke, Jay contended that neither the general public nor the abolitionists could countenance such a bold step.[59]

Was Jay being hypocritical or honest? It is difficult to tell whether he helped deny blacks participation in the antislavery society out of prejudice or misguided paternalism. Therein lay the puzzle of abolitionist ambivalence. Jay knew that, whether free blacks participated in the organized calls for emancipation or not, the mere rumor of their presence was a catalyst for violence. The New York City riots of 1834 were sparked by Tappan's actions and the rumors of an integrated Fourth of July celebration at the Chatham Street Chapel. For the next two years, in Massachusetts, Ohio, and upstate New York, mobs spurred on by newspapers and the speeches of leading citizens sought to defuse the threat they perceived as emanating from the abolitionists. When they could not find abolitionists to punish, they focused their rage upon the local black community.[60] North or South, the threat of physical violence to black citizens was frighteningly real, and the avenues of legal redress narrow. Black inclusion in some organizations would have created combustible circumstances in many regions besides New York, which had witnessed few prior racial disturbances.

Owing to poor health, distance from New York City, and work, Jay seldom left Bedford for long periods of time. Lewis Tappan's diary reveals the presence of a number of prominent abolitionists in the city, but hardly ever mentions Jay. Still, the New York antislavery movement found ways to involve Jay and keep him active, even if only in a symbolic capacity. In October 1835, abolitionists in Utica, New York, sent out a call for an antislavery convention with the aim of forming a state society. Their efforts to hold that convention created a riot led by some of Utica's foremost citizens. The convention was moved to Peterboro, some thirty miles distant. The convention was held, the state society was formed, and William Jay was elected president of the society.[61] In response, Jay wrote a public letter accepting the position. He noted that the distance of his home from the society's offices would have prompted him to decline the post were it not for the continuing assault on the "constitutional, republican" rights of the abolitionists. Abolitionists were clearly being denied their rights of free speech and assembly, and Jay accused politicians of dispersing antislavery assemblies in order to "propitiate" southern voters. In a xenophobic passage, Jay warned that—if politicians were so venal as to mollify slaveholders—they might next succumb to the voices of Roman Catholic foreigners among the population and put down Protestant assemblies![62]

William Lloyd Garrison attended a gathering of the New York State chapter of the Anti-Slavery Society in May 1838. The fact that his brother George thought he should not attend the meeting exposes some budding animosity between the two abolitionist factions that have been aptly described by Lawrence J. Friedman as the "New York stewards" and the "Massachusetts insurgents."[63] Differences aside, Garrison met, and shook hands with, the Tappans, William Jay, Gerrit Smith, and Alvan Stewart, along with many others. That very morning Garrison was treated to a "very animated discussion" between New Yorkers Jay and Stewart regarding the constitutionality of slavery. Garrison believed Jay got the better of the debate. Also in attendance was poet and reformer John Greenleaf Whittier. Whittier noted that Jay's comments were "energetic" and severe, whereas Stewart's defense was "eloquent" but "disconnected."[64]

Prior to this fateful confrontation, in March, Jay had written a letter to Lewis Tappan complaining of the views of "Mr. S" that had appeared in *The Emancipator.* Jay stated that, in his opinion, the antislavery society was increasingly divided on issues of doctrine. Speaking of the upcoming May convention, Jay asserted that "The society will assemble before long, and it must act and act efficiently, or there is end of harmonious action by abolitionists."[65] Jay then forcefully opined that the plan of action suggested by "Mr. S" was not only sinful, but also contrary to the oath of the antislavery society. Jay reminded Tappan that, as a judge, he had taken an oath to support the Constitution of the United States and the Anti-Slavery Society; there could be no compromise on this issue.[66]

Like Jay, Stewart was lawyer and an ardent abolitionist. Based upon his understanding of the Constitution and the Bill of Rights, Stewart had determined that, under the Fifth Amendment, slaves had been denied "of life, liberty, [and] property, without due process of law." Because of this breach, Congress, using a precedent that harkened back to the Magna Carta, had the right to abolish slavery "in every state and territory in the Union."[67] Stewart based his theory on an expansion of the due process clause. His inspiration had come from Joseph Story's interpretation of that constitutional clause outlined in *Commentaries on the Constitution.* Story believed the clause to be but

> an enlargement of the language of the Magna Carta . . . (neither will we pass upon him, or condemn him, but by the lawful judgment of his peers, or by the law of the land.) Lord Coke says that these latter words "per legem terre" (by the law of the land), mean by the due process of law, that is, without due presentment or indictment, and being brought to answer thereto, by due process of the common law. So that this clause, in effect, affirms the right of trial according to process and proceedings of common law.[68]

An individual had a procedural right not to be enslaved unless that person was determined to be a slave under common law proceedings. Stewart insisted that the procedural could be made substantive. He held that, because no person in the United States had been declared a slave by common law procedure, all persons held in slavery had a right to liberty. Therefore, because the rights of slaves had been violated by the denial of due process rights, Congress could eliminate slavery throughout the nation by the mere "enactment of a declaration of law." Determined to press the issue, Stewart submitted a series of seven resolutions to be discussed at the fifth anniversary antislavery conference. If adopted, these resolutions would have amended the second article of the society's constitution, which stated that the organization would not interfere with the rights of the individual states to legislate upon the legality of slavery according to the discretion of those states.[69]

According to legal historian William Wiecek, Stewart's arguments were defective for three reasons. First, Stewart had attributed the presence of the due process clause in the Constitution to a "benevolent conspiracy" theory. He believed that the framers of the document felt compelled to offset the concessions that they had made to slavery. They did this by insisting that the victims of those concessions were only those that were meant to be held as slaves by due process of common law. Second, Stewart somehow believed that the due process clause had been drawn up at the Constitutional Convention of 1787! A position he apparently never altered. Third, Stewart ignored the Supreme Court decision in *Barron v. Baltimore*

(1833), which declared that the first eight amendments to the federal constitution did not serve as restraints on the states.[70]

Jay's direct, "animated" response to Stewart was not recorded for posterity. A revised version of his views did appear later in *The Emancipator* however, and they were uncharacteristically impatient for a man of Jay's usually reserved nature. He responded that, if Congress were granted such extraordinary powers under the Fifth Amendment, then that fact had escaped everyone except Stewart to that point in history. The presence of these powers had escaped the authors of the *Federalist Papers,* men who were intimately acquainted with the dialogue that had spawned the Constitution. So too it had eluded the erudition of jurists and legal scholars James Kent and Joseph Story, who were unaware that such a grant had been bestowed upon Congress. Invoking the Magna Carta concept that freemen were entitled to due process through indictment ignored the fact that due process was daily overlooked in chancery courts throughout the Union. These courts obtained convictions without grand or petit juries, so accepting Stewart's interpretation would "sweep away" the civil jurisdiction of the U.S. courts. If Congress had the right to free a Georgia slave because he was denied due process, then it could also free a suitor in New York chancery court.[71]

Jay also countered the potential argument that the due process clause applied only to certain criminal cases, not chancery courts. If that were the case he said, then the clause could not be applied to the slaves because they were not deprived of life or liberty as the result of a crime. "Property is placed under the same constitutional protection that life and liberty are . . . it is as unconstitutional to take away a man's farm without due process as it is to take away his life." Jay then chided Stewart that:

> Forty-nine years ago, it seems a fundamental law of the republic was adopted, abolishing slavery, but the framers of that law, although commiserating those unfortunate persons known by the name of slaves, kept their commiseration a profound secret, and instead of framing their act of emancipation in intelligible language, adopted a phraseology so occult that no court ever suspected its true meaning; and they selected their phraseology in preference to calling things by their right names from their observation of the practical operation of that phraseology under Magna Carta.[72]

Jay's rebuttal to Stewart was supported by a bipartisan group of Boston and New York delegates who felt that Stewart presumed too much and endowed Congress with too much power. Evidence also exists that Jay and Joshua Leavitt, editor of *The Emancipator,* were in agreement on the rebuttal that appeared in that paper; for Leavitt confided to Jay that Stewart's views were "dangerous and seductive sophistry."[73] Stewart's opponents believed that, if they amended the constitution of the society, they would violate the public trust and put the organization at odds with the majority of the Union. This was not a path upon which they wished to embark. Jay did not equivocate. He clearly stated his belief that the fundamental changes Stewart proposed for the society's constitution were a matter of "life and death" for the antislavery cause.[74] When the debate closed, Stewart's motion was defeated. Jay and Stewart would continue to work together again in the future to promote the antislavery cause, but Theodore Dwight Weld wrote in a letter to Angela Grimke that he felt "bad blood" existed between the two men over this issue.[75]

In October Jay and Gerrit Smith coauthored a letter to the candidates running for governor and lieutenant governor of New York. The two men queried whether the candidates would support laws that deprived the colored people of New York their constitutional rights. They also asked whether fugitive slaves should be granted a trial by jury. Finally, they wanted to know if the candidates supported the law permitting the importation of slaves into New York, and allowed them to be held in that condition for nine months. Although they mentioned that a growing segment of the population was interested in the answers to these questions, the two abolitionists assured the office-seekers that the letter was not an attempt to "wring out a pledge."[76] The letter was a prime example of the abolitionist practice of "questioning." Questioning of politicians was employed to bait office seekers into revealing their true positions to the public.

In 1839 William Jay published his second major work on slavery in that decade. *A View of the Action of the Federal Government in Behalf of Slavery* would not see as many reprints as *Inquiry,* but perhaps no other work of that period reveals just how real and justifiable abolitionists felt their fears of a slave power conspiracy were. But while their anxieties frequently found expression in the imagination of chimerical plots against the Union by proslavery interests, Jay did not perceive any shadowy machinations by covert conspirators.[77] Rather, he found enough evidence to accuse the U.S. government of being openly involved in promoting the interests of the slaveocracy.

View's effectiveness depended upon proving two major points. One, that the U.S. government promoted slavery interests at home through the manipulation of domestic policy, and two, that the need to protect slavery influenced American foreign policy and diplomatic relations with other nations. In all, Jay presented twenty-one points to underpin his accusations, with relevant facts, figures, and quotes to support each point. Jay's approach employed an inductive reasoning that bore a distinct resemblance to Enlightenment empiricism. His twenty-one points provided a framework for the presentation of data that eliminated alternative explanations, and hopefully left the reader with only one logical conclusion.[78] That conclusion was that a "slave power" did exist, and sustained its vitality by existing within the American body politic that served as its willing host. But what were the origins of this power?

Jay understood that the slave power had its Genesis in that bundle of compromises known as the federal constitution. Among its "guilty" compromises, the Constitution had permitted the continuance of the African slave trade for another twenty years after its ratification, had pledged to suppress servile insurrection, and had provided masters with the legal right to pursue and reclaim their slave property throughout the nation. But the true key to slave power, as guaranteed by the document, lay in the formula for proportional representation known as the three-fifths compromise.[79] The three-fifths compromise enabled the South to wield undue influence in several key political areas. The first was the House of Representatives. At the time Jay wrote, representation was divided among twenty-six states; thirteen were slave and thirteen free, but the representation based upon population was far from proportional. The slave states, possessing a free population of 3,823,389, had 100 representatives, while the free states, claiming a population nearly double that figure, at 7,003,451, had 142. One representative was permitted per 47,000 inhabitants; therefore the total number representing the slave states in the House would have stood at seventy-five without the added advantage of a federal ratio that counted slaves as fractional constituents. Jay did not suggest that the Constitution should be altered, but he did wonder why the holders of "human chattels . . . have greater privileges awarded to them than to the holders of any other kind of property."[80] The Senate, being restricted to two members from each state regardless of population, was not open to representational tinkering. But in the House, the South, with only half the free population of the North, was rewarded.

The three-fifths formula also meant that slave states held an unequal influence on electoral votes. Pennsylvania, for example, held thirty electoral votes; the states of South Carolina, Georgia, Alabama, Mississippi, Louisiana, and Kentucky—with an aggregate free population of 189,791 fewer inhabitants—held fifty-three. This disproportionate advantage permitted the slave states, which invariably acted in concert, to force potential presidential candidates to bow to their wishes in order to be elected. Jay pointed to the example of Henry Clay—a politician who repeatedly neglected to say the proper soothing words to slaveholders—as an example of the slave power in action. Did such political power translate into de facto control of the government? Since the adoption of the Constitution the slave states had provided five U.S. presidents, compared to two from the North. In fact, not counting the Van Buren administration, which was in power as Jay wrote, the South had furnished the nation's president for forty out of forty-eight years. With this preeminence of presidential power came the ability to forge policy and control patronage through the rewards of departmental appointments. The slave states also held a distinct advantage in securing the position of Speaker of the House, along with the attendant advantages of committee organization that post bestowed.[81]

Jay's anger over the inequities of the three-fifths compromise was evidence of his Federalist convictions. The three-fifths measure had indeed given the South an unfair political advantage. Federalists and their descendants were convinced that, if slaves had not counted toward representation and the Electoral College, John Adams would have retained the presidency in 1800. Subsequently, in their resolves of the Hartford Convention of 1814, Federalists demanded that only free persons should count toward representation. Nor was Jay alone in his criticism of the three-fifths compromise; other sons of Federalists had made it an issue. Wendell Phillips, an abolitionist of Massachusetts Federalist descent, claimed that the three-fifths compromise "gave the South extra political muscle."[82]

Even with a president from the Northeast, the South continued to hold a disproportionate number of powerful political positions. Jay reinforced this accusation by citing the composition of the Van Buren administration. Long considered a "Northern man of Southern principles" by abolitionists, Van Buren had filled his cabinet positions with slave state politicians. His vice president was Richard M. Johnson, a slaveholder from Kentucky. The attorney general was Felix Grundy of Tennessee, and the secretary of state was John

Forsyth of Georgia. Additionally, the secretary of war, the secretary of the navy, and the postmaster general all hailed from slave states. Further, there had been no less than five appointments to the Supreme Court since 1830. Each of those appointees came from a slave state.[83]

Jay believed that thus ensconced in the seat of power, Southern representatives embarked early upon a course to maintain blacks in a subservient status through the passage of national legislation designed to degrade them based upon the litmus of race. The obsequious acquiescence of their Northern political counterparts aided them in their efforts. In 1790, for example, Congress passed an act that made whiteness the criteria by which aliens might be naturalized and granted the rights of American citizens. Two years later another act passed prescribing that militias should be organized to include every "free, able-bodied, white male citizen." An Act of 1810, organizing the Department of the Post Office, clearly stipulated that none other than free whites should be employed in carrying the mail.[84] The federal government was also implicated by its provisions for the territories that were under its exclusive jurisdiction. Not only had the government permitted slavery into some territories by virtue of the Missouri Compromise, but it had also continued to tolerate slavery's continued existence in the nation's capital. In the District of Columbia, Congress had dictated that white citizens should elect white politicians, thereby making whiteness the requirement for suffrage. Further, the government allowed the District to continue to abide by the archaic slave codes of Maryland and Virginia. Under these laws, a slave caught setting fire to a building was to be beheaded and quartered, and his various body parts then put on display in public places.[85] That slavery should be permitted to exist in all its barbarity under the authority and aegis of the U.S. government outraged Jay, but his litany of culpability was by no means complete.

Jay derided the Fugitive Slave Act of 1793 that permitted slaveholders to pursue fugitives, capture them, and demand their return before a Justice of the Peace without oath or due process of any kind.[86] And if the government could not aid slave owners in the recovery of their property through the expedient of the law, then it would resort to military adventure or diplomacy to accomplish its nefarious goals. A perfect example of this had occurred with the destruction of a slave fort during Andrew Jackson's Florida campaign against the Creek Indians in 1816. The fort, situated on the banks of the Appalachicola River, allegedly served as a militant maroon community from which runaway slaves and their hostile Creek allies could induce Georgia slaves to escape and join them. Jackson instructed the officer entrusted with reducing the fort that the primary objective was to return the fugitive slaves to their owners. Unfortunately, the zeal of the officer in charge prompted him to order red-hot cannon shot poured into the fort, which hit the powder magazine and exploded the fort along with the vast majority of its 300 defenders. Interestingly, twenty-three years later the government awarded $5,465 in prize money to the "heroes" of the "Negro Fort" conflict. Jay speculated that the money would serve as an inducement to those soldiers and sailors placed in similar circumstances to do their proslavery duty even if influenced by growing anti slavery sentiment.[87]

There was more. Through the medium of smuggling, the African slave trade continued unimpeded after 1808. The federal government was guilty of collusion in the smuggling because so little was done to stop it. Should Jay's readers doubt the veracity of his accusation, he pointed to the Treaty of Ghent, negotiated at the conclusion of the War of 1812. In that treaty, the United States and Great Britain pledged to expend their "best endeavors" to end the traffic in human cargoes. But while the United States had expressed a desire to see slave trading declared an act of piracy when practiced off the coast of Africa, the nation balked at signing a joint declaration with Britain pronouncing the practice piracy off the American coast.[88] Britain had managed to extract such a commitment from Spain and other European nations, but with the connivance of the Spanish government in Cuba the trade in human beings to the United States continued. Citing the observations of fellow abolitionist and British commissioner to Cuba, Sir Thomas F. Buxton, Jay noted that the illegal slave trade on that island was so flagrant that it was possible to name the vessels involved, many of which flew the American flag.[89] Little wonder that the U.S. Senate, charged with the ratification of any treaty, had been eager to exempt vessels off of the coast of America from search and seizure!

Jay exposed other ways that foreign policy and diplomacy were beholden to, and protective of, the institution of slavery and its political allies. The concept of an independent nation of former slaves was abhorrent to many American politicians, particularly Southerners. Based upon fears that diplomatic recognition of a black republic might have a deleterious effect upon the morale of supporters of slavery at home, the U.S. government had not only refused to recognize the new government of "Hayti" [sic], it had pressured other Latin American governments to refuse recognition also. This in spite of the fact that, in 1833, imports to America from Haiti exceeded those from Sweden, Scotland, Ireland, Spain, and the British West Indies—among others—in value.[90] In the slaveholding Republic of Texas however, the federal government's acknowledgment of that fledgling nation's independence was accomplished at the behest of northern land speculators and southerners eager to expand westward and take their slave property with them. Recognition of Texas was a legal necessity, a precursor to annexation. Twelve months after Texas achieved independence, that nation, with a constitution that recognized slavery, won diplomatic recognition from the government of the United States. Thirty-seven years after its independence, Haiti had yet to be recognized.[91]

Of all the evidence Jay had presented to this point, none of it, no matter how distasteful, was illegal. The government could recognize or ignore other nations as it saw fit. The Senate could, with its constitutional powers of advice and consent, gut or refuse to ratify a treaty. Most abolitionists, including Jay, believed that each state had the right to decide for itself whether to be slave or free. But when the government attempted to deny its citizens their constitutional rights at the urging of special interests, something was badly amiss. That the slave power feared open debate on the issue of slavery was evident, for as one Southern senator had candidly admitted: "Every agitation of this subject (slavery) weakens the moral force in our favor, and breaks down the moral barriers which now serve to protect and secure us. We have everything to lose and nothing to gain by agitation and discussion."[92] That fear of disintegrating "moral barriers" had led Southern representatives, with the full cooperation of most of their Northern colleagues, to suppress one of the most basic of constitutional freedoms granted the American people: the right of petition. What Jay referred to was the infamous "gag rule," which attempted to throttle open debate in a House of Representatives inundated by a rising tide of antislavery petitions in the years after 1835. Jay deemed it understandable that Southern representatives wanted to stifle debate upon the subject of slavery, but he found it intolerable that they succeeded in their efforts and were joined in their movement by so many Northerners. What better evidence could there be for the pervasive corruption caused by slavery?[93]

Jay concluded that the South was incapable of acting alone. He stressed that in every Southern victory, "in every wicked and cruel act of the Federal Government in behalf of slavery, the people of the

North have participated" for the love of Southern commerce and the money it provided. The Northern representatives who had aided and abetted the South were not solely to blame for their actions; they were merely acting as the representatives of their constituencies. Only when the people of the North repented and renounced their cupidity would morality triumph and justice be done.[94] Beyond promoting business ties with the South, Northern legislators had also long been held in thrall by Southern threats of secession. They had indeed, in the words of John Randolph, been "frightened by their own doughfaces!" Jay believed that the South would have been craven to accept any meddling by a government that overstepped its constitutional bounds in attempting to regulate slavery. But he also stressed that Southern threats of secession were more a result of "passion" than "mature determination." What possible advantages would accrue to the South if it removed itself from the Union?[95]

In 1839, only a minority of Americans held abolitionist views. However, Jay predicted that abolitionist sentiment would swell in reaction to any attempt at secession by the South. And should the South secede, slave owners would lose the protection of the federal government. Not only would they be unable to retrieve their fugitive chattels, but they also would lose the aid of the federal government in suppressing servile insurrection. A region already living in fear of black rebellion would grow increasingly insecure as many whites migrated northward and the ratio of black to white grew increasingly disproportionate. The coastal slave trade would cease, and its practitioners would be treated like the pirates that they were. What of the vaunted Southern power and wealth? Jay argued that a nation's population, industry, and commerce determined its power and wealth. The population of the United States was already migrating westward, not southward, and Southern industry languished as a consequence. Certainly commerce would continue with a separate South, but the world would purchase Southern cotton in the manner that it bought Haitian coffee, with the "least possible intimacy." The South would be rendered a pariah and excluded from the companionship of other nations.[96]

View was an appeal to reason and an attempt to persuade the South to consider its actions carefully. Jay believed that—if the abolitionists ever succeeded in prompting their federal representatives to intervene against the sovereignty of the individual states in legislating against slavery—the Union would be sundered.[97] And even though the federal government had overstepped its constitutional restraints in the promotion of the slave interests, it was highly unlikely that it would overstep its legal limitations in the cause of emancipation. Armed with this knowledge, the South needed to consider its actions prudently. Any advantages that the South thought it might conceivably gain through the tragic act of secession were illusory.[98]

Jay's document once again drew its rationale from his most deeply held beliefs. These tenets were grounded in his understanding of the Constitution and the federal government that had been erected upon it. The government, in so far as it was allowed to do so by law, could act positively for the common good; it could eliminate slavery from the District of Columbia. But as far as tampering in the affairs of state legislation, the government's attitude had to be laissez-faire.[99] This did not mean that Jay subscribed to the emerging rubric of "negative government," whereby almost any action of the central government was deemed intrusive. But rather that the government could not extend itself beyond the restraints legally placed upon it by the Constitution.[100]

Jay grasped the prevailing political thought and economic mood of the nation. The "common" man in the United States had for decades been sold upon the carefully cultivated myth that touted the virtues of self-sufficiency and individuality.[101] Americans absorbed these doctrines through the pleasing philosophy of Jefferson and Jackson, and the abolitionists themselves were urging free blacks to adopt the philosophy. But conditions in the nineteenth century had moved beyond the mere desire on the part of the individual to survive with a mere modicum of comfort; individuals now sought to acquire greater material wealth. In order to acquire more wealth, individuals had to enter the market and subject themselves and their families to the vagaries of supply and demand. Wise individuals understood the need to protect their interests and insulate themselves from the capricious economics of the market economy. Slave owners and northern businessmen turned to the halls of government to promote their own selfish interests, for as Bryce noted: "For . . . managers as well as for intriguers there is no such paradise as the lobby of a state legislature."[102] The lobby of federal government also provided fertile ground for the advancement of special interests. There was certainly collusion involved here, but Jay understood it to be part of the political process, not a clandestine conspiracy orchestrated by the slave owners.

Following hard after *View,* in almost supplemental fashion, came *On the Condition of the Free People of Color in the United States.* Here again, Jay avoided what he saw as unproductive criticism of the South, preferring to concentrate upon the condition of inequality that oppressed free blacks in the North. It was not merely in the "rice-swamps of Georgia" or the "sugar-fields of Louisiana" where prejudice reared its head; it was also abundantly evident in the "valleys of New England" and the "prairies of Ohio." It was shocking to realize that, while Southern laws against black people may have been severe, the "prejudice against their persons" was not as great as in the North.

Free black people were discriminated against in every imaginable way north of the Mason-Dixon Line. The laws of Connecticut and New York were contemptible enough, but the laws passed in Ohio, in direct violation of the state's constitution, were "pre-eminent" for their "wickedness."[103] Jay then proceeded to show how each of these states discriminated legally. In documenting the restriction of freedom of movement, inequality of education and religious freedom, and exclusion from participation in the meting out of justice, Jay contended that black people in the North were not "free" by any definition.[104] The promotion of hatred based upon the color of a person's skin was a disgusting perversion of God's commandment to "love one another." When colonizers and earthly divines suggested that an innate inequality of the races existed, they made a "mockery" of God's law.[105]

Jay's circular seemed to indicate a clearer definition of his own views on race, one untarnished by class considerations. If human beings could not at least "love one another," then the law should provide them with the tools with which to attain equality. In each instance that he cited, Jay lucidly argued that blacks were being denied the ability to advance themselves socially. Betterment through education, religion, and economic acquisition paved the pathway to democratic participation in American society. To bar those doors to one race, while freely admitting "white scavengers," was an affront to justice. The possibility of social equality was conducive to productivity. *Condition* provided an interesting and revealing slice of environmentalist dogma commingled with Jay's opinions on how best to advance racial harmony.

Jay did not tilt his lance at windmills. The racial inequalities that helped to sanction slavery set the nation upon a dangerous course. These injustices had to be portrayed clearly if unselfish men were to reach agreement upon a pragmatic solution to America's racial woes. Americans were expanding westward aggressively. Jay opposed this unrestrained migration because he understood the cost, not only at the individual level, but for the nation as well. America would be forced to grapple with the divisive issue of how to regulate slavery in each new territory. Jay clung to a Christian sense of community and mutual responsibility. He had initially balked at involvement in the Anti-Slavery Society because the organization had no concrete plan. Immediatism, in and of itself, was an ambiguous program that revealed a dissatisfaction with the inadequate efforts to eradicate slavery.[106]

Jay's belief in moral suasion extended to his constitutional arguments in a concatenated fashion. In spite of all of the evidence that he himself had accumulated, he still believed that governments could be induced to behave in a humane manner. And if one level of government might reveal itself to be just, the other levels would follow. Jay had to believe this. His father had helped to pen the *Federalist Papers*. To Jay's mind at least, his father had not only been a patriot, but a paradigm of republican virtue. Political involvement by the antislavery forces would become increasingly plausible to Jay. Political engagement would have to be implemented so that abolitionists could compete with the influential powers arrayed against them. Recognizing the situation for what it was would not be sufficient. Difficult times lay ahead, times that would severely challenge many of Jay's most cherished beliefs as his ideals clashed with the changing realities of attempting to forge a united effort to cleanse the nation.

3

"I Am an Abolitionist, and I Thank God I Am"

And think you that this is the country, and this is the age, in which the republican maxim that the MAJORITY must govern, can be so long and barbarously reversed? Think you that the majority of the PEOPLE in the cotton states, cheered and encouraged as they will be by the sympathy of the world, and the example of the West Indies, will forever tamely submit to be beasts of burden for a few lordly planters?
— William Jay to the nonslaveholders of the South, 1843

In 1840, the American Anti-Slavery Society (AASS) was torn asunder, experiencing the "end of harmonious action" that Jay had predicted. Historians have offered up myriad explanations as to what finally precipitated the fragmentation that had loomed, quite literally, since the organization's inception. Undoubtedly the unconventional William Lloyd Garrison alienated many potential antislavery converts with his methods. There was also increasing dissatisfaction over the realization that Garrisonian philosophy remained an impediment to the greater political involvement proposed by many members outside of his Massachusetts circle.[1] There was also the "woman question." Portraying this element of the debate as the cynosure of the increasing factionalism within the society is erroneous, but it certainly contributed to the process of the society's disintegration.

Moving from the protofeminism of the moral reform movement, activist women had found that Garrison's willingness to include them, even granting them positions of authority within the society, provided a framework for the development of feminist thought.[2] Women advanced from auxiliary antislavery work to active participation in the Massachusetts chapter of the society. For those in the immediate Garrison circle, the increasingly vocal—and socially visible—involvement of the women was acceptable; those outside the circle found the trend unsettling to say the least. It defied the concept of separate gender spheres defined by the Cult of True Womanhood. Women's involvement in the antislavery cause could therefore be cast in a socially disruptive light. Many abolitionists claimed women's participation was a side show that would deflect attention from the true issue of emancipation. Many evangelical reformers who sought more damning arguments against women's direct participation in the cause could couch their objections in biblical terms, for Paul had demanded the silence of women.[3] Whatever the argument, by 1838 the issue of women's involvement in the antislavery movement had caused a split in the Massachusetts society. This occurred when a resolution to receive women into the society on equal terms with men prompted the resignation of some influential clerics.[4]

In May of 1840 at the New York society convention, the American Anti-Slavery Society shattered. The rift was precipitated by the ongoing debate over active political involvement by abolitionists in national elections, which was opposed by the Garrison clique and by the New York City faction.[5] William Jay did not attend the convention, but like Lewis Tappan he advocated a church oriented approach based upon piety and rooted in a firm institutional foundation. Many upstate New Yorkers and westerners were tired of this seemingly ineffective doctrine, and sought political participation. But even if Tappan and his supporters agreed with Garrison that politics was a corrupt bargain, they supported the orthodox clergy who opposed the participation of women. When Garrison's loyalists proposed the nomination of a Quaker teacher and antislavery speaker, Abby Kelley, to the AASS business committee, their motion led to the walkout of most of the conservative members. The conservatives were led by Lewis Tappan, who along with Amos Phelps had been nominated for the same seat as Kelley.[6]

In a belated letter to his father, John Jay described the atmosphere of the convention as one of confusion. "There was great excitement, loud cheers," and numerous calls to order. Francis Jackson of Massachusetts (described by John as a "great friend of Garrison") chaired the meeting and then "kept it among friends, evidently favoring his own party." His favoritism added to the confusion, and numerous claims to the floor were exchanged "to no purpose" by both sides. Ultimately a business committee was nominated, and one of the members nominated to serve on the committee was Abby Kelly. This prompted a debate that lasted half the day. Kelly herself addressed the meeting and gave her views, which—according to John—"did not exactly coincide with those of St. Paul." Kelly delivered her speech "in a tone of voice resembling a scream." John attributed this to shrillness, but by his own descriptions of the agitated proceedings, Kelly must have had to shout in order to be heard. When the vote was taken at least 500 of those present voted in favor of Kelly, while 400 voted against. Tappan, nominated to serve on the same committee, now declined, saying that Kelly's nomination was "contrary to Christ" and destroyed the "efficacy of female action."[7]

A rapprochement was not possible. The factions went in their separate directions, while attempting to downplay the acrimonious breakup. *The Liberator* acknowledged the rift, and understood that the result would be separate organizations. But the journal believed events had transpired for the best. Ever optimistic, the journal predicted that "if the secession will take such a course as Christian love and Christian prudence dictates, they (the separatists) may combine a very large proportion of the North against slavery. We do not expect them to surrender any principle."[8] In the wake of the convention, Tappan's faction almost immediately formed the American and Foreign Anti-Slavery Society (AFASS), which was aligned with the newly formed British and Foreign Anti-Slavery Society. Indeed, prior to the fatal May convention, the New Yorkers had already sent delegates to England to approach one of the English society's founders, Joseph Sturge, about the possibility of an Anglo-American antislavery association.[9]

Just before the convention, Jay had outlined the reasons for his personal dissatisfaction with the AASS. In a letter to the AASS Committee of Arrangements, Jay declined an invitation to speak before the Connecticut branch of the society. Jay explained that his refusal did not betray a flagging commitment to the cause, but reflected his view that the society had begun to promote "wholly different objects" than the abolition of slavery. Jay reaffirmed his adherence to the constitutional approach and his vow to uphold that document. He also believed that the society was intent upon violating its own constitution ("Mr. S" was once again mentioned), and because of this Jay would never again take part in meetings. Jay then went on to complain that the antislavery societies—the auxiliaries of the AASS—were being used to advance theories about the rights of women, and insisted that the society had not been formed to "alter relations between the sexes." Finally, he explained that the proper path to follow was still that of moral suasion. For when the society had previously exhibited a "pattern of Christian and disinterested benevolence," it had even commanded the "secret admiration" of its enemies.[10]

Jay's letter to the Connecticut society is instructive because it defines the major disagreements confronting the abolitionists leading to the breakup of the society. It is possible to analyze how Jay as an individual reacted to each point of contention, and to speculate on his motives for supporting the society's division. There is the distinct possibility that lingering personal animosities conflated with philosophical differences, and colored Jay's reasoning and opinions. An examination of Jay's letters prior to the split reveals his thoughts on each point. Examining the Connecticut letters is worthwhile because it helps to underscore the point that, no matter how principled and philanthropical these members of the antislavery society were, they were individuals. Because of their individuality—and in spite of their apparent rationalism and their moralistic exhortations—they were capable of pettiness and egotism. These too human traits did not serve to inspire the sense of altruism and community required for concerted action; they also belie the abolitionists' constant protestations that the cause of emancipation transcended all other considerations.

Jay's position on the "woman question" was not new and, like his position on free blacks joining the society, was entirely consistent with principles he had earlier avowed. Jay had already informed his friend Tappan that attempts by the Garrisonians to "alter the relative social condition of the female sex" were "unwarrantable."[11] In another, later letter, Jay wrote to Tappan and expressed his opinion that "Garrison with his women, and our abolition friends with their nominations, are doing more to retard and injure the abolition cause than all the politicians in the land."[12] These statements are quite clear, and thus it would be tempting to ascribe Jay's disaffection with the society to the women's issue.

Jay's opinion on women's participation in the society was not related to any sort of misplaced chivalry, or to the desire to protect the "fairer sex" from the brickbats and jeers of the mobocrats. Far more likely it derived from the realization of the need for concentration upon the antislavery issue. Introducing the question of women's rights would distract from the antislavery issue in much the same manner that permitting the membership of free blacks in antislavery societies would, and Jay had earlier threatened to resign the society over the issue of black minister Theodore Wright. The United States William Jay inhabited was intensely conservative, and appeals to conservative society required conformity to accepted social conventions, so that those pleas did not prompt a negative reaction and the abolitionist message become lost.[13] In deference to the social atmosphere (as much as to his own beliefs on social structure), Jay maintained the firmly held social belief about the "place" of women.[14] But Jay never threatened to resign the society over the women's issue, or even to leave the organization regardless of the harm he felt women's participation was causing.

Jay's letter to the Connecticut branch of the AASS also reiterated his continued insistence upon the viability of moral suasion as a matter of principle. Debates over the effectiveness of methods such as moral suasion ultimately led to larger debates over issues such as political involvement. Moral suasion was a benign method of persuasion that attempted to convince slaveholders to abandon their sinfulness, while reassuring them that the abolitionists would never resort to extralegal strategies to deny them of their property. Of itself, the practice of moral suasion never created enough friction to generate any real heat between abolitionists. Any suggestion that Jay would have joined his fellow New Yorkers in leaving the AASS over the issue of moral suasion is ludicrous. Where Jay truly parted company with many of his abolitionist brethren was over the issue of constitutionalism. Jay most definitely disparaged Garrison's inclusion of women in the society's activities, but he frowned even more upon the contumacious, unconstitutional casuistry of the ineffable "Mr. S"—Alvan Stewart.

Within abolitionist circles, the issue of constitutionality was increasingly linked to the debate over political participation. In the early half of the nineteenth century, political participation in the United States had burgeoned alongside the impulse for social reform. For many pious evangelicals and reformers, politics was a corrupt bargain. The electioneering process was rife with the dissolution engendered by alcohol consumption, and tainted by the influence peddling that could only divide communities and the republic, a potential consequence that could not have gone unrecognized by a follower of the old Federalist school such as Jay.[15] Yet there was also ambivalence. Enlightened political participation could provide the influence needed to galvanize a Christian nation, and lead it to salvation.[16] For postmillenarian abolitionists, the purifying process of emancipation was inseparable from the salvation of the nation. Politics, with its broad appeal, held the potential to be the instrument through which emancipation could be realized.

By 1840, the subject of political participation removed the true Garrisonians from this discussion, and from Jay's ire. Even as many abolitionists turned to the possibility of political activity to enact their aims, the Garrisonians were distancing themselves from political involvement. Increasingly inspired by the possibility that the practice of nonresistance was essential to the attainment of human perfection, Garrison and many of his followers removed themselves from active involvement in government through nonparticipation in the political process. Their reasoning was that the U.S. government served as a source of oppression through its sanction of force to maintain its viability. This inherent, and all too frequently misguided, threat of governmental force ran counter to the teachings of the gospel. This pattern was incompatible with the practice of pacifism required to realize true Christian enlightenment.[17] The Garrisonians insisted that slavery continued to exist within the nation because the institution was supported by the threat of force through the U.S. Constitution. Like Garrison, Jay was possessed with a healthy respect for nonviolence. His letters and pamphlets never revealed any criticism of Garrison and his followers for their practice of pacifism or nonparticipation. So while he disagreed with the Garrisonians over women, Jay sympathized with their continuing call for a moral campaign against slavery, and remained on good terms with most of them after the convention.

Alvan Stewart was another story. Jay disapproved of Stewart in no uncertain terms. Not only did Stewart's interpretation of the U.S. Constitution irritate Jay, his unconventional theories were also a clear violation of Article VI of the constitution of the AASS, which upheld the right of sovereign states to legislate in their own interest regarding slavery. Just prior to his confrontation with Stewart in the spring of 1838, Jay had written Joshua Leavitt questioning Stewart's implications that slavery was inconsistent with the sentiments expressed in the Declaration of Independence and the Constitution. For Jay any such sentiments or allusions were immaterial, and even if they existed they possessed no legal weight. What was important was whether or not the Constitution delegated power to Congress to abolish the institution. In a clear slap at Stewart's legal acumen, Jay confided to Leavitt that Stewart's argument was the "most extraordinary" he had "ever heard from a lawyer." Only a month later Jay had taken his attack a step farther in a letter to Elizur Wright, impugning Stewart's opinions as a "vile heresy."[18]

Jay continued to seethe after his open debate with Stewart, heedless of the fact that the vast majority of his peers on both sides of the issue thought that Jay had taken Stewart to the proverbial woodshed. In November, Elizur Wright wrote Jay to inform him that the executive committee of the AASS had asked him to write a letter to English Whig reformer Henry Brougham to clarify the position of American antislavery advocates on the limits of Constitutional power regarding the abolition of slavery. Jay flatly refused to comply, but not without explaining that the issue of constitutionality was becoming increasingly divisive. A noted abolitionist, whom Jay did not name, had recently castigated those of his brethren who operated under the belief that constitutional power was limited or that slave owners could be influenced by moral suasion. Such views were, in Jay's eyes, a direct violation of the AASS constitution, by which they had all sworn to abide.[19] Because of these recent actions, Jay felt that his views were no longer representative of the society. He closed saying:

> I hope, by the grace of God, to live and die; but after the experience I have had, it would not be safe, nay it would not be honest, to tell Lord Brougham or anybody else that those doctrines are believed by the members of our society: by some, and I hope by many they undoubtedly are; but we have had most painful proof that there are abolitionists with whom profession and principle are not inseparable.[20]

Jay's complaint was a consequence of the impatience many abolitionists were beginning to exhibit. Methods such as moral suasion and questioning of political candidates were neither efficient nor expeditious enough for a growing number within abolitionist ranks. Their increasing agitation led to a call for political action. Jay remained suspicious of political action, even though he had, in the case of Gilbert Horton, led the drive to petition government at the national and state level. He had also collaborated with Gerrit Smith to question the New York gubernatorial candidates about their views on slavery. And Jay was well aware that a group of upstate moderates were beginning to push for the creation of a political party by antislavery forces. One of those advocates was friend Gerrit Smith; another was Alvan Stewart. What was even more aggravating, some people were beginning to listen to Stewart and adopt his heresies. With typical drama, Garrison's *Liberator* proclaimed Stewart as "This gigantic abolitionist . . . stirring the heart of the West to its deepest foundations. He harrows the human soul with the originality of Shakespeare."[21]

To Stewart's credit, he was as committed to abolition as any of the foremost advocates of the antislavery cause. He was a tireless organizer and an effective fund raiser. Stewart and Jay parted company when the younger lawyer contended that the Constitution was a benign document created with personal liberty as its primary intent. Stewart wondered, "if slavery expired on the 4th of July 1776, how has it come down to us . . . claiming the assistance of the Constitution as its great patron?" For Stewart, abolitionists were never to make admissions that would weigh against the oppressed, something that Jay's assertion of the constitutional legality of slavery certainly did. If the intent of the Constitution was liberty, then the American people should decide at the ballot box whether or not slavery was condign.[22]

His feelings about Stewart aside, Jay had never hidden his opinions about the political involvement of abolitionists. In a letter written to the Vermont Anti-Slavery Society in 1836, Jay had admonished the members not to abandon religious for political antislavery. The removal of slavery should be sought in the "States through the voluntary action of the masters," he wrote, so there would be no danger to the Union. Should antislavery forces seek to attain their goals by forming a political party however, they would blunt their moral influence and feeling. They would then be joined by a "corrupt and selfish herd," and could inadvertently prove a danger to the stability of the republic.[23]

By the summer of 1840, abolitionists were divided into three distinct groups. They were the nonparticipatory Garrison clique, the institution-bound New York City conservatives exemplified by Jay and Lewis Tappan, and the moderate promoters of political action from New York State, led by Gerrit Smith, James Birney, and Alvan Stewart. Gerrit Smith seemed unfazed by all the internecine philosophical bloodletting, preferring instead to begin working toward the creation of the antislavery Liberty Party. While many members of the Tappan circle would eventually come to realize the necessity of political action, they initially rebuffed overtures from the upstate group to join them.[24] In July, with the angry dissension of the convention barely cooled, Smith wrote to Jay soliciting his candidacy as an abolitionist candidate for governor of New York. Jay declined the offer, replying that his "mere professions of abolitionist sentiments" did not render him a qualified candidate. The effort to forge a political party required a common cause that ignored peripheral issues and Jay believed the abolitionists did not yet possess the unity to make such an entity work; it would only serve to deepen divisions. Jay asked Smith if he, as a member of the general public, would vote for a pure abolitionist candidate whose platform ignored other issues.[25]

Unquestionably Stewart's involvement in helping to forge the new political movement contributed to Jay's reluctance. But more important, and symptomatic of Jay's conservatism, was the fact that he would not merely jettison the ideals and methods that he had adopted because they were no longer fashionable or convenient. To Jay it was of the utmost importance that abolitionists maintain the dignity of their cause; an ideal he emphasized in an address to the Young Men's Anti-Slavery Society of New York City. Jay challenged anyone who might suggest that there was any affinity between the principles of the abolitionists, which were as "fixed as the polar star, ever emanating from one high source," and those of politicians. While the abolitionists were steadfast, politicians were "fickle and wavering," their principles "so faintly exhibited that it is impossible to define them with exactness."[26] The tergiversation of politicians in the name of expediency was a grievous fault, for it had prompted those opportunists to discard the fundamental principles upon which the nation was founded.

For Jay, Whigs and Democrats alike were trampling on the most cherished beliefs to which he was heir. He stated his conviction that while both parties professed fealty to the principles of the past, "claiming to be identical in characteristics with those that preceded [sic] them," they played by very different rules. If the two national parties shared any common ground it was through their mutual rejection of the "appellation and principles of the old Federalists, whose head was Washington, the framers of our Constitution, the founders of our government." "The very name [Federalists], once so honored, is bandied between them as a term of reproach."[27] The difference between the expediency of the politicians and the principles of the abolitionists created a wide gulf between the two. "Resistance to tyranny ... and a consistent adherence to the maxim of 'equal rights,'" which all politicians espoused and failed to practice, prevented even "an approach to affinity between abolitionists and politicians."[28]

Jay then again invoked the ideological heritage that had been bequeathed to him as the son of a founding father and patriot. The consistency of the abolitionists, their "fixedness" upon their goal, ensured the "disinterestedness of their labors and the purity of their ends." The implications could not have been clearer. Politicians, "from the veriest demagogue that fawns upon the great, and blusters in the tavern," to those who sought the highest office, were "intrinsically selfish." Politicians, through their pursuit of their own interests, were unworthy of the ideological heritage they continually invoked. Conversely, the stigma of being charged with selfishness could never adhere to the abolitionists, even though the press often branded them as "incendiaries," or "fanatics." Theirs was the cause of humanity, of altruism.[29] Because of their concern for the whole of the nation, rather than the promotion of their selfish personal interests, abolitionists were the logical inheritors of the nation's republican heritage. Emancipation was the cause of the "patriot, the philanthropist, and the Christian."[30]

In both *Inquiry* and *View*, Jay had used the carrot of liberal self-interest, in conjunction with the potential for financial loss, to convince slaveholders to surrender their chattels of their own volition. That some individual gain could benefit the whole of society was contended by Mandeville and Adam Smith. The difficulty of making Jay's appeal viable lay in the fact that slavery had long ago aligned itself with politics, a fact that had been acknowledged in *View*. The concerns of politics meant the concern of party, which Jay's forebears had viewed with suspicion. And the problem with the "paltry concerns" of party, were that they originated in "self" above all.[31] The arrogance and conceit of the slaveholder rendered party and partisanship secondary to self-interest. Therein lay the classic conflict of attempting to balance commerce and virtue, the duty of the Christian with the voracity of the purse. Without realizing it, Jay was exposing the impracticality of moral suasion.

Debates over politics and principle would continue as the decade of the 1840s progressed, but other events transpired that also demanded considerable attention. After Jay and his Tappanite compatriots separated from the AASS, they had considerable difficulty stirring interest in their newly organized American and Foreign Anti-Slavery Society. *The Emancipator* no longer spoke for the old society; the journal had been transferred to the proprietorship of the New York Young Men's Anti-Slavery Society just before the AASS split. But *The Emancipator's* editor, Joshua Leavitt, was independent and combative, so Tappan and others attempted to launch a new publication dubbed the *American and Foreign Anti-Slavery Reporter.* The effort was underfunded from the start. Letters between Jay and Lewis Tappan in the fall of 1840 year express disillusionment with the inability to enlist more than 400 subscribers for the periodical.[32]

Jay had opinions as to how the business of the new society should be run. A committee of funds was created, with the purpose of determining how best to invest the contributions the society would receive. Jay told Lewis Tappan that, in his opinion, anti-slavery societies were ill-equipped to act as trustees or as "savings banks." A more edifying use for the funds would be to institute scholarships for promising young blacks. He stressed that the society should have as little as possible to do with "public meeting," especially those "for business." Too often such gatherings became forums for the airing of differences that would promote the perception that the antislavery cause was losing vitality. Jay pointedly noted that the abolitionists had already proved the maxim about "too many cooks." Difficulties aside, Jay believed that the best hopes for the revival of the cause rested with the AFASS.[33]

Even as abolitionist factions wrestled for control of the hearts and minds of their followers and fellow Americans, events continued to unfold. The *Amistad* case illustrated this clearly. Seized in Long Island Sound in June of 1839, and escorted to New London, Connecticut, by the U.S. Coast Guard, the *Amistad* was a Spanish vessel out of Havana. En route to Puerto Principe, on the northwest coast of Cuba, the slaves on board the vessel had rebelled and seized her. It was only through the exemplary efforts of Lewis Tappan and others that the slaves eventually won their freedom after a long legal battle. Jay's involvement in the case, as ever, was through his pen.[34]

In a personal letter, Jay wrote Tappan to complain that *The Emancipator* was too involved in politics to notice the *Amistad* case. The efforts of the U.S. Government, which had been aimed at keeping the matter out of the public eye while attempting to return the slaves to their Spanish masters, had been "vile." The government's intention obviously was to sacrifice the slaves for Southern sensibilities.[35] What Jay referred to was the maladroit handling of the

case by Martin Van Buren's secretary of state, Georgia slaveholder
John Forsyth.[36] For this individual, Jay reserved special vituperation in the antislavery press. John Quincy Adams, who defended
the *Amistad* slaves before the Supreme Court, noted with no small
delight in his diary that, in a recent conversation with Mr. Forsyth,
he had found him "smarting under the scourge of Judge William
Jay's comments on his conduct."[37] The final victory over the government prompted a reprinting of Jay's *View,* with an appendix
written by Joshua Leavitt. The addition took particular note of Van
Buren's executive order to send the former slaves back to Spain.
Leavitt wrote with relish that the order should be "engraved on his
[Van Buren's] tomb, to rot only with his memory."[38]

In October of 1841 another vessel, the U.S. brig *Creole,* left Rich-
mond harbor bound for New Orleans. On board were about 160
people, at least 135 of them slaves. On the evening of November 7
the slaves, led by one Madison Washington, rose up and commandeered the ship. John R. Hewell, who had been charged with the
supervision of some of the slaves, was killed in the uprising, and
several crew members were seriously wounded. At first the ship's
new masters demanded that the vessel be sailed to Liberia. Dis-
suaded from that course of action on the premise that the *Creole* did
not have enough provisions on board for such a lengthy journey,
the Bahamas became the next destination of choice. The *Creole* sailed
to Nassau, where the British authorities, under considerable local
pressure and in recognition of their own emancipation act (1833),
ultimately permitted the slaves to debark. British authorities later
returned the ship to the original crew, who promptly sailed to New
Orleans.[39]

The incident incited the outrage of the ever truculent slaveholders in Congress, who bellowed that the Nassau authorities had
deprived American citizens of their property without their consent.
In the Senate, John C. Calhoun served notice that British actions in
the *Creole* affair represented "insidious" and "presumptuous attempts to interfere with our Southern institutions." On at least three
occasions he introduced a resolution aimed at forcing the executive
branch of the government to initiate aggressive action against the
British for "the indignity" that they had "offered the American
flag." Calhoun was especially sensitive to criticism in the antislavery press that naturally weighed in on the side of the slaves and
defended their actions. He was joined in his umbrage by William
R. King of Alabama, who railed at the "miserable, contemptable

[*sic*], and wretched fanatics in our country" who were determined to "embarrass the government and invade the rights of the South."[40]

All of this placed Secretary of State Daniel Webster in a difficult position. It was diplomatically imperative that he mollify the representatives of the slave states and quiet their fulminating rhetoric. As the *Creole* debate raged, the United States wanted to define its eastern borders between Maine and Canada, and quell disturbances along the New York border where Americans were aiding Canadian rebels against Britain. Lord Ashburton would soon be arriving in the United States from Britain to hopefully negotiate a treaty regarding that and other pressing issues. Ashburton was a banker and an experienced diplomat who had served in the cabinet of Sir Robert Peel. Aside from American borders, the other issues he was to negotiate with Webster included extradition, a mutual effort to halt the slave trade, and the rights of American vessels blown off course in the Bermuda Channel.[41] Any incidents or posturing that had the potential to foster further ill-will with Britain had to be blunted. Meanwhile, Calhoun continued to cavil in the Senate that resolution of the *Creole* dispute was as important as Maine's boundary.[42] There could be no question that Southerners had real political clout, but Webster also faced potential criticism in his native Northeast if he were to appear intimidated by their threats. Webster weighed his political and diplomatic considerations, and then responded. In late January of 1842, he wrote to Edward Everett, U.S. ambassador to England, and asked him to inform Lord Aberdeen of the gravity of the *Creole* case.[43]

Webster's options were limited. Relations with Britain were being sorely tested by the *Creole* affair and American debts owed to British banking interests. Webster advised Everett to invoke comity and hospitality between nations. Comity was the essential concept that each nation, in legal intercourse with another, should recognize and respect the laws of that nation in good faith. Webster believed the United States had a right to demand indemnification for the slave property freed in Nassau. He cited the cases of three other vessels, the *Comet, Encomium,* and *Enterprise,* which had also fallen into British hands. In those instances, Lord Palmerston had stated that the claimants were entitled to compensation because they were in lawful possession of their slave property at the time of the interdiction. The passengers upon the *Creole* were Americans, Webster complained, lawfully passing from one point to another. They had only come under British jurisdiction momentarily, and then by an act of violence.[44] He argued that the former slaves, whom he dubbed "mutineers and murderers," should have been returned to the United States to stand trial. But the former slaves' return could not be seriously demanded because, by the time Webster wrote, they had been dispersed among the populations of New Providence and Jamaica, making extradition impossible. Although Americans would eventually be compensated for their lost "property," it would take all of twelve years to reach a settlement.[45]

Abolitionists published several essays examining the *Creole* affair from various viewpoints. Dr. William E. Channing, who had been Lewis Tappan's spiritual mentor, wrote a pamphlet titled *The Duty of the Free States.* An eloquent writer of poetry and prose, Channing took advantage of the incident to remind residents of the Northeast to defend their rights and resist the constant bullying of the Southern representatives. He asserted that the time had come to reunite politics and morality in America.[46] Other abolitionists defended the right of the slaves on board the *Creole* to mutiny in order to gain their freedom, even to the employment of deadly force. William Jay joined in the antislavery chorus of approval for the actions of the *Creole* slaves, and also questioned the efforts of Webster to defuse the issue with British authorities. In *The Creole Case and Mr. Webster's Despatch,* originally published and later reprinted by the *New York American,* Jay presented his objections to Webster's actions and reasoning. Here, Jay rejoined, "we have the Federal Government, putting forth and pledging all its powers to protect slavery."[47] Taking issue with Webster's invocation of comity, Jay stated that there was no precedent for the return of men who had become "free of their own act" under the "comity of nations." No extradition agreement had existed between the United States and Britain since the insertion of an article in the Jay Treaty, and that had been allowed to lapse after twelve years. Even in the recently decided *Amistad* case, the Spanish had not appealed to comity, but to a specific stipulation in a treaty between the United States and Spain.[48] Jay's argument was exhaustive and complex, but at its core was a statement of the immutability of natural law, a concept that had been upheld in the *Amistad* case.

Jay stressed that all of the legal debate that was taking place between United States and British authorities regarding the *Creole,* tended to ignore the fact that a third party was involved in these negotiations: the slaves themselves, who were subject to the laws of neither nation. Jay then unfolded his natural law defense for the slaves. He stated that no man could be subject to the law of any country without his own positive consent. That consent revealed an individual's agency in helping to craft the laws he was subjected to. Slaves had never even given their consent to American law— even by implication—and therefore were not subject to it. Because they did not remain under the rule of American law voluntarily, slaves had a right to ignore that law, and gain their freedom, when they were beyond the coercive limits of its jurisdiction. The British had, in fact, acted properly, because they could only enforce the jurisdiction of American law upon those who were subject to it.[49] As far as English law went, the slaves had committed no crime.

Like Jay's other works, the value of *The Creole Case* did not necessarily reside in its profundity, but in its immediacy. *Inquiry* was a defense of the abolitionist cause against one of its chief opponents. For modern students of the antislavery cause, that work's value lies in its exposition of moderation; the work was written in a tone that epitomizes the ideal of moral suasion. *View* does not seem truly profound until readers realize that Jay is illuminating a theory that was well known to his contemporaries, but that modern historians have claimed as their own. Far from simply accusing proslavery politicians of a "conspiracy theory," *View* was an investigation of their overt efforts. Because *The Creole Case and Mr. Webster's Despatch* deals in legal theory it might seem a departure from its antecedents, but it was not. Jay wrote *Inquiry* as proslavery mobs ravaged American cities. He wrote *View* to explain why and how the U.S. government chose to impose a gag rule on the abolitionist's right of petition, thus depriving them of their civil rights. These were works written at liminal moments in the abolitionist movement, and so was *The Creole Case.*

As a jurist, Jay was in a prime position to recognize trends and potential conflict in the law. The custom of comity that Webster cited did not merely apply to international relations; comity also applied to relationships between the individual states of the Union. The legal powers of states and nations were limited to their own borders. Recognition of the laws of other states, however, could be granted beyond territorial borders provided that recognition did not impinge upon the rights of the compliant state government and its people. By 1834, Joseph Story's *Commentaries on the Conflict of Laws* defined comity as it applied to the United States. The concept was crucial because comity determined the ability of slave owners to move about the nation freely with their property, and even reside in those states where slavery was illegal. But were those states— or nations, as in the case of Britain and the *Creole*—required to recognize the existence of a form of property that they did not sanction? Increasingly, it was being argued that they did not. Paul Finkelman has noted that comity, as it applied to slavery in the United States, had begun to break down in the 1820s. By the 1840s, comity was coming apart.[50]

In the West, the legal disintegration of comity brought conflict between proslavery forces and those whom they rightly viewed as the allies of the slaves themselves, the abolitionists. In at least one instance, these events brought a response from Jay. In June of 1841, the Ohio Supreme Court ruled that slaves brought voluntarily into the state were free under Ohio law. The judgment was a bitter pill for slave owners, many of whom traveled to Cincinnati on business and brought their slaves with them. Tensions escalated during the summer, as slaves fled to the black section of the city for sanctuary. Local businessmen anticipated a loss of trade, and the familiar irrational charges of amalgamation were once again directed toward antislavery forces. When open conflicts between blacks and whites erupted in Cincinnati on September 3, it was only a matter of time before the offices of the antislavery journal *The Philanthropist* were destroyed by a mob. The editor, Gamaliel Bailey, escaped unharmed along with his family, but the destruction was a heavy blow to a periodical already in financial difficulty.[51]

Abolitionist forces responded to Bailey's difficulties, and he received donations from Lewis Tappan, Gerrit Smith, and John Greenleaf Whittier to help replace the printing press. Jay sent a donation of fifty dollars.[52] In an accompanying letter, Jay warned that the gentlemen of Cincinnati and elsewhere, who assaulted abolitionists and their property to gain a little trade with the South were in for a rude awakening:

> Such gentlemen would do well to remember the fate of Philip Egalite. A Prince of the blood—pre-eminently a gentleman of standing and property, he thought it expedient to excite and employ mobs to advance his own selfish purposes. He succeeded in establishing a reign of terror, and was stripped of his property and led to execution by the very scoundrels upon whom he had fawned.[53]

Jay's letter was published in *The Liberator*.

William Jay's stature as a champion of the abolitionist cause was, by now, unassailable in antislavery circles regardless of their allegiance. Of course, this meant that even one as reclusive as Jay could be threatened with potential violence. Even in his hometown of Bedford, many of Jay's fellow New Yorkers found his position intolerable. David Lee Child, reformer and husband of Lydia Maria Child, toured New York and Connecticut in 1841 and made some interesting observations. While visiting Bedford, Child took shelter and food at a local inn, where he recorded the following vignette.

It appears Child was not long at his table before he overheard a conversation between his hostess and a patron who was quaffing "Santa Cruz" at a nearby table. Their talk centered on "one of our most excellent and useful anti-slavery writers," Judge Jay. Child began talking to the patron, who related that William Jay had nearly been ridden out of town on a rail for a recent antislavery speech at the Bedford Court House. The man, whom Child described as a "tall toper, in a fear-nought coat and tarpaulin hat," then revealed that while Jay was speaking, the crowd had begun to chant "nigger baby! nigger baby!" "What did they mean by that?" queried Child. The man replied that "a dead baby, as black as ink," had been sent to Jay in a mahogany box. Child observed that that was no discredit upon Jay, nor was it particularly humorous. "No," answered the stalwart, "but it was a good joke upon him [Jay] for this nigger business."[54] Such were the rewards of the abolitionist.

Even as other events demanded the attention of the attention of the antislavery forces, their political involvement at the national level grew. The Liberty Party had emerged more clearly defined, and even managed to field a presidential candidate in 1840: former Alabama slave owner James G. Birney. Differences of opinion on issues that were peripheral to slavery, such as tariffs, plagued the party, but core principles were evident. The party stood behind the U.S. Constitution as the blueprint for the redress of national maladies. From the ramparts of the law, many abolitionists believed they could battle the slavery interests that dominated the government. Once slavery was defeated, a nationwide free labor system could be adopted. The Liberty Party recognized the importance of the other reform issues, but the abolition of slavery remained the primary objective throughout its fleeting existence.[55]

The Liberty Party was able to attract abolitionists because it offered an alternative to the corruption and expediency they felt was characterized by the Whigs and Democrats. When Jay had spoken to the Young Men's Anti-Slavery Society of New York, he had forcefully characterized the abolitionist's goal as a moral one. Jay's sentiments were not unique; they resonated in many a reformist's ear. The Liberty Party was not intended to be politics as usual, but politics with purity of purpose. To this end, while some abolitionists continued to resist politicization, others began to see it as a moral duty. Such a call to action was formulated by evangelicals like Gerrit Smith to appeal to evangelicals. Elizur Wright, formerly a Garrison adherent but now a promoter of political antislavery, contended that the political involvement of the righteous could only serve to ennoble politics and humanize religion. Increasingly seen as a more practical alternative to moral suasion, political activity still represented little more than an attempt to influence public opinion and morality.[56]

Hurriedly organized, the Liberty Party's first election results were predictably dismal, or as the politically withdrawn Garrison characterized them with some satisfaction, "ludicrous and melancholy." Most political abolitionists remained committed to the Whigs in 1840, and the Birney ticket garnered a scant 7,054 votes out of more than two million cast. During the campaign, Jay had written to Lewis Tappan to express his concern over the political movement and its potential effect upon the image of the abolitionists. "I much fear that Birney's canvass will render abolitionists contemptible in the eyes of politicians, and perhaps their own." When abolitionists had previously stood on principle they had "talked loud" and gained recognition. Now, Jay feared, "we shall exhibit our real weakness."[57]

Despite Jay's reservations, 1842 found him drawn into political antislavery. Many Ohio Liberty Party partisans had become disenchanted with the lack of charisma and political sagacity displayed by Birney. Salmon P. Chase of Ohio, who would later serve as Abraham Lincoln's secretary of the treasury, began making overtures to other potential candidates. His first instincts led him to established political entities John Quincy Adams and Governor William Seward of New York. Adams declined and Chase, still burning to replace the incumbent Birney, fired off a letter to Lewis Tappan asking him to approach Seward. Again, Chase's appeals came to naught as Seward also refused the honor.[58]

Chase approached Tappan because Tappan had warmed to political abolitionism since the breakup of the AASS. Like chase, Tappan was tired of Birney, who had spouted some decidedly antidemocratic rhetoric in the wake of his defeat. Further, the Liberty Party needed abolitionist voters from other parties to defect, and the perception among many was that Birney was not flexible enough to woo voters of other affiliations. At this juncture the Ohio Liberty Party was vibrant and people with talent, among them Gamliel Bailey, whose printing press had been destroyed by the Cincinnati mob. Bailey was a recent convert to the Liberty cause.

He was attracted to its moralistic tone, even though he retained reservations about political antislavery. As late as 1839 Bailey had advocated the Whig Party as the best champion for the antislavery cause. Indeed, many Ohio Liberty men sought a Liberty-Whig alliance with its potential benefit of offering the Liberty Party greater visibility. Such a merger would not be easy to achieve however, for the Whigs saw the Liberty Party as a potential threat.[59]

But before the Liberty Party could tender any appeal to Whigs such as the Western Reserve's Joshua Giddings, the party needed to be seen as more than a regional movement. To this end, Chase realized that a more congenial alliance of the eastern and western Liberty factions could only strengthen the antislavery effort. Further, an eastern presidential candidate, one with broad appeal, would strengthen that alliance and make the Liberty Party truly national. Already spurned by Adams of Massachusetts and Seward of New York, Chase once again turned to Tappan and asked about replacing Birney with William Jay. A voracious reader and collector of antislavery materials, Chase had already read *View*. In a glowing letter to Tappan, Chase extolled Jay's virtues. He mentioned Judge Jay's "irreproachable character" and opined: "To nominate such a man would not seem like a burlesque." Beyond character Chase also believed that Jay had "sufficient" ability and a good knowledge of State affairs. Of course, Chase did not fail to notice that Jay was "connected with the revolution by his relationship to the first Chief Justice."[60]

Once again the task of playing recruiter fell to Tappan. Tappan wrote an enthusiastic letter to Jay, and enclosed an introductory letter from Chase. "I confess," Tappan told his friend, "the proceedings of the Ohio Liberty Party interest me more and more, and I feel almost induced to unite with them." He then added hopefully: "What say you?" Tappan admitted that an abolitionist candidate might never be elected to "high office." However, the voices of the Liberty Party supporters could influence the government to end all accommodation to the institution of slavery. He assured Jay that the party was national in its "principles," and that its sole purpose was to "divorce" the government from "all participation in slavery and the slave trade." Tappan asked Jay to ruminate upon the proposal and let him know his "reflections upon the subject."[61]

Throughout all of this maneuvering, Birney was well aware that a movement was afoot to unseat him. As soon as Birney had been renominated in 1841, Chase openly suggested that he step aside in favor of a more appealing candidate, preferably an antislavery

Whig. Chase's proposal must have injured Birney's pride to some extent; it had been Birney who had converted an apolitical Chase to the antislavery cause in the mid-1830s. Gamaliel Bailey was less enthusiastic than Chase about replacing the incumbent, and wrote Birney a lengthy letter outlining his feelings on the attempted draft of Jay. "I doubt not, that you would cheerfully give place to a man, whom you believed more eligible than yourself," wrote Bailey. But Bailey was not sure that a more eligible candidate existed, and did not want Birney to step down unless Birney himself felt a more qualified candidate was available. Bailey then compared Jay's strengths to those of his friend:

> Judge Jay had been named. In most respects he can claim no superiority over you—in some respects he is not so well fitted—in others, he has, I think, the advantage. I will mention the last. He is associated with the revolution, through his distinguished father. He has filled an important office, before the public for many years. He is more known to the public, as a political writer on the slavery question. He has made himself popular with the peace party, by his little tract on war. He has not rendered himself obnoxious to any class of abolitionists, having taken no active part in the division of the American A.S. Society.[62]

Judge for your self, Bailey advised. If Jay possessed adequate prudence, judgment, and self-possession—if Jay had any prospect of securing a larger vote—then Birney should "cheerfully" resign.[63]

Like Bailey, not all Liberty men yearned to remove Birney. *The Emancipator*'s editor, Joshua Leavitt, viewed Chase as a newcomer to the Liberty Party cause, and as a neophyte, Chase's attempts to dictate strategy were an affront. To boost Birney's morale, Leavitt wrote him that Chase truly had no one to name as an alternative candidate. Yes, Chase had been considering William Jay, but had "no better reason for it only that he is son of John Jay." In an interesting postscript, Leavitt added: "Alvan Stewart says, 'Tell Birney to stand his ground until he is shot down.' I shall vouch for it." Meanwhile, Elizur Wright wrote directly to Chase: "Judge Jay is good in his place, very; but he has neither courage nor scope. He was not born for all mankind but for a very select class. Knowing him perfectly as I do, I should, if he were our candidate, eat and sleep only on a hatchet lest he should fall into a fit of prudence and *disclaim* us all to death."[64] Wright's assessment was perhaps a trifle harsh, but it was not wholly unfair.

Jay was *not* for everybody. Tappan and Jay so often seemed to understand and support each other because they thought so much alike. Both men were rooted in an older political understanding of what was required to be a contributing member of American society, an ideal republican. Their devout Christianity merged with their commitment to that ideology. Men performed their Christian duty was for the love of humankind; political duty—only if required—for the elevation of the nation. Both Jay and Tappan subscribed to government led by men who could exhibit the correct disinterestedness. A proper republican possessed enough education and wealth to do his duty without needing accolades or emoluments. The example of Phillip Egalite, whom Jay had referred to in his earlier letter to Gamaliel Bailey, was a civic and Christian object lesson. Inviting the approbation of the unwashed multitudes, Egalite had surrendered to the deadly sin of pride and met his just fate.[65]

Chase's reverential references to Jay's "patriot" lineage intimate a lingering sense of deference toward the icons of the past. Lewis Tappan, in his innumerable letters, could quite comfortably summon up the familiarity to begin correspondence to his peers, "Brother Leavitt," or "Brother Weld." But even in the briefest and most inconsequential note, it was exceedingly rare that Tappan addresses his close friend Jay as anything less than the formal, "My Dear Sir." So Elizur Wright was essentially correct. The idea of a disinterested man of position and principle might appeal to some of a certain class, but what about a broad based appeal? Americans of every class were increasingly involved in politics and enjoyed the distractions it provided. Could the staid Jay compete any better than Birney, or entertain Americans in an era of "hard cider" campaigns?

There was a more elementary, pressing question to be answered. Was Jay on board as a Liberty man or not? No one could tell; signals were mixed. The conservative Judge Jay was deliberating. He had told Tappan that he appreciated the constitutional foundation of the Liberty Party, but what did Jay mean when he told Tappan that, "what little virtue there is in politicians is with the Whigs"? Those same inconsistent Whigs who, along with the Democrats, had besmirched the memory of the hallowed Federalists? All of this left the man in the crosshairs, James G. Birney, to contemplate his fate. In spite of his uncomfortable position, Birney did not squirm, but handled the entire affair with quiet dignity. He knew Jay personally,

for the two men had corresponded for years. Much of their correspondence was devoted to organizational minutiae, but there was
also a sympathetic letter from Jay when Birney had just lost his
seventeen-year-old son. The two men were on cordial terms, even
if Jay frowned upon Birney's politicking.[66]

Birney wrote to Charles Stewart and Joshua Leavitt expressing
his desire to avoid enmity at the upcoming Liberty Convention. If
Jay was anointed, if Jay was unanimously nominated, if Jay was
truly a Liberty Party man, then Birney would withdraw his name
from the ticket. Birney then delivered the following homage:

> If Judge Jay has become a Liberty party man—of which, however, I
> have heard nothing decisive—there is no one in our ranks equally
> well known, who would better represent us in our coming struggle.
> His own qualifications for any station calling for integrity and in-
> telligence are so ample, that I would not disparage them, by the
> additional one sometimes spoken of—but that ought never to be
> spoken of, by abolitionists, that he is the son of his excellent and dis-
> tinguished father.[67]

It was a remarkable testimonial from a man who refused to be
embittered by events. A statement of respect rather than deference,
which removed Jay from his father's shadow and valorized him.

In the end, Jay declined the nomination and recommended that
it go to Birney. At the 1843 Liberty Party Convention in Buffalo,
New York, Birney was renominated with Thomas Morris as his
running mate. The party also nominated Alvan Stewart to run for
governor of New York. Jay's decision to remove himself from consideration helped to avoid a potentially divisive and damaging situation. Chase took his defeat philosophically, writing to Tappan that
"the thing is as it is and we must make the best of it." At least, he
continued, Birney was "an honest man . . . and a devoted friend of
the cause." In Chase's opinion, Birney would not collect as many
voters as Jay, and certainly not as many as Adams. But Chase still
thought Birney superior to anyone the Democrats and Whigs had
to offer. "We must give him what votes we can," he sighed.[68]

At their convention, the Whig Party nominated Henry Clay as
their presidential candidate, with Theodore Frelinghuysen as his
vice presidential partner. Frelinghuysen was a former New Jersey
senator with an impressive history of involvement in Protestant
moral reform movements. He was president of the America Tract
Society, had opposed Andrew Jackson's Indian removal policies,
and was a long-standing member of the American Colonization

Society. During the campaign, Frelinghuysen had written a re-assuring letter to Joseph G. Hall of Hernando, Mississippi, deny-ing that he was an abolitionist and claiming that he never had been. Frelinghuysen vouchsafed his credentials as an "ardent friend" of the colonization society, while declaring his belief that Congress had no power to legislate against domestic slavery. The letter was made public, and appeared first in the *Louisiana Chronicle*.[69]

Jay wrote an immediate response to Frelinghuysen, reminding him of his Christian duty and advising the candidate that his posi-tion gave him a unique opportunity to do good. His previous benevolent works had stamped him as a representative of the Chris-tian, rather than the political, interests of the nation. But Jay added that Frelinghuysen had shirked his duty. The candidate's letter to Hall contained sentiments that could have been uttered by "any driver on a southern plantation," or any "common trafficker in human flesh." His disclaimer of abolitionist sympathies had been neither "honest, "manly," nor "Christian," and failed to recognize that proslavery interests viewed colonization and emancipation as a common enemy. If Frelinghuysen was the Christian he professed to be, did he not realize that slavery insulted "all the attributes of God . . . and the rights of man"? Frelinghuysen had announced "great principles" before "Temperance Societies and Sabbath Union," but needed to realize that: "Unless the principles of justice and humanity, and the precepts of our religion, are all reversed in their applications to men with dark complexions, you stultify your-self every time you open your lips on the platform of a religious society." Jay hoped that a better acquaintance with the subject of slavery would lead Frelinghuysen to proclaim in the future: "I am an abolitionist, and thank God I am!"[70]

The letter to Frelinghuysen bore no resemblance to the polite "questioning" letter on which Jay and Gerrit Smith had earlier col-laborated. In fact, it exhibited a clear tone of moral intimidation in-dicative of an increasingly confrontational Jay. But a shift in attitude did not denote a change in method, for Jay still remained commit-ted to moral suasion. And even as he considered greater political activism, Jay had penned a work that revealed his commitment to the old appeal.

Address to the Non-Slaveholders of the Slave States (1843) was exactly what the title inferred, a direct appeal to that majority of the south-ern population that did not hold human property. The style of the work was reminiscent of *View*, and appealed to the self-interest of the nonslaveholders. Jay argued that the South languished behind

the North in industry, education, population, and military preparedness. In each of these instances, Jay supplied statistics to support his claims. But there was more. Jay also believed that the
quality of Southern religion, and its ability to furnish the moral
sinew essential to the community, had been vitiated due to its association with slavery. The direct result of this connection was a
society rife with wanton violence and coincident disregard for human life. If the South suffered under moral and economic disadvan-
tages, this was surely due to the efforts of the planters, "the great
capitalists of the South," to promote their beloved institution at the
expense of all other considerations.[71]

The abolitionist press frequently appealed to the sensibilities of
Northern artisans and mechanics when attempting to stave off
antiabolitionist violence. The idea was usually an attempt to make
the laboring classes feel common cause with the antislavery forces
as opposed to those "gentlemen of property and standing" who manipulated them for their own cynical ends. More than just a fear of
the mob, these entreaties were also represented a recognition of the
growing political power of the working classes. Now Jay felt the
time for the abolitionists to ally themselves with those who were
exploited in the South: the "mean whites." In a land where the
"great mass of the laboring population" toiled under the lash, he
noted, "bodily labor" became "disreputable from the mere influence
of association." The power of the slaveholders rested upon the acquiescence of the rest of the white population in their region, and
because of this, it was in the interest of the slave power to keep the
majority of the population in ignorance. Jay cautioned the be-
nighted majority that the Southern aristocracy cared not one whit
for the lower classes. In order to remote their own interests, the
planters would not hesitate in "crushing" the industrious poor "to
the earth."[72]

The difficulty upper- and middle-class reformers had in crafting
an antislavery argument that would be palatable to a class of people
with whom they had little in common remained. But at least when
they were spared the disadvantage of having to respond to charges
of promoting amalgamation, or of seeking to disrupt the harmony
of the republic, abolitionists and reformers could craft a credible
appeal. The thrust of Jay's pamphlet was to convince nonslaveholders and small slaveholders that slavery existed by their "suf-
ferance," and could be eliminated by their "mandate." Nothing as
drastic as an uprising needed to be encouraged, nor would Jay have
suggested such a measure. But practical measures, the reclamation

of those liberties to which American citizens were entitled, would weaken slavery in his opinion. The mere reinstitution of a free press in the South, for example, would have gone a long way toward speeding the demise of slavery in a region where debated upon the subject was forbidden.[73]

Jay's *Address to the Non-Slaveholders* reveals that his recent experience with political antislavery had him thinking about the power of the ballot box. The power of the vote went beyond the tacit approval implied by common cause. Certainly Jay's call for a "mandate" of the people to depose the planters is a recognition that the lower classes, those people whose intentions were suspect, now held considerable influence. Here is a clear indication that Jay was willing to overcome his distrust of democracy, and its companion disorder, to achieve the desired goal of abolition. It is tempting to see his call to action as reciprocation. In abolitionists' eyes, the planters and their business partners to the North had long called upon the lower orders to silence the antislavery message. But there is no threat of mob violence in Jay's work. There is only the orderly participation of people empowered by their legal, constitutional rights.

Students of Southern history would find startling similarities between Jay's *Address* and a work that appeared some fourteen years later, Hinton Rowan Helper's *The Impending Crisis of the South*. Helper, too, dedicated his book to the nonslaveholding whites of the South. He remarked upon the degraded state of their labor and education, while noting the superiority of the North in industry and agriculture. Printed in 1857, Helper's work gained some notoriety in the North, and many readers interpreted it as evidence of growing antislavery sentiment in the South. Interesting because Helper, as the son of a North Carolina yeoman farmer and small slaveholder, was exactly the class of person Jay targeted in his appeal. Censorship of antislavery materials was stringent in the South, but Jay's pamphlet sold briskly in the North. Lewis Tappan wrote Jay to say he wished he had 5,000 more copies.[74]

The debate over whether or not abolitionists belonged in politics was not the only question bandied about in antislavery circles in the 1840s. Many abolitionists believed that their churches—if not giving open support to slavery—gave tacit approval to the institution. Further, churches of all denominations frequently frowned upon, or disciplined, those with dissenting viewpoints. As with politics, many abolitionists sought to remove themselves, to "come out from," the corrupting influence of institutions that were associated with slavery, or did nothing to combat the evil. Although often, and understandably, associated with the anti-institutional Garrisonians, this "come-outerism" movement actually had a broad based appeal. In 1845, Liberty Party organizer William Goodell wrote a popular pamphlet titled *Come-Outerism: The Duty of Secession From a Corrupt Church.* So too, Gerrit Smith and James G. Birney left the Presbyterian Church to form an independent, antislavery congregation.[75]

While come-outerism had a divisive effect on the Methodist and Baptist Churches in the years 1844–1845, Episcopal bishops used their considerable powers and influence to ward off any potential debate on slavery in the church. As an Episcopalian, in addition to being an officer of the AFASS and other benevolent societies, William Jay was an anomaly. In examining the religious affiliations of 502 officers of four abolition societies in the years 1833–1864, John McKivigan could only find eight Episcopalians. Jay's strong belief in the importance of institutional organizations in the promotion of good works meant that he would not be infected with come-outerism. To disengage from the church of his ancestors would have been difficult enough, but he also would have lost his voice in church politics. Thus Jay remained a member of the Episcopal Church and, as he had with Bishop Hobart, remained an unhesitating critic of the church's hierarchy and its policies.[76]

In 1846, even as many abolitionists were leaving their various churches, Jay wrote two opinions critical of the Episcopal Church and its leaders. The first was in an introduction to Samuel Wilberforce's book a *History of the Protestant Episcopal Church in America.* Wiberforce, who was in fact bishop of Oxford, had penned a work critical of the American church and its inaction on the slavery issue. Finding a publisher to furnish an American reprint of Wilberforce's work had been a protracted affair. Jay believed, in fact, that the American church had attempted to suppress the work. To Jay the efforts to stifle the offending tome revealed that Episcopal bishops and clergy were in collusion with slave owners in their attempts to "wring from the Bible a title" to their slaves. Further, through the rejection of black applicants to seminaries, and by denying the right of free black churches to participate in church conventions, the Episcopal Church had made second-class citizens of black Americans. In short, the Episcopal Church was supporting a caste system.[77]

But even as Jay defended the rights of blacks to participate in the church—his church—he felt the need to defend social structure. He needed to ensure that none of his readers confused rank, which was "sanctioned" by the Bible, with caste, which was "heathenish" in origin. Rank was "founded on condition, and usually connected with personal distinctions and acquirements." Rank may have "conferred privileges," but it was not "inconsistent with the claims of justice and humanity." Caste in America was based upon racial criteria, "irrespective" of the merits of the individuals who composed those races. Jay observed that in "Hindostan," a more pliant caste system could at least elevate or depress individuals. But in America the only effects of caste were "degradation, cruelty, and wretchedness." How interesting (and mentally gymnastic) that Jay was at once able to defend logically the social order he esteemed, while at the same time decrying a system that denied equal opportunity for advancement based upon race.[78]

That same year, Jay responded to an address delivered by the bishop of the Episcopal Church in North Carolina, L. Sillman Ives. At a convention of his diocese, Ives told of having spent a goodly part of the Lenten season in an area of the state that had received neither religious instruction nor services for the better part of the year. The bishop found the experience gratifying, and had viewed with approval the system of religious training employed on the plantations he had visited. On Good Friday he had witnessed a halt to all labor, and a "cleanly clad multitude" crowding the chapel. But the events of Easter morn prompted Ives to launch into a shimmering paean to slavery rendered benevolent through religion. His homily is no less remarkable over 100 years later:

> And when I saw on the blessed Easter morn, the master with his goodly number of servants kneeling with reverent hearts and devout thanksgivings to take the bread of life at the same altar—I could not but indulge the hope that ere long my spirit may be refreshed by such scenes in every part of my diocese; while I could not help believing that, had some of our brethren of other lands [England] been present, they would have been induced to change their wailing over imaginary suffering into the heartfelt exclamation, "Happy are the people who are in such a case; yea, blessed are the people who have the lord for their God."[79]

Ives continued that, if only his friend the bishop of Oxford (Wilberforce) could have witnessed the rustic but inspirational Easter service, then he surely would have apologized to the American church for his harsh criticism of it. How much better the Church in England would be served if it would recognize its own complicity in helping impose the factory system upon the English people.[80]

Jay considered Ives's address as the first response to Wilberforce's *Reproof of the American Church*, and Jay responded to Ives in a withering public letter. It was bad enough that many Episcopal clergymen owned slaves and benefited from their labors, Jay fumed, but at least they kept silent. They had the good sense not to reveal the discrepancy between their religion and their practice. But Ives had thrown down the "gauntlet to the whole of Christendom beyond the slave region," introduced the subject to his church councils, and regaled his convention with a portrait of the "blessedness of North Carolina slaves." Worse, Ives had sneered at fellow Christians for their "wailing" over the "imaginary" suffering of those slaves. Was Ives making a solemn declaration that "southern slavery is unattended with real actual suffering"? Jay looked askance at Ives's interpretation of the events he had witnessed. How much religious instruction had the slaves been given? If all toil had been suspended for Good Friday, was that not more out of "civility to the bishop by the masters"? Were people to suppose that during the bishop's visit, the slaves were going to "throw down their hoes" and don clean clothing to spend Good Friday "dancing, or roaming over the plantations"? No, said Jay, it was "far easier to see a large gang of slaves standing in a church, than to see the motive which brought them there."[81]

Further, Jay wanted to know what manner of Christianity the slaves learned, for it seemed to be Christianity of a "very peculiar character." Speaking of Christians, he observed that, when treated cruelly, we know "we [white Christians] suffer in violation of the precepts of our religion." What did the slave learn? That one race is privileged to turn another into "merchandise"? That God confers favors—marriage, parental relations, and the knowledge of salvation—upon one group while withholding it from the slave? That while one favored segment of humanity learns industriousness so that they might better themselves and provide for their families, the lot of the slave is ceaseless toil for the benefit of his "happier brethren"? The very inequities that could only "outrage" the moral sensibilities of the slave, were essential components of the religion he learned. Why should he give his heart to a creator that demanded his obedience to his oppressor?[82]

Jay scoffed at the idea that a slaveholder who could sell someone's mother in the marketplace, or "plough her back with the lash," should squeeze out so many tears over the inequities of the English factory system. In what was, for Jay, a surprisingly emotional plea, he concluded by asking if Christians learned to regard the least of those among them as pastors taught us to regard slaves. Should blacks be kept out of seminaries? Should black people, "however decent their deportment, be excluded from our stage-coaches, packets, and railroads"? William Jay, who had refused to hear a black minister address the AASS, was now preaching racial acceptance. Then Jay turned his attention to his fellow abolitionists. Having vented his spleen on Ives, Jay suddenly felt compelled to excoriate the come-outers. Those deluded people had understandably been dismayed by the efforts of the ministry to promote slavery and caste, but they failed to make "due allowance for the frailty of our fallen nature." They vainly believed that by removing themselves from the "restraints of ecclesiastical organizations, they might partake of the benign impulses of Christianity" more freely. But by turning their backs upon the "appointed means of grace," they had instead made a "shipwreck of their faith."[83]

It was an odd—not to mention totally out of context—conclusion to Jay's impassioned supplication on behalf of the enslaved. Once again on the threshold of a more radical commitment, Jay balked and defended the order he cherished. The church, his church, might promote misery and its clergy might be deceivers, but the institution was still the source of saving grace, and those who believed otherwise were misguided. Likewise, politicians might prate and greedily promote themselves at the expense of the nation's honor, but that did not mean that the system that created them was evil. The social order, the institutions upon which it rested, had core values that were sacrosanct and could not be corrupted. Jay repeatedly defended society and its institutions, even as he strove to alter aspects of its more by exposing inherent injustices. Apparently there was nothing that could shake Jay's faith. Or was there?

The decade of the 1840s was tumultuous, and Jay's reforming efforts were necessarily diverse. While his antislavery remained of the utmost importance, Jay began an attempt to help the world realize the most difficult reform of all: the peaceful resolution of disputes among nations. Although the decade began in promise, events loomed upon the horizon that would make it difficult for Jay to maintain his optimistic demeanor. Those events, particularly the war with Mexico, were going to lead Jay in some surprising directions.

4

"On the Altar of Moloch"

Free institutions are called for in expectation that they will lighten
the public burdens; but in vain will nations seek for prosperity in
political revolutions so long as they trust to the sword for peace and
security.

—William Jay, *War and Peace*, 1842

Although the antislavery campaign was always of paramount importance to Jay, he continued to devote himself to other reform efforts. In the early 1840s, Jay found himself increasingly involved in
the American Peace Society (APS). Centered in the northeast, the APS
adopted its constitution on May 8, 1828, in New York City. The association moved its operations to Hartford, Connecticut, in 1835, and
then to Boston in 1837, where it remained throughout Jay's lifetime.
The APS attracted a constellation of luminaries to promote its agenda.
Among the earliest members were Dr. William E. Channing, Josiah
Quincy, and Lewis Tappan. By the early 1840s the organization could
boast the support of Gerrit Smith, poet John Greenleaf Whittier,
future U.S. senator Charles Sumner, and William Jay.

Like other reform movements, the APS was born of an impetus
to direct religious energies into tangible social improvement. The
peace movement was especially attractive to the urban middle class

of the Northeast, and that is indeed where the organization maintained its greatest strength. In the years following the War of 1812,
the movement gained momentum, spawning many small, local efforts such as David Low Dodge's New York Peace Society (NYPS),
founded in 1815. But as with other noncentralized benevolent
societies, the efforts of these disjointed organizations lacked cohe-
sion and frequently broke down into intramural bickering.[1]

Enter William Ladd. A graduate of Harvard and a wealthy sea
captain from Minot, Maine, Ladd envisioned a national peace society as early as 1826. Combining unlimited enthusiasm with tireless organizing effort, Ladd managed to have the New England area
peace societies united behind him by 1827, and the APS formed by
1828. The society became increasingly popular with reformers because it appealed to Christian millennial sensibilities that regarded
the attainment of world peace as a triumph of Christianity. To best
achieve this glorious goal, many in the organization suggested
spreading their arms wide and receiving "into communion all who
seek to abolish war." These open admission standards would per-
mit politicians to take their place as society members alongside
abolitionists, and would also sow the seeds of dissension over a
doctrinal issue considered by many pacifists to be of the utmost
importance.[2]

The controversy over the legitimacy of defensive warfare had divided peace advocates before the APS had even been formed. The
dispute was not only philosophical, but also—as was often the
case—regional. One group, best represented by NYPS founder
David Low Dodge, argued that war, even in self-defense, was contrary to scripture, and that Christians needed to adopt a more
"lamblike" demeanor to realize would peace. Another group, represented by the Massachusetts Peace Society (MPS) leadership of
William E. Channing and Josiah Quincy, realized that the majority
of the American public was not yet prepared to "turn the other
cheek" in submission to aggression. They sought to mute the debate over the issue of defensive war, so that a national peace effort
might engender wider popular appeal. To this end the Declaration
of Sentiments of American Peace Society did not address the issue
of defensive warfare.[3] The decision to shelve debate on the issue
angered one member of the society in particular: William Lloyd
Garrison.

Garrison, along with his father-in-law, George Benson, was an
early member of the APS. But by 1838, Garrison's increasingly
nonresistant beliefs clashed with the all-inclusive approach of the

society. Garrison sought to broaden the social agenda of the APS, and confront issues that he felt the society had avoided in its circumspection. The dissentient Garrison's mind, ever febrile in its intensity, conjured up a plethora of auxiliary issues that he claimed cried out for immediate discussion. He argued that standing armies, conscientious objection, and the rejection of capital punishment all needed to be addressed before the society could ever launch a united peace effort. A rupture was inevitable. In September of 1838, two years before the New York antislavery factions divided from the AASS, Garrison and several hundred of his faithful met in Boston to form the New England Non-Resistance Society (NENRS).[4]

The purpose of recounting these events is not to belabor the point that dissension was rampant in antebellum reform societies; that is apparent. Expediency and principle grappled eternally in the effort to impress upon the American public the pressing need for reform. But there was also the fundamental issue of whether to disengage from American institutions or work within them. Garrison and his fellow members of the NENRS viewed themselves as radical pacifists, and thought the APS too timid to address controversial issues. Members of the NENRS vowed to refuse service in militias. They would never serve in offices that enforced penal laws, nor would they vote for public officials who might exercise force as a component of their authority.[5] For Channing and others, the court of public opinion was the best vehicle by which they could influence the very structures Garrison rejected. Public opinion could sway politicians, and political cooperation was essential to the creation of an international system destined to adjudicate disputes among nations.

The APS strove to promote would peace through the voluntary cooperation of Christian nations. The best way to attain this desired unity was through the creation of a "Congress of Nations," and initially the society's efforts were devoted to seeking ways to make such a body a reality. In 1833 the APS sponsored a contest soliciting essays that would outline workable plans for the creation of such a congress. The society appointed two committees to select the winning essay, and among the notable personages chosen to select the winner were William Wirt, John Quincy Adams, Daniel Webster, and William Ladd himself. Forty participants submitted essays to the society, which then published the five best works. At the behest of the society, Ladd then took the best elements of the unpublished dissertations and amalgamated them into his own, *An Essay on the Congress of Nations*.[6]

Although Ladd borrowed extensively from the submissions, he could claim some exclusive intellectual property as a result of his task. While reviewing the essays, Ladd formulated an original plan that divided any proposed congress into a tripartite body with independent functions. The first element provided a diplomatic contingent, and would be a congress of ambassadors filled by the representatives of those "Christian" nations that chose to furnish them. The second branch would be a court of nations charged with adjudicating disputes. These two bodies would respectively act as the legislative and judiciary branches of government. The most novel branch of government was that of the executive. That office would not be filled by an individual, but would be provided by public opinion, which Ladd felt could best guide the efforts of the congress.[7] Ladd's essay was published in 1840, but he died a year afterward. His efforts to create and maintain a national peace society had been little short of Herculean, and the strain extracted a heavy toll. Over the span of fourteen years he had annually traveled hundreds of miles on speaking engagements, raised funds, edited the society's journal, *The Calumet,* and wrote for other newspapers and periodicals. All of that in spite of steadily declining health and bouts of temporary paralysis. Ladd had been elected president of the APS in 1838; upon his death he was replaced by Samuel E. Coues of New Hampshire.[8] The expiration of the society's founder did not slow its efforts.

Jay became vice president of the society in 1842. He, too, had been working on a plan for the promotion of world peace, and in that same year introduced his plan in a slim volume titled *War and Peace.* Jay approved of the idea of a Congress of Nations in principal. After all, "extensive national alliances for the prosecution of war" had been formed, why not alliances for the "preservation" of peace? Implementing the plan for such a congress would take time, however; public opinion would have to be enlightened and directed, and diplomatic guarantees and treaties drawn. Europe, with its history of incessant warfare, would benefit tremendously from the creation of a mediating congress. But could the nations of that continent be expected to cease their constant conflict simply because a call for "universal peace" went forth? No, a practical, workable framework for peace required a plan that could be implemented immediately, and without protracted negotiations.[9]

Jay opened *War and Peace* by informing his readers that they lived in an age of moral revolution, an age when a few "obscure Quakers could set events in motion which would result in the abolition of slavery in the British Empire." Similarly, temperance societies had emerged, and fought the good fight to free the world's societies from the influence of the "fell destroyer" alcohol. True, human nature remained unchanged by these events; but even if immutable, the "powers" of human nature could be "developed and directed," and its self-destructive "propensities controlled by the influence of reason and religion." While these heady moral victories were reason for optimism, Jay cautioned that there was yet another villain that needed to be confronted. War, the "remorseless tyrant," still extended "his bloody scepter over the nations of the earth."[10]

But mere rhetoric was insufficient to prepare Jay's audience for the task at hand. Before the court of public opinion could deliver a verdict against warfare, it had to be made aware of the cost of war in both human and monetary terms. "He is a superficial inquirer," said Jay, who "in investigating the evils of war, confines his observation to the scenes and consequences of actual hostility." War was pervasive; its influence was felt at all times and in all places. Even as the United States rested at peace, the nation was prepared for war. Militias stood ready, military schools produced officers trained in carnage, and the navy patrolled the oceans. How many millions of dollars were subtracted from America's "annual labors" in anticipation of future conflicts, how much time was thus squandered and sacrificed "on the altar of Moloch"?[11]

Jay's then launched his disquisition into a compulsory exposition and comparison of statistics punctuated by biblical references. He presented a comparison of national revenue expenditures for 1838. In that year the total revenue of the United States was $24,309,299; of that figure, payments for maintenance of the navy amounted to $6,403,551. Total military expenditures, including pensions, came to $12,665,210, for a combined total of $19,068,761, or 78¢ of every total revenue dollar! America's allocation for military adventure was far more lavish than any European nation expended that same year. But of course, Jay noted with stinging sarcasm, in 1838 the United States was at war with the Seminoles in Florida. The nation was therefore compelled to "expend millions" to drive "from the Peninsula a few hundred Indians, that they might no longer harbor fugitive slaves from the plantations of Georgia and Alabama."[12]

For Jay, war and the abominable institution of slavery were inextricably linked. War created a situation where the rights of the people had to be subsumed to the will of the ruler (or dictator) in order to prosecute the conflict more efficiently: "Civil liberty requires the substitution of laws for the will of the ruler; but in war, the will of the ruler and his subordinates becomes the source of legitimate authority. *Salus populi* is acknowledged as the *suprema lex;* and the bulwarks erected around the civil rights of the citizen are leveled on the proclamation of martial law."[13] Two forms of slavery therefore existed in the world according to Jay; the personal slavery of the bondman and the political slavery that wars imposed upon the citizens of belligerent nations. In order to realize its full potential, humankind had to be liberated from the physical and moral constraints that the horrors of war imposed.[14]

The events surrounding the ill-fated brig *Creole* were transpiring even as Jay wrote, and he used those events to buttress his argument. Recounting the tale, Jay noted the truculent behavior of Southern congressional delegates and how their irrational passion had led Britain and the United States to the brink of war. Jay then turned to a lengthy reassessment of European wars and their cost, lavishing special attention on the Napoleonic contests between Britain and France. There was a paradox at work here. Military preparedness, designed to enhance a nation's security, could not guarantee a nation's peace. Military power could not disseminate virtue, education, or freedom. Those nations best prepared for war and gifted in the martial arts were those who invariably suffered the greatest from war's consequences—"folly, cruelty, and wickedness"—but what could be done to prevent its reoccurrence?[15] Jay believed that war was incompatible with Christian virtue and teachings, and humanity could not sit by and await the coming of the millennial prophecy. The "prevalence of Christian principles" exhibited by so many nations of the earth, must act to eliminate war. Jay believed that the time to begin the experiment was propitious, because Christianity was diffusing its influence throughout the world. Soon the sins of slavery, intemperance, and all manner of crime would be banished from the face of the earth. With such wondrous work afoot, was it unreasonable to believe that the forces of Christianity and philanthropy could not mitigate or conquer war?[16]

In the midst of describing the lunacy of war, Jay found reason for optimism. The question that remained to be answered was: Which of the world's nations was so altruistic and infused with Christian spirit that it would hoist the standard and lead the way toward world peace? Because it had been the first to abolish the slave trade, because it had taken the lead in convincing men of the dangers of liquor consumption, Jay felt the honor should fall to the United States. The American "republic" was at peace with the world, and its extended territory and expansive commerce favored the United States as a world leader. No nation had "less reason to covet the possessions of others, or to apprehend the loss of her own." The world watched America, and it was "the first of the nations of the earth by whom the sword is to be sheathed, to be drawn no more."[17]

As Jay wrote *War and Peace,* two visions of an American mission were gaining distinct form. Both visions had some of their strongest proponents in the northeast. John O'Sullivan, editor of the *Democratic Review* and later the *New York Morning News,* promoted one image. O'Sullivan's concept was continentalist in application, and remains known as "Manifest Destiny." As America continued to spread westward, many in the press and in Congress could envision an American Colossus standing astride the North American Continent. New territories existed for Americans to "subdue and fertilize," new races (once subdued themselves) would be "civilized." In O'Sullivan's exuberant racist vision, the "white race had received the divine command, to subdue and replenish the earth." Those races that resisted the joys of white civilization faced certain "extinction."[18]

Jay too had a mission for America. But while O'Sullivan's vision was jingoistic and militant, Jay's was pacifistic and millenarian. Like O'Sullivan, Jay too had been to Pisgah, but he had viewed a much different Promised Land from the heights. For Jay and many evangelicals, the beacon of Christian reform emanated from America, and it was in an enlightened, pious America that the Millennium would begin. America furnished a standard of piety for the rest of the world. The moral influence of America's shining example would radiate outward to alter the course of international events. Reverend Harvey Miller believed that those individuals who immigrated to America could not help but become converts to, and disciples of, the blessed American mission. For Miller the very presence of those immigrants provided "a gathering of nations within our borders," and from that gathering "a reflex influence shall go out from this land to bless the nations of the earth."[19] Ralph Waldo Emerson expressed similar sentiments in his 1838 *Address On War:*

> Not in an obscure corner, not in a feudal Europe, not in an antiquated appendage where no onward step can be taken without rebellion, is this seed of benevolence laid in the furrow, with tears of hope; but in this broad America of God and man, where the forest is only now

falling, or yet to fall, and the green earth opened up to the inundation of emigrant men from all quarters of oppression and guilt; here, where not a family, not a few men, but mankind, shall say what shall be; here we ask, Shall it be War, or shall it be peace?[20]

Emerson's passage reveals his belief in the superiority of America, a land recently wrested from nature but eminently progressive and suited to lead. The verdant hills of this lush, new Canaan could provide balm for a battered mankind, and held the hope of the world.

The centerpiece of Jay's peace plan called for stipulated arbitration. Stipulated arbitration required the appointment of a neutral nation, by mutual consent of contracting nations, to act as a mediator in resolving differences between those nations. Jay believed that the plan could be affected immediately, and that a mediating nation could be appointed in all future treaties between belligerents. But the plan did not need to be restricted to warring nations. Jay suggested that no nation enjoyed such harmonious relations with the United States as its "first and ancient ally, France." What if, in their next treaty, the United States and France agreed to name a friendly power to adjudicate any future disputes that might arise between the two? Naturally both parties would have to resolve that they would not resort to arms, and would abide by the decision of the appointed power.[21]

Jay defended his call for stipulated arbitration from both a Christian and political standpoint. He felt his proposal was in accord with the precepts of Christian virtue, for Jesus proclaimed: "Blessed are the peacemakers, for they shall be called the children of God." But even though Jay believed that the age was "propitious to the enterprise," and "open to the reception of new truths," he was also realistic enough to realize that Biblical incantations alone would not provide sufficient motivation. How could humankind be induced to tread the path toward righteousness? Like William Ladd before him, Jay did not believe governments could be trusted to take the lead; the appeal needed to be made directly to the citizens of the world. Moral suasion could influence public opinion, and the tools to accomplish the task were readily available through "voluntary associations, the pulpit, and the press." "Let the friends of peace," Jay continued, "concentrate their exertions in peace societies . . . and call upon their hearers to engage in this blessed work." Present the world's rulers with petitions from their subjects, and convince the press to portray the horrors of war unflinchingly.[22]

Having hopefully convinced his audience of the Christian virtue of his plan, Jay defended its practicality. To those individuals who would condemn his plan as "visionary and impossible," he replied that it was not. The plan "violated no principle of human nature," and required no adjustment in the "passions and prejudices of mankind." The proposal was based upon past national policy experience, and immediately adaptable to the current "state of civilized society." Further, and perhaps most important for Jay, the plan was not only "consistent with the precepts of Christianity," but "also in accordance with the selfish dictates of worldly policy."[23]

What were the sources of Jay's peace plan? From where did the idea of stipulated arbitration emerge? Many of Jay's peers, as well as some modern historians, have pointed to John Jay as the source of William's inspiration. Richard Cobden, the British member of Parliament who promoted William Jay's plan to the House of Commons, noted precedents in the Jay Treaty of 1794. Historian and chronicler of the American peace movement Merle Curti has also remarked on the influence John Jay's diplomatic work had upon his son.[24] William had an intimate knowledge of John Jay's treaty, because he had defended it fiercely and effectively in his biography of his father. However, to cite the Jay Treaty as the sole source of William's inspiration diminishes the originality of his idea.

Arbitration appeared in the Jay Treaty in Articles 6 and 7. John Jay proposed it in order to rule upon questions of pre–Revolutionary War debts owed British merchants, and on questions of captures and confiscations that had occurred during the conflict, usually involving American merchant vessels. In accordance with those articles, the United States and Great Britain created two attendant commissions to overhear complaints. Both sides deemed this mediation far less prejudicial and—in the case of captures and confiscations by the British Navy—more expedient than the long, drawn out procedures of Admiralty courts. English merchants directed their appeals through American courts, which referred them to the American commission. The U.S. government agreed to pay debts to businessmen validated by the commission. Both panels were composed of five commissioners, with two appointed by each side, and one agreed upon. According to the treaty, arbitrators were to rule according to the principles of "justice, equity, and the law of nations."

The commission on damages to American shipping convened in London in 1796. The commission on debts owed English merchants was convened in Philadelphia in 1797. How well the system worked is open to question, although both sides received cash settlements. When the commission on confiscated debts met in 1797, one of the English appointees was a Mr. MacDonald. McDonald had the quaint habit of haranguing the commission with opinions critical of the United States. In one incident, he introduced a resolution declaring that the American colonies had been in a state of rebellion from 1776–1783, and had not been independent states as claimed by the Declaration of Independence. The American commissioners stormed out.[25]

Shortcomings aside, the Jay Treaty furnished a useful precedent for the viability of arbitration as a diplomatic tool. But proving that it exerted any special influence on the plan William Jay outlined in *War and Peace* is difficult. Although he pointed to several historical examples of stipulated arbitration, William Jay never referred to, or examined, the Jay Treaty in any depth in his work. He cited the intervention of the Russian emperor in bringing the United States and Great Britain together to negotiate the Treaty of Ghent, which ended the War of 1812. He also mentioned, without much analysis, the appointment of William I, king of the Netherlands, to help resolve the Maine boundary dispute as a result of that same treaty. In this instance the results were hardly inspiring. William I was unable to find the boundary in dispute, and essentially told the two nations to resolve their differences among themselves. Jay also referred to the more recent involvement of the king of Prussia in forming a commission to arbitrate American claims against Mexico following the Texas war for independence.[26] But these minor interventions hardly served as ringing endorsements for the practicality of arbitration. Jay could not admit it, but the history of stipulated arbitration was obviously short and flawed. Such minor details seldom discouraged reformers and true believers.

One work that Jay referred to while crafting his argument was the work of eighteenth-century Swiss jurist and author Emmerich de Vattel. Vattel's *Law of Nations* was a work that Jay found sympathetic to his philosophy. The passage Jay quoted, that "arbitration is a method very reasonable, very conformable to the law of nature," was an assessment that supported Jay's beliefs. The quote did not, however, reveal the depth of philosophical affinity between Jay's views and those of Vattel. Like Hugo Grotius and Jean Jacques Burlamaqui, Vattel had attempted to find common legal principles for a Europe divided between Catholic and Protestant states. Vattel believed that all laws had their origins with man in the state of nature. Because nations were formed of men, the resolutions and laws of nations were created by men. Therefore, nations were subject to the same laws of nature as men. This was what Grotius had referred to as the "international law of nations." The laws of those nations varied from state to state as they would from individual to individual. But society itself became a moral entity—a body politic—upon the adoption of the codes of its individual members. The body politic was therefore a reflection of the morality of the people who comprised it. Vattel was an antecedent, an example of the mutual responsibility preached by republicans, evangelicals, and reformers, but leavened with enough individual agency to make the principles palatable.[27]

States, like their citizens, were perfectly free to do right or wrong. Even though individual nations were endowed with the agency of choice, Vattel stressed—in a sentiment that Jay would have assuredly applauded—that virtuous behavior was the "most certain road to prosperity and happiness." There were other concordances: when Jay had argued for the rights of the slaves on board the *Creole* to free themselves, he echoed Vattel. Vattel clearly asserted that, because men were free by nature, they could not lose their freedom without their consent. John Locke, whose philosophy is often credited with having been influential in defining the arguments that led to the American Revolution, had also linked slavery and warfare. In his *Two Treatises on Government*, Locke concluded that when one man attempted to put another under his absolute power, then a state of war must necessarily exist between them. The arguments that American colonists found so compelling in their struggle to overthrow a corrupt and despotic Parliament were also used by the abolitionists in their war against slavery. So too, the linkage between war, slavery, and the suppression of humankind's ability to realize its most elevated aspirations was plain.[28]

Of course the concept of natural law was not unique to Vattel, or Jay, and the political philosophers who had linked slavery and warfare were legion. For a goodly portion of literate Americans, the arguments of those philosophers, and the emotions they evoked, were familiar and readily accessible as part of their personal intellectual investigations. Certainly John C. Calhoun could understand Jay's arguments, even if he did not subscribe to them or admit their justice. *War and Peace* was tightly focused. It was the art of the broad-based appeal directed at the court of public opinion of which Ladd had spoken. To this end the work was never purposefully abstruse. If Jay descanted upon Cicero or Vattel, he immediately supported their observations with quotes from unimpeachable American sources such as Franklin or Jefferson.[29]

In 1841, Joseph Sturge toured the United States. The English industrialist and Quaker abolitionist had been instrumental in cataloging the abuses of the apprenticeship system that supplanted slavery in the British West Indies.[30] Sturge was also extremely active in the cause of promoting peace, having founded the Birmingham Peace Auxiliary in 1819. At the time of his American tour, Sturge was serving as president of the London Peace Society, and was acquainted with Jay through the earlier formation of the American and Foreign Anti-Slavery Society (AFASS). The two men dined at Jay's Bedford home in May of that year, and Jay presented Sturge with a portion of the manuscript outlining his peace plan. Sturge was favorably impressed, and offered to get the entire work published and distributed in England, an offer that Jay gratefully accepted. Later that summer, Sturge met with members of the American Peace Society in Boston, and suggested that a convention should be staged in London for the free exchange of ideas on how best to promote world peace.[31]

When *War and Peace* appeared, it converted many adherents away from Ladd's idea of a Court and Congress of Nations. Even those who remained unconvinced of the efficacy of stipulated arbitration believed that its implementation might provide a step toward the ultimate creation of a Congress of Nations, and therefore promoted its adoption. Beginning in 1843, with the first international peace congress in London, stipulated arbitration was promoted as either the panacea for war, or as a tool that could ultimately result in the formation of a Congress of Nations. Jay was unable to attend that first peace congress, but Lewis Tappan did, and he promoted Jay's little work assiduously.[32]

As a member of a delegation sent from the London peace convention, Tappan met with British prime minister Robert Peel and King Leopold of Belgium. Upon meeting Leopold, Tappan presented him with a copy of *War and Peace* that bore the following inscription: "Presented to His Majesty Leopold the 1st King of the Belgians by Lewis Tappan of New York, U.S.A. July 5th, 1843." For his part, Leopold assured Tappan that he would read Jay's work "attentively," and Tappan breathlessly took the monarch at his word. "You may, I think, depend upon King Leopold's promise about reading your essay," he reported back to Jay. "He seemed sincere. Ministers of the crown are more apt to be insincere than their royal masters." Still, Tappan fretted that he had only been able to present Leopold with a pamphlet, for that "looked rather shabby." The New Yorker did atone for his perceived breach of protocol, however, by making the king "a low bow" upon presenting him with the work.[33]

Jay probably enjoyed Tappan's unintentionally humorous description of his royal encounter. In fact, he needed an infusion of good humor, because apart from the distractions of his crusading, 1843 was a difficult year for him. On a personal level, Jay's brother Peter died in February. The eldest of the Jay siblings, twelve years William's senior, Peter had died of what one obituary described as an "affection of the lungs."[34] That summer, tragedy struck the Jay family again when William's grandson John died. But there were other concerns. The winds of change were wafting through the ever agitated realm of New York politics, and Jay would be a victim of the subsequent maneuvering.[35]

In June, Jay was removed from his judgeship in what antislavery newspapers termed a blatantly proslavery reaction to Jay's abolitionist efforts.[36] William C. Bouck had been elected governor. New York State politics were in transition; Martin Van Buren's Albany Regency, which had directed the fortunes of the Democratic Party in New York for some twenty years, was disintegrating. But even though Bouck was himself a Democrat, and had been elected by a huge majority, he failed to take advantage of his mandate. Unity in the Democratic Party evaporated soon after the gubernatorial election, and Bouck's removal of Jay was an attempt at conciliation with the proslavery wing of his own party. The governor was remarkable for his unrestrained nepotism and distribution of political favors even in a time when such practices were the norm; Jay's seat may have provided an attractive favor. The *Emancipator and Free American* excoriated Bouck and his pliant legislature for their act of "infamy," in removing one of the "wisest judges and worthiest of men."[37] Later, Jay wrote a mild letter of thanks to the paper for their defense in his behalf. He also thanked those citizens he had served and offered a bit of reflection. He mused that he had always avoided party politics, not only because the two major parties were so corrupt, but also because he felt it unethical for a judge in the proper execution of his duties to be so involved.[38] In a letter to Merritt Mitchell, however, Jay was less restrained. He declared that his removal "illustrated one of the numberless, accursed, influences of slavery." He had long fought against slavery, and he swore that "the leisure Governor Bouck has given me, shall be faithfully devoted to the prosecution of the [continuing] warfare."[39]

Jay took advantage of the "leisure" Bouck gave him in other ways also. His proscription left him free to sail to Europe in November, and then move on to tour Egypt. Prior to Jay's departure, the ever effusive Tappan sent him a London itinerary recommending a boarding house, giving the addresses of several shops, and the names of those who could prove helpful. Tappan also included letters—not an uncommon practice in an era of indifferent postal service—for Jay to deliver to Joseph Sturge and other English reformers. Knowing that Jay would sail from England to Egypt, Tappan expressed the hope that he would do his part to spread the antislavery gospel in the Mediterranean. He closed his letter: "I rely on your taking to Malta" copies of "your *Inquiry* [and] *View* to present to the heathen there." Tappan also noted that he was sending along his own offering of a "few pamphlets" for distribution.[40]

Ostensibly Jay made the journey to improve his health, but the first part of the trip did not have a salutary effect. His ship, the *Victoria*, was overtaken by stormy weather accompanied by heavy gales. Jay complained that the violent rocking of the ship deprived him of sleep and had been the cause of severe bruises upon his body. Still, he had to confess that his lungs felt better, and he did display good recuperative powers. Arriving in London on November 22, he addressed a meeting of the British and Foreign Anti-Slavery Society the next day.[41] Jay remained overseas with his wife Augusta and his daughters until the summer of 1844. While he was enjoying his sojourn and rubbing elbows with his fellow reformers across the Atlantic, events in the United States advanced the controversies between pro- and antislavery forces to a still higher level. As these events unfolded, they only served to further convince Jay that the bond between warfare and slavery was inviole.

In 1837 the newly independent nation of Texas had been formally recognized by the U.S. government, but the new republic's subsequent appeals for annexation were rebuffed. The issue did not lie dormant, however; proslavery forces viewed annexation as an opportunity to protect and expand the institution of slavery. Antislavery forces also perceived annexation as a chance for proponents of slavery to expand their political influence. For them, annexation could only lead to war with Mexico or England, and culminate in the partition of the Union. Both sides crafted their arguments and hardened their positions until 1843, when the administration of John Tyler openly sought congressional approval and support for annexation.[42] Now the confrontation between the two sides intensified.

The issue of Texas annexation is often portrayed as yet another event that exacerbated and defined sectional differences along the road to the Civil War. But the dispute over Texas entailed far more than a debate between regional factions within the United States. The question was complicated by foreign policy issues, particularly in matters that concerned Mexico and Great Britain. After its "war for independence," the newly emerged nation of Texas was thinly populated and destitute. In the words of one rather arrogant American agent, the fledgling nation's security depended, "more upon the weakness and imbecility of her enemy [Mexico] as upon her own strength." Texas could also be thankful that Mexico was distracted by its relationship with Great Britain. Since 1820, Mexican governments had received large infusions of British credit, upon which they later defaulted. Mexico was also beholden to the British because British capital and expertise propped up the ailing Mexican mining industry. After Texas's independence, the British believed that annexation of the new state by the American government might be inimical to British interests. Owing to the large scale of its investment in Mexico, Britain wanted to be sure its capital was secure and its commercial advantages were maintained. The unfettered growth of an emerging American empire could only serve to slow British economic expansion in the Western Hemisphere. But Britain also feared that annexation would lead to the perpetuation of slavery in Texas, and that was something to be avoided if possible.[43]

Britain itself had profited greatly from the slave trade. But between 1806 and 1807, the British put the slow squeeze on slave trading. They first made it illegal for Britons to trade in slaves with other nations, and then abolished the traffic within the empire. In subsequent treaties with other nations, Britain made sure to add clauses whereby the signers agreed to end their own slave trading. This tactic worked well with Germany and Austria, but as was shown with the *Amistad*, some nations proved less than enthusiastic about enforcing their end of the bargain. With the religious fervor that only a convert can display, Britain set about enforcing its own rules. Britain could. Blessed with a powerful navy, the nation dispatched zealous Atlantic slave squadrons to rescue Africans from slave ships and transport them to Sierra Leone. By 1834, slavery itself had been legislated out of existence within the empire, and an apprenticeship system set in place to accustom the former slaves to civilization.[44]

By 1843 most Americans suspected British intentions; Anglophobia reigned. No matter where one resided, there seemed to be an issue that brought British claims into direct conflict with the interests of an expanding America. In the Northeast, the Webster-Ashburton Treaty had only recently resolved the Maine border dispute, many Americans felt shamefully. To the northwest, troubles with the borders of the Oregon Territory loomed. Slave owners of the southeast and their allies also believed that they had reason to view British intentions with a jaundiced eye. Britain may have purchased large quantities of southern cotton, but it was decidedly unfriendly to the means of production. Britain had the unsettling habit of freeing slaves on board American coastal traders that might be blown off course and into the ports of her majesty's possessions.[45] In the case of the *Creole* they had even freed slaves from a vessel that had been commandeered by the slaves themselves. In 1842, Texas suggested that the United States, Great Britain, and France serve as intermediaries to broker a deal that would secure Texas's borders from Mexican harassment. The idea had fallen through but, in the spring of 1843 Britain offered to use its good relations with Texas and Mexico to help negotiate an agreement. Now rumors spread, hinting that Britain planned to extract an unthinkable concession from Texas as part of the cost for its intervention. If Britain could lure the financially strapped republic into a deal by using lucrative commercial incentives, then Britain might demand that Texas abolish slavery as part of the bargain. The South and slavery would then be confined, cut off from westward expansion. Equally disconcerting was the fact that a free and independent Texas west of the Mississippi would create a vacuum into which slaves would be encouraged to escape.[46]

Most of the allegations about purported British intentions in Texas were spread by an agent of the Tyler administration in London, Duff Green. Green was the Maryland-born editor of the pro-Calhoun *United States Telegraph.* An ardent racist who had invested heavily in Texas bonds and Missouri lands, Green exposed British designs in a letter to Secretary of State Abel Upshur. Through the dissemination of this information, Green intended to rouse anti-British sentiment, and create support in America for annexation. Green's actions could be attributed to a wider pattern of southern mendacity designed to control events and advance their proslavery agenda.[47] In fact, there was at least a kernel of truth to Green's allegations.

In the summer of 1843, when Lewis Tappan traveled to London attend the peace convention, he had not gone alone. Nor had he gone there merely to genuflect before royalty and promote Jay's book. Tappan was accompanied by Stephen Pearl Andrews, a

Massachusetts-born lawyer who had earlier migrated to Texas. Once there, Andrews's antislavery convictions made him an unwelcome eccentric in the Lone Star Republic, so he fled to New York with a plan that he presented to Tappan. The plan began with Tappan introducing Andrews to important abolitionists in London. Once presented, Andrews planned to work with the British abolitionists, and approach their government with a plan to buy out Texans' interests in keeping their slaves. The idea was for British investors to buy up large tracts of Texas's readily available land. The proceeds from those sales could then be used by the nearly bankrupt nation to purchase all slave property. Once freed from the yoke of slavery, Texas could convert to free labor. The plan was typically visionary, and the British ministers declined the honor of suggesting it to the Texas government. Still, the efforts of the antislavery interests to prompt English involvement in Texas remained operative.[48]

Lewis Tappan believed that the mission that he and Andrews had undertaken while in England was bearing fruit, if only because the knowledge of it had instigated yet another overbearing response by the proslavery interests. When Abel Upshur died in an explosion on board the U.S.S. *Princeton* in February of 1844, John C. Calhoun became secretary of state. The Tyler administration had been making a painstaking effort to convince northerners that a Texas treaty was in the best interests of the United States, based upon advantages to be gained in security from, and economic competition with, Great Britain. The administration seemed to be eliciting its desired response when Calhoun undid its work with a few maladroit strokes of his pen. Writing to British foreign secretary Lord Aberdeen, Calhoun informed him that what the British did in their own empire regarding the emancipation of slaves was their business. The United States, however, and especially the South, would take a dim view of any British efforts to eliminate slavery in Texas. In the secretary of state's view, any such attempt would be injurious to Southern interests. Calhoun then went on to lecture Lord Aberdeen about the merits of slavery, claiming that it was beneficial to white and black alike. The overbearing correspondence to Aberdeen had been sent through British minister to Richard Pakenham of the United States, and became known as the "Pakenham Letter." When the letter's contents became public, the margin of support needed in the North for a Texas treaty vanished.[49]

Jay was in Egypt viewing the pyramids when Calhoun committed his blunder. But in a packet from Jay's son John, Lewis Tappan tucked a brief letter that informed him of the incident, and gleefully took a share of credit for it: "The anti-s[lavery] cause is advancing with rapid strides. Tyler and Calhoun have disgraced themselves by their insinuation and precipitate development of the Texas plot. Surely Andrews and myself did not visit England in vain and we provoked this early show of hands on the part of these political gamblers."[50] Tappan urged Jay to keep the Texas issue before the British, because he feared that the annexationists had suffered only a minor setback. If the Tyler administration could obtain Texas peacefully, it would. But if Mexico continued to present an "obstacle" to annexation, the administration would, in all probability, disregard that obstacle. The inescapable conclusion was that war would soon follow.

Tappan continued to apprise Jay—who remained curiously silent during his European tour—of political events at home in America. Just before Jay's return in the summer of 1844, Tappan sent him a letter that revealed exactly how turbulent the American political and domestic scene had become. He noted that the Methodist council of New York had met and deposed a Bishop Andrew because his wife was a slaveholder. Naturally, Southern Methodist leaders were furious and threatening separation. Tappan mentioned that the slavery interests were becoming desperate politically, and had taken up the cry "Texas or ruin." At their convention meanwhile, the Democrats had rejected Van Buren and placed James K. Polk at the head of their presidential ticket. Polk had a proannexation policy, and many Northern Democrats hesitated to support him. Because of that opposition, Tappan believed that the ranks of the Liberty Party would swell with new supporters. Ironically, he also predicted that the actions of the Democrats would lead to the election of Henry Clay. Little did Jay's friend realize that the growth of the Liberty Party would transpire, with the unforeseen consequence of taking votes from Clay and leading to his defeat in the 1844 presidential election.[51]

There was more news. A new, "cheap" reprint of Jay's *View* was selling rapidly. And there was also a tidbit of that Tappan could not have realized related directly to Jay's evolving opinions on Texas. If many in the South had taken up the cause of "Texas or ruin," many Northern abolitionists had increasingly adopted the stance of Texas and disunion. Indeed, Tappan told Jay that the Garrisonians had "hoisted the flag of disunion." Clergy had deserted Garrison's ranks—save for the Universalists—"and by their dissensions, fanaticism, and violence," the Garrisonians were harming the abolitionist cause and dishonoring their country. But for once Jay and his confidant were not of one mind. Of all of the abolitionists, Tappan should have been aware of Jay's thoughts. And Tappan must have been cognizant of a letter that Jay had written to the *Liberty Press* in October of 1843, suggesting that disunion was preferable to the annexation of Texas.[52]

Jay's correspondence was voluminous and addressed to numerous peers, and among those many correspondents was Henry Ingersoll Bowditch. Abolitionism was as varied as the individuals who promoted it. Not all New Englanders were hod carriers for the Garrisonian point of view, and Bowditch, Boston patrician and Liberty Party man, reflected that diversity. Polk's election in 1844 virtually assured annexation of Texas, and Bowditch wrote to Jay attempting to solicit his opinions upon the impending Texas statehood. About three years earlier Jay had intimated to Bowditch that, should Texas be annexed, he would become an advocate for disunion. Bowditch wondered: Did Jay still maintain his earlier stance?[53]

Bowditch's letter to Jay came soon after Congress had done everything in its power to provide the Polk administration with the tools to ensure annexation. In January, a resolution was proposed in the House authorizing that territory properly included in and belonging" to Texas be created into a state and admitted to the United States. That bold measure lacked the support to pass the Senate. President-Elect Polk now convinced the Senate to broaden the measure, and give the president the prerogative either to accept the House resolution or enter into new negotiations with Texas. The resolution passed in its modified form and Tyler, not waiting for the incoming Polk to make the decision—and feeling the crop of the omnipresent Calhoun upon his flanks—seized the opportunity to implement the annexation process. Save for some negations, Polk inherited Texas.[54]

Jay agonized over Bowditch's question for several weeks, and actually began to write another pamphlet, or "little book," in response. What Bowditch received however, was a succinct response that Jay termed more of a "table of contents" for the "little book" he had begun. Arguing from a constitutional standpoint, Jay contended that every violation of that document did not provide grounds for the dissolution of the Union. The toleration of slavery by the Constitution did not necessitate the dissolution of the Union, because the "evil was partial, and confined within certain limits."

While slavery remained confined within those limits, the ultimate demise of the institution "was inevitable." The issue of Texas was another matter.[55]

As a straw target for his riposte, Jay used Secretary of State John C. Calhoun, and Calhoun's famous *Exposition and Protest* of 1828 provided the bull's-eye. Jay attacked Calhoun's strict interpretation of the Constitution that deemed the Tariff Act of 1828 unconstitutional. Calhoun's formulation had allowed that the tariff was permissible as a revenue act, but not as a measure that allowed the government to do indirectly what it could not do directly: promote domestic manufactures. To Calhoun and other South Carolinians, the tariff had potentially been grounds for armed resistance and dissolution of the bonds of Union. Yet Calhoun, execrable hypocrite that he was, according to Jay, had made plain his belief that the U.S. government should annex Texas for the protection of slavery! Calhoun was suggesting that the U.S. government perform exactly the service that had been the basis for his protest against the tariff: promote the slavery interests of the South to the disadvantage of the North.[56]

For Jay the tariff had not been a "violation of the express provisions of the Constitution." The annexation process however, was not only "detestable" in its design, it violated the Constitution in its form. Under the old Articles of Confederation, provisions provided for new states to be admitted out of the national territory. According to Jay, those same powers and provisions later transferred to the Constitution. Obviously Texas was not part of the national territory, and that was where the real problem lay. Under the proposed resolution of the Congress, the president had the right to enter into negotiations with the government of Texas to conclude a treaty of annexation. Once negotiations were concluded, the president could then send the treaty to either the House or the Senate for ratification. In other words, the president could use his prerogative to guide the treaty in the direction where he felt it had the best chance for passage. To bypass the Senate would be a clear violation of that body's constitutional power to ratify treaties. The Senate's prerogative of ratification was nullified by allowing the president to treat the treaty as "articles," and present it to the House if the chance for passage there was better.[57]

This iniquity, this "wound" to the Constitution, was being perpetrated by a slave power that sought to "burst the bounds within which it was sure to perish." The slave region had secured a majority in the Senate, and once ratified, annexation would be impossible to repeal. Thus directed by southern interests, the course of annexation violated the "mutual compact" that bound the United States together. Yes, slavery was recognized as a part of the constitutional compromise, but that recognition did not grant the government the power to abolish, "nurse, cherish," or "protect it as a national institution." Under the annexation plan proposed by the machinations of the slave power in government, the Constitution had become an "instrument of cruelty, oppression, and wickedness." "It has ceased," said Jay, "to be the Constitution, which I have, on various occasions, sworn to support."

What were the consequences if the North sat idly by and allowed annexation? The end result could only be the control of the government by the slave power at the sacrifice of Northern political rights and interests. This would coincide with a rapid corruption of government and American society as the slave power tightened its hold on the nation. The extension of slavery and Southern boundaries, and the plunder of the Spanish provinces would ensue. Northern citizens were already denied their constitutional rights by the arrogance of the slave owners in government. Congress had instituted the gag rule, and should any individuals have the temerity to speak out for human liberty on Southern soil, they faced the death penalty. Colored citizens in the South were enslaved or jailed at pleasure. How much more would the citizens of the North endure? Jay answered his rhetorical question by replying that the ultimate consequence of Southern actions could only be a bloody Northern rebellion against the slave power "taskmasters." Why? Because the nation as it existed, this "connection," as Jay referred to it, was far more likely to "enslave the North . . . than free the South."[58] The time to separate was the present, before the South had the chance to augment its power. Perhaps Jay, as a man of peace, also saw separation as having the potential to avoid any such conflict.

Jay then offered some surprising suggestions as to what the duties of the North were so long as the cords of Union remained intact. He held that all constitutional privileges regarding the apprehension of fugitive slaves should be suspended, and that those engaged in the apprehension or return of slaves to their masters should be punished. Further, any person in northern territory with a deed to slave property should also be punished. "Punished" was Jay's own wording; what the punishment should be was unspecified. Most astounding was Jay's belief that, whenever a colored citizen was imprisoned in the South, a like number of residents from the state where the imprisonment took place, who might be residing on Northern soil, should be imprisoned and held until the release of the captive in the South could be secured. For all of Jay's fine legal distinctions, constitutional niceties were clearly absent in this suggestion. Finally, citizens had to petition the Congress and state legislatures for an "amicable dissolution of the Union."[59]

The revelation that Jay may have harbored dissolutionist ideals is, at first blush, shocking. Did this mean that he had gone over to Garrison's camp? No. It would have been inconceivable for Jay to tear up a copy of the Constitution as Garrison did; his views on separation of the Union were distinctly different from Garrison's, more a matter of utility than idealism. True, both were based upon conscience. But Garrison's position, that the Constitution supported slavery and therefore abolitionists could not support the government, while not necessarily mere political posturing, strove to produce a desired effect. That effect was to shock the American public into the realization that the government's association with slavery had led to its moral contamination. But Jay did not believe that the toleration of slavery by the Constitution warranted disunion. As long as slavery remained within the limits of the Constitution, the extinction of the institution was unavoidable. The limits of slavery lay within the borders of the slave states themselves. The Constitution had compromised with slavery, but a compromise merely indicated "the absence of a grant of power." The government could defend the slave owner from servile insurrection, but constitutionally the federal government had no legitimate license to advance the cause of slavery.[60]

Jay did not cast any stones at the slaveholders themselves, explaining to Bowditch that they had acted in accordance "with the habits and principles of their ancestors." Jay understood filial obligation as well as any Southerner. And besides, what ever offenses the Southern representatives had committed, had been done with the full cooperation of their Northern counterparts in Washington. However, the actions in behalf of Texas annexation had violated the Senate's right to ratify treaties. Rather than the North continuing to supplement the growing strength of the South, it was just as well that the sections separate at this point.[61]

Jay's Bowditch letter was reprinted in numerous newspapers and journals through out the nation. And while many abolitionists criticized Jay and looked upon the communiqué with opprobrium, for Garrison it was sweet vindication. With its usual florid rhetoric, *The Liberator* trumpeted Jay's views while putting its own spin on them. The paper suggested that the compact between North and South was iniquitous, and that each individual should withdraw from the federal compact.[62] That was, most assuredly, not Jay's contention. Having given the impression that Jay had come around to the Garrisonian point of view, the rest of the column spent itself attacking two of his critics, Gamaliel Bailey and Gerrit Smith.[63] For Garrison's part—and *The Liberator* was, above all, the voice of Garrison—the column was a grotesque travesty and trivialization of Jay's stance. It was an unnatural and unsolicited alliance.

Did Jay's new willingness to consider disunion mean that he had been radicalized by events? In spite of his obvious agitation over the legality of the annexation process, the answer is no. For a conservative such as Jay, governments were created by societies of men for their own survival. The binding agent of society and government was the constitution. If that constitution, the foundation upon which government was structured was weakened, then the consent of the governed was eroded and the fabric of that society would begin to fray. The danger to the stability of the United States as a republic—and Jay assuredly believed the United States to be a republic—was that it could be undermined by special interests.

The South continued to demand concessions that would continually revitalize the institution of slavery, and malleable Northern politicians complied. In *View,* Jay had clearly stated that the Constitution's three-fifths clause had been a guilty concession.[64] But it was now being proposed that Americans once again grant indulgences to the special interests of the slaveholders so they might expand their power and representational influence through the acquisition of Texas. To do this it would be necessary to circumvent that section of the Constitution requiring a two-thirds majority of the Senate to ratify treaties. The separation of North and South would represent a tremendous change, but it would at least protect the Constitution from further depredations by a slave power concerned only with its own expansion, and a power that had violated the social contract represented by the document it sought to undermine.

Other Northern conservatives had proposed separation of the North and South. As president, John Quincy Adams had been an advocate of annexation. Later, as a congressman, he realized that annexation meant the extension of slavery, and he joined eleven other abolitionist Representatives in threatening disunion if annexation were to occur. The Federalists had contemplated breaking the Union thirty years earlier over Jefferson's desire to purchase the Louisiana Territory, and the reasons and sentiments were similar.

The debates over the Louisiana Purchase revealed a desire for Constitutional balance inflamed by sectional jealousies. On that occasion a New Hampshire senator had noted, in words that rang remarkably similar to those of Jay and his peers: "I hope the time is not far distant when the sound part will separate from the corrupt."[65]

Naturally many of those closest to Jay called upon him to clarify his position. To Tappan he reiterated his stance that his position did not mean that he had turned his back on the Constitution. An abolitionist could support disunion and remain true to the document. In a letter to E. M. Davis, Jay cited Congress as the source of "tyranny." The North had equal representation in the Senate and a majority in the House. "Hence our rights are trampled under foot by our own representatives. They hasten to open their jaws and receive the gags of the slaveholders." As long as America could escape the embrace of the "pirate republic" of Texas, then Jay promised to "cherish our federal Union." Without Texas the influence of the slaveholders would gradually wane. But if Texas was admitted to the Union, well, Jay loved his family and friends too much to leave them "prey to the accursed government which will follow."[66]

Late in February 1845, members of the House and Senate cast their votes to annex the Republic of Texas. Mexico, of course, had already lost Texas in 1836 but remained unreconciled to the reality of finally losing the territory. The Mexican minister to the United States was recalled, diplomatic relations were broken off, and war seemed the next step. Diplomatic contact was restored by November of 1845, and President Polk sent James Slidell to negotiate for the demarcation of a Texas border. Slidell had also been instructed to refuse any arbitration by a European power in resolving the dispute. The demands of the American government included payment to U.S. citizens for damages suffered in Mexico's repeated revolutions. The Polk administration agreed to assume the demands for damages—and provide an extra $5 million—if Mexico would extend the Texas border to include the New Mexico territory and California. In fact, if California was included in the settlement, the American government would pay an additional $25 million. The Mexican government was badly divided, but it was also incensed by such exorbitant demands. Slidell soon returned home having failed in his mission.[67]

The southern border of Texas itself was in dispute, and it was here that the Mexican-American War began. Mexico insisted that the Texas border to the south was at the Nueces River. Texans claimed that the border was further south along the Rio Grande. Texans wanted the more southerly boundary because it would give them a buffer zone between themselves and Mexican settlements. They also wanted to extend their border westward along the Rio Grande to enhance their claim to Santa Fe. Even before the failure of Slidell's mission, Polk had sent troops into Texas. Perhaps he wanted a display of force to impress Mexico at the bargaining table. Whatever his reasons, Polk definitely supported the claims of the Texans, and on January 13, 1846, he sent General Zachary Taylor to occupy the land between the Nueces and Rio Grande Rivers. Taylor's progress was leisurely; he reached the Rio Grande on March 28. By April 24, Mexican and American troops clashed. The war with Mexico had begun.[68]

In December of 1846, the American Peace Society offered a prize of $500 for the best essay describing the causes and evils of that conflict. The essays were to be 150–250 pages in length and they were to be submitted within four months of the conclusion of the war. Twelve essays were received by November of 1848 and judged by a panel of three. In 1849, the panel of judges awarded the prize to New Hampshire reverend Abriel Livermore. Jay, who was now serving in the capacity of president of the society, had also submitted a tract that he decided to have printed at his own expense. Having done this, he donated the plates used in the printing to the society, which printed and distributed some 21,000 copies of the document.[69]

Bereft of the buoyant optimism of *War and Peace, A Review of the Causes and Consequences of the Mexican War* was the brooding work of a man who has seen his worst fears realized. Jay labored sedulously to portray the injustice perpetrated against Mexico by the United States. He also wanted to be sure to reveal that Southern intentions to expand slavery westward were the primary concern in pressing the war effort. If Americans had been deceived into engaging in an unjust war, then it was though the auspices of southern interests that they had been beguiled. How these ambitions were realized was the subject of Jay's examination. He carefully explored the perfidious means by which Mexico had been duped, denied good faith bargaining, and repeatedly violated as a sovereign nation.[70]

But Jay, ordinarily straightforward in his exposition, dispensed with any pretense of objectivity. The good judge detected a legion of scoundrels at work in this business, and he took the time to bring each of them before his bench, providing them with no counsel for the defense. He accused Powhatten Ellis, the minister to Mexico in 1836 and a Mississippi slaveholder, of being sent to precipitate a breach with Mexico through demands for reparations.[71] Andrew Jackson had done nothing to arrest the tide of volunteers from the United States that flooded into Texas during that state's war for independence. Thus Jackson had perpetrated the crime that Aaron Burr had only designed: the seizure and creation of a western empire. John Calhoun's suggestion that Texas would have to be annexed in self-defense was an exercise in mendacity.[72] Martin Van Buren, Abel Upshur, Waddy Thompson of South Carolina—each of these heretics was tried before the inquisitor Jay and the *auto da fe* pronounced. Jay's spitefulness was somewhat understandable—his feelings about annexation were no secret—but given his usual moderation it was surprising.

Having assailed his reader with the human and monetary costs of the war, Jay concluded with a promotion of his plan to promote peace. He reiterated that to keep the peace by preparing for war was a fallacy, for the natural and bitter fruits of conquest were pride and arrogance, a condition fatal to peace.[73] Under every form of government the people lost their wealth by their own consent because of their "insane admiration of glory, and their own foolish idea of the necessity of military preparation."[74] Charles Sumner of Massachusetts wrote to Jay lauding his work and opined that "the just historian hereafter will be compelled to adopt your views."[75]

In fact there was nothing new in Jay's review of the Mexican-American War, this in spite of the fact that the work ran thirty-seven chapters and easily exceeded the APS-imposed limit of 250 pages. The book—for that was what it was—occasionally rambled, and managed to include a eulogy for John Quincy Adams. For all of Jay's apparent anger, he avoided any mention of disunion. He arrayed his usual facts, statistics, and political observations, in accordance with his philosophy of putting the facts before the public in hopes of persuading it to his point of view. Jay had once threatened: "Rather than be in union with Texas, let the confederation be shivered. My voice, my efforts, will be for disunion."[76] Yet by 1849, that "accursed republic" was a part of the United States, and Jay's talk of regional separation seemed as much bluster as the secessionist vitriol of many slaveholders.

The United States acquired the New Mexico territory and California as a result of the war with Mexico. Fearing that proslavery forces would attempt to introduce slavery into the new western territories, abolitionists appealed to the residents to reject any such efforts. In 1849, in cooperation with the AFASS, Jay issued his *Address to the Inhabitants of New Mexico and California, on the Omission by Congress to Provide Them with Territorial Government and on the Social and Political Evils of Slavery.* Twenty other members of the AFASS endorsed the work. Save for a brief introduction, the "address" was nothing more than Jay's *Address to the Non-Slaveholders of the South,* recycled and reprinted verbatim. The expedient of merely reissuing an older work suggests lassitude on the part of Jay and his peers, or a general complacency emanating through the organizational structure of the AFASS.

Suggesting that such dedicated individuals were otiose in their efforts seems absurd. A more cogent explanation for Jay's sudden loss of vitality might have been fatigue. In the winter of 1849, James Fenimore Cooper visited the Jay family and wrote down this somber report: "I have seen [William] Jay, his wife and children, Mrs. Bruen [Jay's daughter Sarah Louisa], Eliza . . . I have also seen Mrs. Banyer and Miss Nancy, the latter looking very ill . . . Jay, thin, old and white-headed. He keeps his color however, pretty well. Mrs. Jay looks old and care worn."[77] Cooper noted that the Jays did not venture out much, and that Jay's daughter Anna Balch had died the year before. Jay, Garrison, Tappan were all private citizens, not professional politicians. Regardless of whether or not their efforts were occasionally misguided or smacked of hypocrisy, they did what they did out of a sense of Christian duty. Many conjoined that with a sense of disinterested republican obligation to the nation. They balanced family, business, and philanthropy in a variety of causes, often under a palpable threat of physical violence to themselves and their loved ones.

Age also had to be a factor. While Lewis Tappan and Jay were born within a year of each other—in 1788 and 1789 respectively—many of their collaborators and contemporaries were younger. William Lloyd Garrison was born in 1805, Gamaliel Bailey in 1807. The 1840s had been a decade of intense reforming activity coupled with bitter disappointment at events such as the annexation of Texas. It would have been understandable if these elder representatives had given in to disillusionment by 1850, but they did not. Jay had assuredly not lost his passion for his numerous causes, but he must have needed a respite.

"The Time Has Come for Christians and Churches to Act"

All these evils might have been easily avoided by a law satisfying every requirement of the Constitution, and yet treating the alleged fugitive as a MAN, and granting him the same protection as is accorded to an alleged murderer.

—William Jay to Samuel Eliot, 1850

Henry Clay's Compromise of 1850 attempted to address the issue that increasingly threatened what little sectional harmony remained. The compromise confronted questions of slavery in the District of Columbia, slavery in territories acquired in the war with Mexico, the boundaries of Texas, and the return of fugitive slaves. So controversial and acrimonious were many of these issues that Clay failed to get the legislation passed in omnibus form. Now seventy-three years old and having spent an abundance of his political capital on the measure's passage, Clay departed Washington and Stephen Douglas guided the bill through Congress in piecemeal form.[1]

In recent years historians have looked upon the compromise as more of an "armistice" that failed to address or defuse long-term questions such as popular sovereignty. A compromise would have something to please everyone; the legislation of 1850 merely had something to infuriate everyone. Sectional differences were beginning to harden, and the plan exposed the increasing tensions between Americans in the North and South. But regardless of the settlement's merits, or lack thereof, the stories surrounding the passage of that legislation have continued to furnish political historians with the components of high tragedy. It was truly the last flourish for the Great Triumvirate of Henry Clay, Daniel Webster, and John C. Calhoun. For Clay, alias "The Great Compromiser," or "Harry of the West," it was a chance to burnish his political legacy by healing the Union. As part of the political wrangling over the plan, Clay's political influence may have helped elevate supporter Webster to secretary of state upon the death of President Zachary Taylor. Opposition to the plan was also the last act of a dying John C. Calhoun. Barely an account of the proceedings exists that fails to mention Calhoun. Too weak to read his speech opposing the compromise, and so having it delivered by James Mason of Virginia, Calhoun sat listening in the Senate like a baleful apparition.[2] And it was also Mason who authored the portion of the compromise that would galvanize abolitionists like Jay.

A senator from a slave state bordering on the free North, Mason was worried about the number of slaves annually lured to escape North by the propinquity of freedom. Most slave owners in the border states believed—and not without some justification—that antislavery Northerners were involved with the theft of their valuable slave property. Even if abolitionists were not involved in directly inducing slaves to flee, they were at least willing to aid and abet the fugitives in retaining their freedom once they escaped North. Either way it amounted to theft. To facilitate the retrieval of their valuable property, and ensure its return, Mason designed that portion of Clay's compromise that would be the Fugitive Slave Law. The law permitted accused former slaves to be extradited South without trial, testimony, or a writ of habeus corpus. It appointed commissioners to rule on requests for extradition. Those commissioners—usually a justice of the peace—would earn $10 if they decided in favor of extradition and $5 if they found in favor of the suspected fugitive. Commissioners could also force Northern citizens to become members of fugitive-hunting posses upon request of slave catchers. Those citizens who had reservations, or refused to comply with the commissioner's orders, faced a $1,000 fine. When the law passed as part of the Compromise of 1850, it only proved what Jay had long contended: that the slave power was able to maintain its viability with the support of the federal government.[3]

For abolitionists, the central problem of the compromise was the Fugitive Slave Law. Not only did they fear that the federal government supported the interests of slave owners, but they also suspected that slave owners wished to use the government to expand their dominion northward. Lawmakers in Congress did little to ameliorate the abolitionist's trepidation. The abolitionists expected the usual boasting by some Southerners—Robert Toombs of Georgia vowed he would call the roll of his slaves at the foot of Bunker Hill. But they were appalled when elected Northern officials such as Daniel Webster stated that any resistance to the enforcement of the act should be "as an act of clear treason." Constitutionally, the law was enforceable because the government had the right to regulate immigration into the various states. The law also made it impossible for a slave to obtain citizenship by escaping from bondage. But the law also abrogated the right of the states to regulate and protect their own citizens by creating the potential for the violation of the rights of the accused to a trial or to testify in their own behalf opened the door for the transportation of innocents into thralldom.[4]

While the legislation was being debated, Jay wrote a brief letter to his congressman, William Nelson. Although he addressed his concerns over each of the issues involved, Jay reserved his most pungent animadversions for Henry Clay's acceptance of the Fugitive Slave Law as part of the compromise. Likening Clay to a physician, Jay suggested that the proposed law was a panacea. Doctor Clay had recommended this prescription to restore "a general healthful action throughout the present morbid system of the confederacy"! Unfortunately, the good doctor was having difficulty convincing the patient to take the medicine. Then Jay suggested that Clay was really proposing a game law for the hunting of men throughout the nation. And if Clay was the gamekeeper, then Mason was the hunter, who insisted on expanding the dominion of the hunter's rights to the violation of private dwellings for the taking of the quarry. How long would it be, Jay asked, before "southern ruffians and northern doughfaces" were "roaming through our bedrooms and ransacking our closets in search of prey?" He closed his argument with a bit of doggerel.

Oh! goodly and grand is our hunting to see,
In this "land of the brave and home of the free!"
Right merrily hunting the black man, whose sin,
Is the curl of his hair ad the hue of his skin!
So speed to their hunting o'er mountain and glen,
Through canebreak and forest—the hunting of men![5]

As a Westchester County judge, William Jay had grappled intellectually with the problems he personally would have encountered had he been called upon to enforce the old Fugitive Slave Act of 1793. Would he consign another human being to slavery? Could he, as a public official who had sworn to uphold the Constitution, be required to enforce a law that he found repugnant and "immoral"? In all honesty Jay knew that he would be bound to uphold the law because he could not honestly deny that it was constitutional. His own conclusions so angered Jay that he decided, if called to preside over any case under the fugitive slave law, he would "tear up [his] commission and leave the bench." But events had never come to that turn, so Jay had not been obliged to make that dramatic gesture.[6]

Of course, in 1850, Jay was no longer a judge, and therefore would not be called upon to weigh issues of personal morality against statist duty. Still, others sought his legal counsel. Alarmed by the potential jeopardy that they found themselves in as a result of the passage of the Fugitive Slave Law, a group of free blacks in Jay's hometown of Bedford decided to seek the Judge's advice. They first inquired about the constitutionality of the fugitive law. They then asked about their best course of action should they be made subject to the authority of that law. Without delving into any deep legal discussion, Jay replied that the Fugitive Slave Law of 1850 was unconstitutional. He based this belief upon his conviction that Congress did not possess the constitutional power to pass laws regulating fugitive slaves. He also stated that he opposed the law on moral grounds, because the law violated the laws of "humanity," the "principles of justice," and the "obligations of the religion of Jesus Christ." But having said this, Jay advised his communicants that, in "practical operation," the law had "binding force." He conveyed his fears that the law would be executed, even if it lacked moral force. Here was yet another legislative boon to the South, voted into existence by Northern representatives, one of whom hailed from Boston.[7]

The question of how the free black citizens of the North could protect themselves against the law posed a much thornier problem.

Jay was disturbed by reports that many free people of color were considering arming themselves in self-defense. He had defended the right of slaves on board the *Creole* to use deadly force to secure their freedom. In so doing, he had argued that a black man had the same right to take a life in self-defense as a white man. But now, faced with a volatile situation that held the very real potential for violence, Jay could not sanction the use of force. Violence in opposition to the law would not secure the freedom of the free blacks of the North; it would only be detrimental to their cause. He implored the free blacks of Bedford to practice restraint: "Leave, I beseech you, the pistol and the bowie knife to the Southern ruffians and their Northern mercenaries. That this law will lead to bloodshed, I take it for granted; but let it be the blood of the innocent, not the guilty. If anything can raise the torpid conscience of the North it will be our streets stained with human blood, shed by the slave catchers."[8] Few of those citizens of Bedford who had communicated with Jay could have embraced his recommendation, or taken much solace in his conclusions.

The representative from Boston whom Jay had referred to as having voted for the Fugitive Slave Law was one Samuel A. Eliot. Eliot had been one of only three Northern Whigs who had voted for the law, and he returned home to find himself the subject of public derision for his decision. Being a member of one of Boston's foremost families did nothing to shield him from public reproach. Public reaction to, and criticism of Eliot continued to be so potent that he realized his political future was finished, and refused to stand for the next election. Then, in an attempt to deflect some of the barbs being cast in his direction, Eliot published an article explaining his reasons for voting the fugitive bill into law. He based his defense upon the premise that the return of fugitives was a constitutional obligation, and that the new law was more favorable to the interests of the fugitive than the law of 1793 that it superseded. Once he became aware of Eliot's attempts to wriggle out from under public scrutiny, Jay rebutted the Bostonian's explanations in an extensive public letter.[9]

Even if the Fugitive Slave Law was "arbitrary, detestable, and diabolical," Jay replied, he did not deny the constitutional obligation that Eliot referred to. Much of Eliot's self-defense was based upon a constitutional history lesson, however, and it was here that Jay opened his attack. The erstwhile representative claimed that, at the time of the Constitutional Convention, slavery had been abolished in several states. Because of this, Southern delegates to that convention had realized that their slave property might be tempted to escape northward to freedom. To assuage southern fears, a provision had been provided for the return of fugitives and, according to Eliot, the acceptance of the compact could not have been secured without it. As there were thirteen states at the time of the 1787 convention, Jay asked how many states had, as Eliot claimed, abolished slavery. Jay answered that not one single state had abolished slavery at that juncture. Only Massachusetts could have been considered a free state, and that had been by judicial decision, not by act of legislature or constitutional provision. Jay's exposure of Eliot's error provided him with a salient for his next assault upon Eliot's reasoning.[10]

What about Eliot's assertion that a constitutional accord could not have been realized without some concession regarding the return of runaway slaves? Eliot had clearly stated that this demand was a sine qua non to the acceptance of the compact by the Southern states. Not true, countered Jay. In fact, if the roll of delegates present at the convention were examined, it would be a difficult task to identify more than half a dozen who were not themselves slaveholders. In fact, at the time the convention convened on May 25, nothing was said about the return of fugitive slaves; fugitives from justice yes, fugitives from bondage no. This held true whether Southern delegates or their Northern counterparts held the floor. Finally, on August 29, the fifteenth article had been amended to include a provision for fugitives from slavery. And because of the preponderance of slaveholders in attendance, the measure passed without opposition. Eliot's history lesson was flawed. Jay icily informed Eliot: "I have pointed out your historical mistake, not because it has the remotest bearing on your justification, but because you think it has."[11]

Jay asserted that the true compromise of the convention had not been between North and South, but between the small states and the large. The first compromise of that disagreement had led to representation in one house of Congress being equal, and according to population in the other. Here was where Southern bullying over the question of who counted among the population for purposes of determining representation began. This debate led to the second concession, and was the genesis of the three-fifths compromise. The third compromise, esteemed by Jay the most "wicked," was the one that restricted the ability of the legislature to tax the "migration or importation [of slaves] be prohibited." Debate on this suggestion led to the continuance of the slave trade in the United States for another twenty years.[12]

Jay found Eliot's plea that the new law was more "favorable" to fugitives than the older law of 1793, specious in the extreme. Why then, he asked, were Eliot's idiotic constituents vilifying his efforts when their representative was in fact "loosening the bonds of the oppressed, and facilitating escape from the prison house"? Eliot had apologized to his electorate for not granting fugitives a trial by jury. He rationalized that no greater injustice was done to the accused than before, because the old law had not provided for a trial. "For fifty-seven years . . . we have been living under the laws which provided no such thing." Was a similar law now "cruel and inhuman"? But Jay pointed out that, as a member of the Massachusetts legislature, Eliot had previously voted for a resolution to request that the U.S. Congress take the public sentiment of free states into account when passing legislation regarding claims against those who had "escaped from labor or service" in other states. The purpose of that resolution had been to secure a trial by jury for those individuals against whom such claims were made.[13] Why had Eliot's "moral philosophy" changed so drastically once in Washington?

Jay's letter simply wanted to prove that, if Eliot's history was faulty, then his rationale in voting for the fugitive bill must have been equally defective. Wrong-headedness aside, Eliot had failed to do his moral duty. God had granted him a chance to honor his "Puritan descent by standing forth before the nation . . . an advocate of justice and freedom." Instead, Eliot had sacrificed principle upon the altar of political expediency. In so doing, he had helped degrade perceptions of America's "national character abroad." He had also, under pretense of preserving the Union, weakened the attachment of conscientious men for a confederacy which requires such horrible sacrifices for its continuance."[14]

Although abolitionists and free blacks of the North viewed the Fugitive Slave Law with repugnance and anger, the reaction throughout the North was mixed. Response varied from state to state, but acceptance was the general rule among the majority of whites who could have cared less about what happened to their surplus black population. In places like Boston and Christiana, Pennsylvania, there were instances of resistance to the enforcement of the Fugitive Slave Law. But it is important to remember that the resistance was almost exclusively organized by free blacks in their own defense. Abolitionists might have had legitimate concerns that

Daniel Webster and other politicians sought to put the North to hard labor under "the women-whippers of the South," but they had some difficulty getting the message out. Nor had their influence and stature grown or expanded appreciably, for they remained targets of sporadic violence. In New York, a meeting of the American Anti-Slavery Society (AASS) was mobbed when William Lloyd Garrison and Frederick Douglass were found to be in attendance. The *New York Sunday Era* gloated over the ignominious treatment of "Garrison's Nigger Minstrels" with unreserved relish. Likewise, when British abolitionists George Thompson toured the United States, antiabolitionist demonstrations drove him out of Springfield, Massachusetts. The antislavery forces might have believed that politicians were going to be the ruin of the nation, but those politicians remained more popular than the abolitionists. The problem was just as Jay had earlier realized: politicians were acting as their constituents desired.[15]

Jay believed however, that the Compromise of 1850 had not been the offspring of politicians alone. Politicians and their constituencies accepted bad legislation, and behaved as they did, because they lacked moral guidance. That guidance had to come from the American Protestant Church. The problem was that the churches had abdicated their responsibility to furnish Americans with the proper moral direction. They refused to speak out against—or at least be critical of—slavery. To Jay's way of reasoning, American's "opinions in favor of human liberty [remained] the same." Unfortunately the "expression" of those sentiments had "been stifled by a sudden, mighty, and combined effort of capitalists and politicians, aided to a great extent by ecclesiastical influence."[16]

Jay's accusations revealed an interesting progression of thought. Previously, he had never failed to remind the church hierarchy, such as Bishops Hobart and Ives, about their duties and their failings. But as in his letter to Ives, Jay always defended the institution itself. The church might censure books such as Wilberforce's *History*, and the church might bar blacks from seminaries and conventions, but the church remained the "appointed means of grace."[17] What of politicians? Jay had recognized that their venal natures made them pliant, passing proslavery legislation because it was the will of their constituents in the North and South. But now those politicians had joined with the church in an effort to hoodwink the American public and stifle the debate on slavery. And well they should according to Jay, for if the blinders should be removed, then the American people, with their innate love of liberty, would realize the injustice being done to the black race, and demand redress.

The duplicity of the American church in helping smother—or at least discourage—debate over the immorality of slavery was a recurring theme for Jay in the final years of his life. Acting as a spokesman for the American and Foreign Anti-Slavery Society (AFASS), Jay expounded upon this theme in a brief pamphlet. In *An Address to the Antislavery Christians of the United States,* Jay claimed that the higher laws espoused by the church were subverted by the reluctance of the religious leadership to confront the sin of slavery. Why, he asked, was there such reticence on the part of God's ministers to condemn slavery from the pulpit? They refused to do so for political and economic reasons. In the North there was probably not a congregation that did not have at least one individual attending Sunday services with links to slaveholding interests. Northern ministers—the "Cotton Divinity"—therefore shunned the subject. In the South, where worshippers as well as ministers were directly involved in slavery, condemnation of slavery was not even a consideration.[18]

The consequence of this unhappy state of affairs was moral degradation on a national scale. Churches sent missionaries to "China and Hindoostan [*sic*]" to preach to the inhabitants of their sinfulness, but they ignored the sin that existed in America. Churches had created tract societies for the dissemination of Christian ideals; yet in none of those tracts was slavery rebuked. The church, that great "instrument of moral reform," refused to recognize the tenets of the gospel and apply them to the existing and "popular sin" of slavery. "Do unto others as they should do unto you" was a maxim sufficient to "banish" slavery, yet the lesson was not applied. In his conclusion, Jay called upon Christians to combat the sin of omission by joining the AFASS and contributing to its treasury.[19]

If the American church did not practice the aggressive Christianity embraced by Jay and his associates, there was no lack of it within the ranks of the abolitionists. The Fugitive Slave Law had infuriated them, but other events also commanded their constant attention and led to increased activism. On December 4, 1851, the U.S. mail steamer *Humboldt* cruised into New York Harbor. On board the vessel was Louis Kossuth, leader of the failed Hungarian Revolution of 1848. The plight of Hungary was typical of many European states at midcentury. Movements toward representative government on the continent earlier in the century had been supplanted by a trend toward the reimposition of absolute monarchy. The vast majority of Americans might not have grasped the nuances of the Hungarian situation, but they did understand that Kossuth represented a force for independence and constitutional government.[20]

The United States had secured Kossuth's release from the Ottoman government, where he was being held under protective custody, and transported him to American shores. The primary purpose of Kossuth's visit was to raise funds for another Hungarian revolution, and by funding his efforts citizens of New York and America could become the "Lafayettes of Hungary." A better man could hardly have been entrusted with the task. Handsome and charismatic, dressed in a black velvet frock coat and wearing a sword and feathered hat, Kossuth exuded self-confidence. Americans responded to the dapper revolutionary with unabashed enthusiasm. New York feted him with receptions, speakers delivered hortatory addresses, and a raucous, uncontrolled crowd viewed a parade in his honor. Kossuth went on to tour the American Midwest, where he enjoyed tremendous popularity among German immigrants who had recently come to the United States to escape the reimposition of monarchy at home.[21]

The abolitionists of New York took note of Kossuth's arrival. An exchange of correspondence between Jay and Lewis Tappan reveals that they intended to use Kossuth as a foil, their purpose being to confront the American people with their own hypocrisy. Kossuth settled into the Irving House on Broadway. On the morning of December 9, members of the AFASS waited upon the Hungarian leader to present him with a letter and an address regarding his mission to America.[22] The address asked Kossuth, as a friend and representative of "universal liberty," to exert his influence in the cause of emancipation. The letter and address were both reprinted. Because of their similarities, some confusion existed in the antislavery press over who authored the address and who penned the letter. But according to Lewis Tappan, Jay wrote the letter. Its sentiments were later eloquently revealed to the Secretary of the American Peace Society. In his communication, Jay wondered how Americans could support intervention in the cause of freedom abroad, when we waged war "against the rights and liberties of millions at home." How could the American republic, which trampled "in the dust THREE MILLIONS [sic] of its own people . . . affect a zeal for human rights so ardent, as to make war upon every foreign nation that denies to a portion of its subjects an elective government or universal suffrage"?[23]

By not fully embracing the excitement over Kossuth, abolitionists once again appeared to be outside the mainstream of American public opinion. But for all of the enthusiastic moral support average Americans lent the Hungarian, they were a little more penurious when it came to giving him cash contributions. American politicians were even more reserved; Secretary of State Webster found Kossuth's presence in the states embarrassing. And while he and other Whigs expressed support for the Hungarian leader, they did so more to woo the votes of German Democrats. In reality, there was no way that the Fillmore administration would formally recognize Kossuth as a foreign head of state, much less intervene in Austro-Hungarian affairs. Kossuth called upon Henry Clay and openly appealed for help. Clay acknowledged the amount of American moral support the revolutionary leader had received, but Clay bluntly informed him that material aid was out of the question.[24] Kossuth left the United States in July of 1852, taking with him what money he had been able to raise. His presence had provided a diversion from the increasing troubles that confronted the nation, and his appeal to the nation as a beacon of freedom made Americans feel a little bit better about themselves. Jay's letter had been but a minor component of the whole overblown affair; its intuition had been correct, even if much of the message was lost. The swell of self-esteem over America's pride of place among the free nations of the world would deflate as the nation began the process of confronting its own inequities.

Part of America's process of self-examination began with the publication of *Uncle Tom's Cabin* in March of 1852. Whether or not the work was evidence of growing antislavery sentiment in the North, the importance of Harriet Beecher Stowe's work is difficult to deny. Despite its length, the book was published in serial form by the antislavery newspaper, the *National Era*. Stowe also sent out complimentary copies to leading abolitionists, and Lewis Tappan received a copy almost immediately. Tappan broke his usual rule about engaging in worthless pursuits such as reading novels, and confided in a letter to Stowe that he found the work compelling. What bothered Tappan was Stowe's procolonization conclusions, especially as evinced in the closing letter of the novel's George Harris. The line from the fictitious letter that discomfited Tappan was where George said: "On the shores of Africa I see a republic— a republic [Liberia] formed of picked men." The word *picked* was particularly irksome to Tappan. He wrote Stowe that, far from subjecting their candidates to a rigorous selection process, the American Colonization Society would dump all American blacks in Liberia who they could convince to leave! Tappan was determined to convince Stowe of her error.[25]

Naturally Tappan realized that he could not revise what was already in print. But the success of Stowe's work had created the demand that she produce a "key" that would cite the original documents and stories upon which *Uncle Tom* had been based. If Tappan could get Stowe to reject her colonizing views in the forthcoming key, that would be victory enough. He recommended Jay's venerable comparison of the AASS and the pro-colonization (ACS)—and mentioned *View* for good measure—as a curative to wrong thinking. Tappan then sat back and fretted about whether Stowe would read Jay, and what form the final revision of the *Key to Uncle Tom's Cabin* would take.[26] Ultimately Stowe renounced her pro-colonization viewpoint, and called upon the Christian Church to do its duty in adding the slaves to realize their potential. Did Stowe read Jay's works? It is possible, but there is no evidence to suggest that either *Inquiry* or *View* prompted her conversion.[27]

No matter how much Jay's opinions changed over the years, he had never relinquished the right to remain a member of those organizations that purported to do God's work, even if they fell short of promoting antislavery expectations. He remained an Episcopalian in spite of the fact that his church continued to exhibit little support for abolitionists, and most of them considered it to be a friend of slaveholders.[28] To Jay, separation from the church would have been a dereliction of duty. The church remained the "appointed means of grace," but it needed to enlarge its application of the gospel and address issues such as slavery. Jay believed he could not act as a conscience for the church of his father if he removed himself from it. His previous letters criticizing the church hierarchy were well known. He continued to remind the church of its duties in letters that appeared publicly in antislavery journals.[29]

Rather than endanger their funding, many of the church sponsored benevolent societies refused to confront or condemn the institution of slavery. Such a policy was a double-edged sword, however, for organizations such as the American Tract Society and the American Missionary Society witnessed a goodly number of abolitionists depart their ranks in protest.[30] Some, such as William Jay and George Burrell Cheever, had determined to stay on and fight for change until the battle was won. In 1853, Jay issued letters explaining his refusal to contribute any more money to the American Tract Society for "sins of omission" and the society's avowed policy of spreading the gospel, not politics.[31] The "sins of omission," of course, focused upon the society's steadfast refusal to confront the explosive issue of slavery. Jay could not have come to his decision lightly; his name had appeared on the society's membership roll as early as 1827.[32]

In yet another letter, Jay chided the tract society's willingness to attack only safe targets. Consumers of spirits had been censured, so too had wine sellers, gamblers, and theater-goers, in spite of the fact that many church members attended the theater.[33] Why was the society incapable of unleashing the same sort of rhetoric upon slaveholders as that with which it scorched moderate drinkers? He included some passages from antialcohol tracts as examples.

"The demon will haunt the timid. It is noisy and fiery; attack it and it will roll its eyes and snap its teeth, and threaten vengeance. Attempt to starve it and it will rage like a starving tiger." Jay wondered, would it not be condign to attack slave owners in this manner?[34] The few works on slavery that the tract society had the temerity to print condemned slavery in Africa and Brazil, not the United States, and they were heavily edited before reprinting. It seemed clear to Jay that the society declined comment upon such matters owing to its commercial interests with the South.[35]

Jay also targeted the proslavery rationalizations of the clergy both North and South. The short work that he produced to address this matter: *An Examination of the Mosaic Laws of Servitude* (1854) admirably displayed Jay's skill as a biblical scholar to complement his political and legal abilities. This was indeed a scholarly paper with a clearly defined thesis. His purpose was to dismantle the arguments of the proslavery clergy that "God himself had established slavery among the Hebrews," and that "the slavery thus enacted in Palestine justifies the existence of our own."[36] The debate on the biblical interpretation of slavery was an interesting one to engage in, and it required skill and caution.[37]

To provide a basis from which to launch his attack, Jay examined and defined the legality of American slavery using statutes that upheld the institution in South Carolina and Louisiana.[38] He then began his examination of the Mosaic laws through a scrutiny of the Hebraic language. Paying special attention to verbs and their conjugation, Jay proved that no Hebrew word had existed to represent the concept of slavery at the time of the Old Testament. Because there was no precedence in the laws of God for the application of euphemisms, how could American and Hebrew definitions of servitude be equated with slavery?[39] This was not to say that servitude was unknown among the Hebrews, but according to Jay, the servitude that had existed in ancient times was quite different from American slavery. Jay did not use the term "indentured," but he did portray the Hebrew version of servitude as a fairly mild institution based upon consensual agreement over a limited period of service. The nearest one could come to any indication of slavery in the Mosaic laws was the concept of the "man-stealer," whom the Hebraic laws proclaimed worthy of death.[40]

Overall this was an atavistic work, reminiscent of the Jay of the 1830s. In both the lucid progression of his argument and the scholarly aspects of the debate, Jay shone, but his argument was not unique. The casuistry of justifying American slavery through biblical precepts was examined by Harriet Beecher Stowe in her *Key to Uncle Tom's Cabin*. Naturally, Stowe leaned heavily upon her knowledge of the lectures of her father, Lyman Beecher, on the subject. The knowledge she exhibited was impressive, and bore resemblance to Jay's arguments. The subject would also later be examined by George Burrell Cheever and others with impressive theological credentials.[41] Lewis Tappan, a biased source if there ever was one, proclaimed Jay's version "the best treatise that has ever been published in this country on the subject."[42]

In spite of his impending age, Jay's efforts did not lessen. The year 1853 saw a compilation of Jay's antislavery works published as *Miscellaneous Writings on Slavery*. In that year Jay also addressed the annual meeting of the American Peace Society. Never mentioning his own efforts in that regard, he praised Richard Cobden for his work in promoting stipulated arbitration before the English Parliament. In the U.S. Senate, Henry Foote of Mississippi had brought a similar measure to adopt arbitration before the Committee on Foreign Relations.[43] Jay interpreted these developments—this international recognition of the value of arbitration—as stemming from changing public opinion. These advances were the direct result of free speech and a free press. But there was also reason for caution. In the United States Jay saw an attempt to revive one of war's legacies—the law of treason—and use it to enforce the Fugitive Slave Law. Fortunately, in the case of a man who had refused to participate in the capture of slaves when so ordered by a constable, the efforts to obtain a conviction on charges of treason had failed. If people could be accused of treason for refusing to uphold an unjust law, then surely a state of war existed in the United States over the issue of slavery. The linkage, for Jay, was obvious. But he stated his belief that the man's acquittal revealed progress, and fore-told of a time when war would become an anachronism.[44]

In spite of Jay's renewed optimism, the nation had not charted a course toward islands of tranquillity. Fractiousness continued to grow over the issue of slavery and its expansion. Although he pro-duced no major work to criticize it, Jay found the emerging debates over the opening of the Kansas-Nebraska Territory extremely dis-tasteful. The repeal of the Missouri Compromise and the potential for the expansion of slavery into new territories did not bode well for the nation. Jay was forced to decline an offer to speak before an anti-Nebraska convention in Massachusetts, but he did return a letter of regret, and expressed his opinion of Daniel Webster. Webster's conduct had been unforgivable in his defense of the "atrocious" Fugitive Slave Act, yet his actions had been "raptur-ously applauded by the monied, the literary, and the ecclesiastical aristocracy of Massachusetts" and New England. It was further evidence of the slave power taking advantage of Northern moral "paralysis." Southern trade was again calling the tune, and North-erners were dancing to it.[45]

Jay did not have to look far to realize just how damaging an ef-fect Southern commerce had upon northern moral commitment. New York City was becoming known as "the prolongation of the South." And while there was a social aspect to the relationship be-tween the city and the slave states, the primary link was merchan-dise. Southerners shunned cheaper outlets for goods in Charleston and Savannah and purchased their shoes, furniture, and dry goods for New York merchants. To cement the bonds even further, many New Yorkers were cotton factors, the speculators that served as middlemen between growers and the market. Consequently, in the years leading up to the Civil War, New York dominated every as-pect of the cotton trade "from plantation to market."[46]

Prior to 1850, many New York merchants had declared them-selves free-soil men opposed to the westward expansion of slavery. Many had opposed the annexation of Texas, and snapped their fin-gers at southern threats of secession should slavery not be granted room to expand. But as the political storm clouds loomed over the Compromise of 1850, those same merchants began to find the dark threats of Southern secession and its disruption of business, more palpable. Now the merchants of the Empire City fell over each other in their attempts to urge their representatives to vote for the com-promise and other concessions. They rejoiced when the measure passed, and the stock market soared. For Jay and his merchant friend Lewis Tappan, it was a sad spectacle.[47]

Because of his age and the fact that he had no more official duties to perform in Westchester, Jay began to spend more time in New York City and less in Bedford. Increasingly weak, he was unable to deliver the address he had written for the twenty-seventh anniversary of the American Peace Society in Boston. In May of 1855, Charles Sumner addressed the society and delivered the somber speech for him. With much of Europe participating in the Crimean War, the cause of peace had been dealt a devastating blow. Former British prime minister and now foreign secretary Lord John Russell had declared in Parliament that the war was fought to "maintain the independence of Europe." But Jay believed Russell's statement was false, and that France and England had allied against Russia to maintain the balance of power. Under this rubric, it became the duty of nations to deprive other nations of gaining too much power. Pacifists had long been contending that the public needed to be educated about the horrors and waste of wars. They had begun to indulge the hope that "the increasing intelligence of the masses, and their enlarged influence," would restrain leaders from "gambling away their lives and property for power and territory." But nothing had truly changed. The pacifists had been deluded, and the war proved that this was the case in the most disheartening manner. In England the people had spoken, and public opinion had been overwhelmingly in favor of the conflict. The war in the Crimea had not been fought for the "personal ambition and selfishness of rulers, but in obedience to popular clamor."[48]

Sumner's delivery of Jay's address was not the only collaboration between the two men that year. In New York, Jay introduced Charles Sumner as the speaker at an antislavery anniversary convention, to an audience of mixed "color."[49] The man who had once advised against allowing colored participation in antislavery activities, and had once even threatened to resign the original society should a black minister speak at a meeting, had changed his stance.[50]

Jay revisited England in the spring and summer of 1856, taking his wife and sisters with him. There he entertained and was entertained by churchmen and reformers. He dined with the rector of Liverpool and forged a friendship with abolitionist James Cropper and his wife. Jay continued to take an interest in all manner of efforts at social improvement. He accompanied Cropper on a tour of a reform school where the inmates lived upon an old hulk of a fifty gun frigate that had been transformed into their prison. The converted naval vessel was, Jay noted, "at once school, prison, and playground."[51] The visit was not without cares for the ailing Jays however. Although he noted that his sisters were well, Jay's wife, Augusta, fell ill, and took over a month to recover.[52]

The sojourn in England would be the last Jay family vacation. The children of William's generation were beginning to succumb to age. On November 13, 1856, a couple of months after she had returned from England, Ann Jay died in the New York City home of her sister Maria (Mrs. Banyer). Ann was seventy-three. Maria herself died a scant eight days later, and William was left without siblings. Lewis Tappan sent condolences, likening the "accumulated sorrows" of the Jays to those of the English royal family upon the death of Princess Amelia in 1810.[53]

Still in demand among antislavery factions although he was approaching seventy, Jay received an invitation to a National Disunion Convention at Worcester, Massachusetts, in the summer of 1857. Among others, it was signed by William Lloyd Garrison. Jay wrote back and declined the invitation. He also communicated that the disunion supporters would not realize their goal, and would be "doomed to disappointment." Still, he applauded their efforts, because exposure to the iniquities forced upon the American people by the union would not serve to dissolve it, but render such action unnecessary. When the people of the North ceased to "idolize" the union and let themselves be bullied by trade interests promoted by obsequious politicians, the Union would be saved and the slave power vanquished. On that happy day no one, not even the promoters of the convention, would wish to see the union "severed."[54]

In the winter of 1857, it appeared as though Jay's criticism of the American Tract Society might bear fruit. A special committee was formed to examine the actions of the executive committee and its policy toward the issue of slavery. Jay wrote the special committee to inquire into its deliberations; he was disappointed. The report of the special committee merely recapitulated the old policies of the society. The body would not allow itself to be made the "special organ" of any system of religious or moral reform. Its purpose was to spread "Godliness" while bearing testimony against forms of fundamental error in doctrine and "practical immorality."[55]

Jay's retort highlighted the hypocrisy of the committee's defense. Citing the constitution of the tract society, the committee had argued that the organization's purpose was to circulate publications that met with the "approbation of all evangelical Christians," Jay countered the committee's findings with a few frank questions. Did all Christians truly approve of tracts that singled out, and condemned as sin, alcohol consumption, gambling, and tobacco chewing? Surely there were evangelical Christians who engaged in these activities in moderation, and did not consider them sinful. Why was the tract society oblivious to the feelings of these people, while it coddled the feelings of those were involved in slavery? Was bondage not deemed sinful by many Christians?[56]

Jay's questions were rhetorical. In his many years of crusading, he had never fired a broadside without a firmly established target. In this instance the target was a member of the tract society's publishing committee, and that individual was Reverend Nehemiah Adams. Not only did Adams possess an absolute veto on every submission for publication, he himself had written an extensive apologia and vindication of slavery titled *A South Side View of Slavery*. Adams contended that the "interchange between Africa and the Southern States" had blessed the imported Africans with many "marvelous acts of divine grace." Through that "interchange," multitudes of slaves were saved from their savagery, and it was obvious that the "South had learned to be, and is fitted to be, the protector and friend of the African." Jay countered that the work of salvation and conversion in the South was made all the more miraculous because it had been performed upon people kept ignorant, and denied access to tracts or the Holy Bible. The conversion process was all the more remarkable because the converted were daily exposed to a system that, by its very nature, refuted Christian principles. What sort of Christianity robbed the slaves of the earnings of their labor? Where was the Christianity in a system that denied the slaves the civil right of marriage, thereby "encouraging universal prostitution"? How did Christian enlightenment come to those who were denied the "opportunities of moral and intellectual culture"?[57]

There was more than enough vacillation in Adams's work so that Jay could have found additional arguments to assail it with. Adams openly admitted that slavery was less efficient than free labor, and that the agricultural practices associated with cotton production depleted the soil. He cited instances, based upon personal experience, of children being sold away from their families, a situation Adams contended was as distressing to the slaver owner as it was to the slaver parent. Adams also came out against dissolution of the Union, but his reason for opposing such an action was that the

South would ultimately emerge from separation as the North's superior. And Adams proclaimed that true emancipation was not possible because black and white could not live in harmony unless they intermarried. If emancipation did occur, the freedmen and women—unprotected by the aegis of slavery—would be exploited by the white race. Even worse, they would be placed in direct, bareknuckled competition with that most degraded of races, the Irish.[58]

For Jay, Adams's apostasy as a man of God lay more in the sinfulness of his defense of slavery than in the absurdities of his arguments. Jay's letter was a clear indication that he believed the church (regardless of denomination) could be a solution to the problem of the ignorant and degraded slave. The church could provide the education and spiritual guidance that would help instill values of frugality and piety in the slaves. These were the values so many reformers deemed conducive to full participation in, and contribution to, American society. In his earlier works such as *Inquiry,* Jay had exposed the moral problem that faced Americans. For their own individual salvation and that of the nation itself, slavery had to be abolished. But Jay had also revealed a reluctance to break bread with the emancipated until they were productive members of society, capable of reasoned discourse. Jay had not provided a formula to alleviate ignorance and want, he had merely railed against the system that denied blacks access to the tools of inclusion.

The solution that Jay ultimately endorsed held the church as the key to relieving the problems that would face the freed people, but first the church needed to address the greater sin of slavery. The church could be a vehicle for education. The church could provide lessons in social inclusion through membership, and the church could certainly provide the lessons needed to instill the moral fiber so prized, so essential, to the reformers. It seems a foregone conclusion that Jay the institutionalist, Jay who scorned comeouters as deluded, would arrive at this solution.

Sadly the church failed Jay. Ironically his staunch belief in institutions as the source of redress for social ills went unrewarded. For all the efforts he expended in the last years of his life, the church was not persuaded to conform to its own tenets of moral behavior. Churchmen, high and low, were in many instances as venal and corrupt as the most shameless politician. To illustrate this, one of the members of the committee of inquiry to whom Jay addressed his letter was Theodore Frelinghuysen. Jay's admonishment to

Frelinghuysen to do his moral duty did as little good as when Jay had reminded him of the same obligation as a vice presidential candidate.

The letter was Jay's last major effort to reform a social institution. His heart failing him, Jay began to put his affairs in order. He asked his son John to review a draft of his will and submit it to any heirs for revisions. The Jay land, some of which was in New York City, was divided into fourteen parcels of equal appraised value, and the land of the estates at Bedford and Rye was distributed by lots. Jay then effectively turned over his affairs to his son, and asked him to handle the revision of his will. "On reflection," he told John, "I think the task of writing over and copying your interrogatories . . . may require more labor than I can well bestow."[59]

Jay's wife, Augusta, died on April 26, 1857, and the judge was effectively alone. Friends did come to call at 21 West 37th Street, whenever Jay was staying in the city. Lewis Tappan recounted one dinner that he had with Jay a year after Augusta had died. Jay was pleased that both Lewis and his brother Arthur had come to call. He told the brothers that he tried exercising mornings, but was "quite feeble" and unable to walk more than half a block without becoming "much fatigued." Still, Jay remained intensely interested in the affairs of Congress and the tract society, and the men conversed at length on those subjects. Before the Tappans left, Jay told them:

> In my situation I naturally look back upon my antislavery labors, and I do not see anything to regret. We have had a hard struggle, if the project of forcing slavery upon Kansas is defeated we shall commence a new struggle, one that will be successful. In what I have written for the cause no one has ever been able to convict me of a false statement. It is because I have avoided exaggeration and have been careful to state accepted facts; and because I have acted in the fear of God.[60]

Realistically, it was an extensive quote for Tappan to remember and later transpose to his journal. Either he scribbled it down on the spot, or it was a prepared statement delivered to Tappan for posterity.

Jay returned to Bedford for the summer. He was having increasing trouble breathing, and was confined to either his bed or a chair. His final letter to friend Lewis Tappan recorded that Jay knew death was near. William Jay saw his seventieth birthday on June 16 of that year. In October he died. He was buried in a plot at St. Matthew's Church in Bedford with his wife. The hills around Bedford were alive with autumn color as the funeral procession made its way to the cemetery. The hearse was followed by a number of Westchester County's free black population that Jay had befriended in the past. A simple service without any eulogy was delivered by Reverend Edward B. Boggs, and William Jay was laid to rest. At Jay's request, the inscription on the tombstone read: "Verily, verily, I say unto you, he that believeth on me hath everlasting life."[61]

Jay undoubtedly wanted a funeral devoid of memorials to his passing, but that did not mean that his passing went unnoticed. The next spring, on May 12, 1859, "a meeting of colored citizens" gathered in New York City's Shiloh Presbyterian Church to hear Frederick Douglass eulogize William Jay. Another prominent black abolitionist, Reverend Henry H. Garnet, presided over the service. Douglass's eulogy was predictably glowing. He praised Jay's accomplishments and writings, his virtue and piety, and then Douglass asked his audience how a reformer's life and work should be judged: "To form any just estimate of the character of a reformer, and to comprehend the value of his services, it is important to notice whether he embraced the cause early or late, in the morning . . . or in the refreshing cool of the evening, when the heaviest work is already done."[62] Douglass did not find Jay wanting in his regard, and then he made a remarkable observation. He asserted that "impartial history will accord to William Jay the credit of having affirmed all the leading principles of modern abolitionism." He then proclaimed Jay the father of immediatism.[63]

As evidence, Douglass cited Jay's earliest works: his letter to Elias Boudinot calling for Congress to "stay the plague" of widening slavery. His efforts on behalf of Gilbert Horton in 1826, when Jay wrote the petition forwarded to Congress demanding "the immediate abolition of slavery in the District of Columbia." These were actions that recommended that William Jay, not William Lloyd Garrison, should be recognized as the avatar of American immediatism.[64] Of course Jay was thirty years old in 1819 when he wrote his letter to Boudinot. Garrison was still a young man learning the printing trade at the time, so Jay had a good head start in his antislavery career. Could Douglass have advanced Jay over Garrison because of personal animus? Possibly. Douglass had split with the Garrisonians over the issues of disunion and political participation in the early 1850s. But Douglass also continued to speak glowingly of Garrison on every occasion.

George Burrell Cheever also eulogized Jay before a New York gathering of the American Peace Society on May 8, 1859. Cheever used Jay's own words extensively and compellingly to emphasize Jay's character as much as his accomplishments. This was appropriate. Jay always lauded the efforts of his peers and never mentioned his own. Cheever thus attempted to capture the mind and piety of Jay when he quoted: "The love of personal freedom is a passion, shared alike by the good and the vile; while a disinterested regard for the rights and liberties of others is not the product of the battlefield, but the fruit of a heart purified by influences from above."[65] The quote was an apt choice on Cheever's part, and it served as a reminder of Jay's legacy.

Notes

INTRODUCTION

1. Linda K. Kerber, "Abolitionists and Amalgamators: The New York City Race Riots of 1834," *New York History* 48 (January, 1967), 28–40; Edwin G. Burrows and Mike Wallace, *Gotham: A History of New York City to 1898* (New York: Oxford University Press, 1999), 558–559; Tyler Anbinder, *Five Points* (New York: Free Press, 2001), 7–13.

2. Burrows and Wallace, *Gotham,* 558–559.

3. Kerber, "Abolitionists and Amalgamators," 37; Bertram Wyatt-Brown, *Lewis Tappan and the Evangelical War Against Slavery* (Cleveland, Ohio: Case Western Reserve University Press, 1969), xiii.

4. William M. Wiecek, "Latimer: Lawyers, Abolitionists, and the Problem of Unjust Laws," in *Antislavery Reconsidered: New Perspectives on the Abolitionists,* Lewis Perry and Michael Fellman, eds. (Baton Rouge: Louisiana State University Press, 1979), 231.

5. Howard Zinn, "Abolitionists, Freedom Riders, and the Tactics of Agitation," in *The Antislavery Vanguard: New Essays on the Abolitionists,* Martin Duberman, ed. (Princeton: Princeton University Press, 1965), 417–451; Henry Mayer, *All On Fire: William Lloyd Garrison and the Abolition of Slavery* (New York: St. Martin's Press, 1998), xvii.

6. Ellen DuBois, "Women's Rights and Abolition: The Nature of the Connection," in Perry and Fellman, *Antislavery Reconsidered,* 238–252.

7. Aileen S. Kraditor, *Means and Ends in American Abolitionism: Garrison and His Critics on Strategy and Tactics, 1834–1850* (New York: Pantheon Books, 1967), 16–17.

8. Mayer, *All On Fire*, 7–8.

9. Ibid., 23–24.

10. T. Harry Williams, *Lincoln and the Radicals* (Madison: University of Wisconsin Press, 1941), 5; James M. Banner Jr., *To the Hartford Convention: The Federalists and the Origins of Party Politics in Massachusetts, 1789–1815* (New York: Alfred A. Knopf, 1970), 22–24; Rogers M. Smith, "Constructing American National Identity: Strategies of the Federalists," in *Federalists Reconsidered*, Doron Ben-Atar and Barbara B. Oberg, eds. (Charlottesville: University of Virginia Press, 1998), 19–40.

11. David Lowenthal, *Possessed by the Past: The Heritage Crusade and the Spoils of History* (New York: Free Press, 1996), 34; Linda Kerber, *Federalists in Dissent: Imagery and Ideology in Jeffersonian America* (Ithaca: Cornell University Press, 1970), 53–65. Kerber links Federalist fathers and sons in the promotion of the antislavery cause. She states that "the political abolitionism of an earlier generation was transformed into a humanitarian abolitionism by sons who took fathers at their word. Kerber, *Federalists*, 62.

12. William Jay to James Fenimore Cooper, January 5, 1827, *The Correspondence of James Fenimore Cooper*, 2 vols. (New Haven: Yale University Press, 1922), 112–113.

13. Paul Finkelman, "The Problem of Slavery in the Age of Federalism," in Ben-Atar and Oberg, *Federalists Reconsidered*, 146–149; David Brion Davis, "The Emergence of Immediatism in British and American Antislavery Thought," *Mississippi Valley Historical Review* 49 (1962–1963), 209–230.

14. William M. Wiecek, *The Sources of Antislavery Constitutionalism in America* (Ithaca: Cornell University Press, 1977), 82–83.

15. Peter J. Wosh, *Spreading the Word: The Bible Business in Nineteenth Century America* (Ithaca: Cornell University Press, 1994), 121; John R. McKivigan, *The War Against Proslavery Religion: Abolitionism and the Northern Churches, 1830–1865* (Ithaca: Cornell University Press, 1984), 109–110.

16. Keith J. Hardman, *Charles Grandison Finney, 1792–1875: Revivalist and Reformer* (Syracuse: Syracuse University Press, 1987), 45–48; Joseph A. Conforti, *Jonathan Edwards, Religious Tradition, and American Culture* (Chapel Hill: University of North Carolina Press, 1995), 11–17; George Burrell Cheever, *The True Christian Patriot: A Discourse on the Virtues and Public Services of the Late William Jay* (Boston: American Peace Society, 1860), 15.

CHAPTER 1

1. Richard B. Morris, ed., *John Jay: The Making of a Revolutionary, Unpublished Papers, 1745–1780* (New York: Harper & Row, 1975), 29; Robert Bolton Jr., *History of the County of Westchester From Its First Settlement to the Present Time* (New York: Alexander S. Gould, 1848), 81–83; Elizabeth Blackmar, *Manhattan for Rent, 1785–1850* (Ithaca: Cornell University Press, 1989), 30–33.

2. John Jay, *Memorials of Peter A. Jay: Compiled for His Descendents* (Netherlands: G. J. Thieme, 1905), 7; Robert J. Taylor, ed., *Diary of John Quincy Adams, 1779–1786,* 2 vols. (Cambridge: Belknap Press, 1981), I: 288–301.

3. Blackmar, *Manhattan for Rent,* 30–33; Betsy Blackmar, "Rewalking the 'Walking City': Housing and Property Relations in New York City, 1780–1840," in *Material Life in America, 1600–1860,* Robert Blair St. George, ed. (Boston: Northeastern University Press, 1988), 371–384. Trinity Church leases for favored individuals could run ninety-nine years. Among those who purchased favorable leases were John Jacob Astor and Aaron Burr.

4. Morris, *John Jay,* 29.

5. Robert J. Taylor, ed., *The Adams Papers: The Diary of John Quincy Adams,* 12 vols. (Cambridge: Belknap Press, 1981), I: 288–289; Edwin G. Burrows and Mike Wallace, *Gotham: A History of New York City to 1898* (New York: Oxford University Press, 1998), 270–271, 301.

6. George Pellew, *John Jay* (Boston: Houghton Mifflin, 1899), 205–206.

7. William Jay, *The Life of John Jay: With Selections from His Correspondence and Miscellaneous Papers,* 2 vols. (New York: J. J. Harper, 1833), I: 253.

8. Morris, *John Jay,* 152–154.

9. So much so that twentieth-century biographer Frank Monaghan felt compelled to title his work on Jay: *John Jay, Defender of Liberty Against Kings and Peoples, Author of the Constitution and Governor of New York, President of the Continental Congress, Co-Author of the Federalist, Negotiator of the Peace of 1783 and the Jay Treaty of 1794, First Chief Justice of the United States* (New York: Bobbs Merrill, 1935).

10. Stephen Howarth, *To Shining Sea: A History of the United States Navy, 1775–1991* (New York: Random House 1991). French colonies as well. With some 300 merchant vessels impounded by the British, and lacking a navy of any consequence, America's only recourse was diplomatic protest.

11. Claude G. Bowers, *Jefferson and Hamilton: The Struggle for Democracy in America* (New York: Houghton Mifflin, 1925), 246–247.

12. Jay, *Life of John Jay,* I: 253.

13. Bowers, *Jefferson and Hamilton,* 249.

14. Frederic Austin Ogg, "Jay's Treaty and the Slavery Interests of the United States," *Annual Report of the American Historical Association* (Washington, D.C.: Government Printing Office, 1901), 275–298.

15. Albert J. Beveridge, *The Life of John Marshall,* 4 vols. (Boston: Houghton Mifflin, 1916), II: 113–118.

16. Jay, *Life of John Jay,* I: 357, 361–361.

17. Bernard Bailyn, ed., *The Debate on the Constitution,* 2 vols. (New York: Gryphon, 1993), I: 9.

18. Bowers, *Jefferson and Hamilton,* 248.

19. Lewis P. Simpson, ed., *The Federalist Literary Mind: Selections from the Monthly Anthology and Boston Review, 1803–1811* (Baton Rouge: Louisiana State University Press, 1962), 87, 95–102.

20. William A. Wiecek, "Latimer: Lawyers, Abolitionists, and the Problem of Unjust Laws," in Perry and Fellman, *Antislavery Reconsidered,* 231.

21. Jay, *Memorials*, 23–24; Bolton, *History of Westchester*, 81.

22. Bayard Tuckerman, *William Jay and the Constitutional Movement for the Abolition of Slavery* (New York: Negro Universities Press, 1969), 2–3; Cooper, *Correspondence*, I: 29; Alan Taylor, *William Cooper's Town: Power and Persuasion on the Frontier of the Early American Republic* (New York: Random House, 1995), 399–400.

23. James Fenimore Cooper, *Gleanings in Europe: England* (Albany: State University of New York Press, 1982), 155.

24. Taylor, *William Cooper's Town*, 143–144.

25. Pellew, *John Jay*, 313; Cooper, *Correspondence*, I: 42; Tuckerman, *William Jay*, 5; Henry Walcott Boynton, *James Fenimore Cooper* (New York: Century, 1931), 82.

26. James Fenimore Cooper to William Buell Sprague, Paris, November 15, 1831, in James Franklin Beard, ed., *The Letters and Journals of James Fenimore Cooper*, 6 vols. (Cambridge: Harvard University Press, 1960), II: 155.

27. John Jay, *Memorials*, 10; Taylor, *William Cooper's Town*, 340–341.

28. Boynton, *Cooper*, 30.

29. Ibid., 30.

30. Taylor, *William Cooper's Town*, 340–341; Cooper, *Correspondence*, III; Charles Sellers, *The Market Revolution: Jacksonian America, 1815–1846* (New York: Oxford University Press, 1991), 65. For biographical outlines of all Yale students of Jay's class see Franklin Bowditch Dexter, *Biographical Sketches of the Graduates of Yale College: With Annals of the College History* (New York: Holt, 1885–1912).

31. John W. Blassingame, ed., *The Frederick Douglass Papers*, 4 vols. (New Haven: Yale University Press, 1979–), III: n. 260.

32. William Jay to John Jay, Albany, May 10, 1808; William Jay to John Jay, Albany, August 9, 1808; William Jay to John Jay, Albany, March 13, 1809, John Jay Collection (JJC), Columbia University, New York.

33. William Jay to John Jay, Albany, March 13, 1809, JJC.

34. William Jay to John Jay, Albany, August 19, 1809, JJC.

35. I. N. Phelps Stokes, *New York: Past and Present, 1524–1939* (New York: Plantin Press, 1935), 75. Stokes reveals epidemics of yellow fever occurred in 1795, 1796, and 1798. The disease returned in 1803 to claim some 600 lives.

36. Pellew, *John Jay*, 295–301; Jay, *Memorials*, 34–35.

37. Jay, *Memorials*, 36, 73–74; Monaghan, *John Jay*, 427–428.

38. Jay, *Memorials*, 35–36.

39. Morris, *John Jay*, 246; Monaghan, *John Jay*, 428, 430; Pellew, *John Jay*, 304.

40. Tuckerman, *William Jay*, 8–9.

41. Ibid., 10.

42. Monaghan, *John Jay*, 433; William Jay, *New York Evening Post for the Country*, November 3, 1820. Contains an article relating to the cattle show

and fair of the Westchester Agricultural Society, written by Secretary William Jay. I would like to thank Elizabeth G. Fuller of the Westchester County Historical Society for making me aware of this document in her letter of September 22, 1994.

43. George Adams Boyd, *Elias Boudinot, Patriot and Statesman, 1740–1821* (Princeton: Princeton University Press, 1952), 213–214.

44. Elias Boudinot, *A Star in the West, or A Humble Attempt to Discover the Long Lost Ten Tribes of Israel, Prepatory to Their Return to Their Beloved City, Jerusalem* (Trenton, N.J.: D. Fenton, S. Hutchinson, J. Dunham, and George Sherman, 1816).

45. Boyd, *Boudinot*, 258–259.

46. Creighton Lacy, *The Word Carrying Giant: The Growth of the American Bible Society, 1816–1966* (South Pasadena, Calif.: William Carey Library, 1977), 7.

47. Boyd, *Boudinot*, 259.

48. *American Bible Society Annual Report* (New York: G. F. Hopkins, 1816), 38.

49. Ibid., 4; Lacy, *Word Carrying Giant*, 7.

50. Tuckerman, *William Jay*, 10.

51. John M. Mason, *Essays of Episcopacy and the Apology for Apostolic Orders and its Advocates Reviewed*, edited by Reverend Ebeneezer Mason (New York: Robert Carter, 1844), 1–3. The full title of Hobart's work was: *A Companion for the Altar: Consisting of a Short Explanation of the Lord's Supper; and Meditations and Prayers Properly to Be Used Before, and During the Receiving of the Holy Communion, According to the Form Prescribed by the Protestant Episcopal Church in the United States of America.*

52. William Jay to John Jay, New York, May 10, 1811, JJC.

53. William Jay to John Jay, New York, February 11, 1812, JJC.

54. Craig Hanyan and Mary T. Hanyan, *DeWitt Clinton and the Rise of the People's Men* (Montreal: McGill-Queen's University Press, 1996), 96.

55. Ibid., 96–99.

56. William Jay, *A Letter to the Right Reverend Bishop Hobart, Occasioned by the Strictures on Bible Societies, Contained in His Late Charge to the Convention of New York* (New York, 1823); John Henry Hobart, *A Reply to a Letter to the Right Reverend Bishop Hobart, Occasioned by the Strictures on Bible Societies, Contained in His Address to the Convention of New York, by a Churchman of the Diocese of New York, in a Letter to That Gentleman by Corrector* (New York, 1823).

57. William Jay to Peter A. Jay, November 11, 1820, JJC.

58. Morris, *Jay*, 702; *Heads of Families at the First Census Take in the Year 1790: New York* (Baltimore: Genealogical Publishing, 1966), 133.

59. Morris, *Jay*, 401.

60. Arthur J. Alexander, "Federal Officeholders in New York State as Slaveowners, 1789–1805," *Journal of Negro History* 28 (July, 1943), 326–350.

61. Ibid., 823.

62. Pellew, *Jay*, 217; Richard B. Morris, ed., *John Jay: The Winning of the Peace—Unpublished Papers, 1780–1784* (New York: Harper & Row, 1980), 13–14.

63. Robert Isaac and Samuel Wilberforce, eds., *The Correspondence of William Wilberforce*, 2 vols. (Philadelphia: Henry Perkins, 1841), II: 50, 67.

64. Morris, *Winning of the Peace*, 705–706.

65. Ibid.

66. Richard H. Brown, "The Missouri Crisis, Slavery, and the Politics of Jacksonianism," *South Atlantic Quarterly* (Winter, 1966), 55–72.

67. Alvin Kass, *Politics in New York State, 1800–1830* (Syracuse: Syracuse University Press, 1965), 84–85.

68. Tuckerman, *William Jay*, 28–29; Douglass, *Papers*, 269–270.

69. David A. Carson, "The Louisiana Purchase Debates," *The Historian* (Spring, 1992), 477–491; Steven Watts, "Ministers, Misanthropes, and Mandarins: The Federalists and the Culture of Capitalism," in Ben-Atar and Oberg, *Federalists Reconsidered*, 160–161.

70. Cooper, *Correspondence*, 114.

71. Ibid.

72. William Jay, *A View of the Action of the Federal Government in Behalf of Slavery* (New York, 1839), 238–240; William Jay to James Fenimore Cooper, January 5, 1827, in Cooper, *Correspondence*, 114–115; Don E. Fehrenbacker, *Slavery, Law, and Politics: The Dred Scott Case in Historical Perspective* (New York: Oxford University Press, 1981), 33.

73. Ibid., 556–557.

74. Ibid., 558–566.

75. Douglass, *Papers*, 270–271.

76. Alexander C. Flick, ed., *History of the State of New York*, 10 vols. (New York: Columbia University Press, 1934), VI: 11–12; Alexander, *Federalists*, 326–336.

77. Flick, *History*, 12; Alexander, *Federalists*, 326–335; Finkelman, "Problem of Slavery."

78. Dixon Ryan Fox, *The Decline of Aristocracy in the Politics of New York* (New York: Columbia University Press, 1919).

79. Lee Benson, *The Concept of Jacksonian Democracy: New York as a Test Case* (Princeton: Princeton University Press, 1961); Kass, *Politics*, 5–6.

80. Dexter, *Biographical Sketches*, 132. Dexter provides a convenient bibliography of Jay's works throughout his life, and during the years 1826–1829 Jay seemed concerned with essays. *Essay on the Importance of the Sabbath considered Merely a Civic Institution* (1826) and *Essay on the Perpetuity and Divine Authority of the Sabbath* (1827) reveal that Jay was increasingly being drawn into the groundswell for societal reform.

81. Jay, *Life of John Jay*, II: 463.

82. E. Anthony Rotundo, *American Manhood: Transformations in Masculinity from the Revolution to the Modern Era* (New York: Basic Books, 1993), 56–58.

83. William Jay, *War and Peace: The Evils of the First, and a Plan for Preserving the Last* (New York: Wiley and Putnam, 1842), iii–xiv.

84. Henry Adams, *The Education of Henry Adams* (New York: Modern Library, 1918), 20.

CHAPTER 2

1. Morris, *John Jay: The Making of a Revolutionary*, 4–5; Jay, *The Life of John Jay*, I: iv.

2. Jay, *John Jay*, II: 460–462.

3. Morris, *John Jay: The Making of a Revolutionary*, 3–4.

4. John Quincy Adams to William Jay, October 20, 1832, JJC.

5. David M. Potter, *The Impending Crisis, 1848–1861* (New York: Harper & Row, 1976), 79.

6. Leonard L. Richards, "The Jacksonians and Slavery," *Antislavery Reconsidered,* in Perry and Fellman, *Federalists Reconsidered* 99; Sellers, *Market Revolution,* 404–405.

7. William Jay, *An Essay on Duelling* (Savannah, Ga.: Savannah Anti-Dueling Association, 1829), 8–9, 13.

8. Ibid., 6–7.

9. Dexter, *Biographical Sketches,* 133.

10. *Second Annual Report,* American Tract Society (New York: Society's House 1827), 58.

11. Cooper resided in Europe for several years, in order to give his daughters a Paris education.

12. James Fenimore Cooper to Peter Augustus Jay, Paris, January 2, 1832, in Beard, *Letters and Journals,* II: 171–172, VI: 317.

13. Cooper, *Correspondence,* I: 301–303.

14. Ibid., I: 302.

15. Ibid.

16. Hardman, *Charles Grandison Finney,* 152–153. One purpose of these numerous societies was to promote such an overwhelming groundswell of social piousness as to usher in the Millennium as quickly as possible.

17. Friedman, *Gregarious Saints,* 69; McKivigan, *The War Against Proslavery Religion,* 203–220. Jay's status as an Episcopalian made his involvement in these organizations all the more remarkable. McKivigan lists 583 officers of four national abolition societies from 1833 to 1864. Even with the denomination of 189 of these members unknown, only eight Episcopalians are listed.

18. Harman, *Finney,* 253–254.

19. Ibid., 252–257; David L. Weddle, *The Law as Gospel: Revival and Reform in the Theology of Charles G. Finney* (Metuchen, N.J.: Scarecrow Press, 1985), 261–266, 274–275; Anbinder, *Five Points,* 8–9. Undoubtedly of tremendous intellectual attraction to Jay were the constant analogies between the laws of man, governments, and God's moral law that former barrister Finney indulged in.

20. P. J. Staudenraus, *The African Colonization Movement, 1816–1865* (New York: Columbia University Press, 1961), 227–230.

21. Wyatt-Brown, *Lewis Tappan*, 78–79, 257–258.

22. Ibid., 104–105. The work that Jay made an indirect reference to was Garrison's *Thoughts on African Colonization* (1832), a skillfully manipulative diatribe that used portions of colonization society literature taken out of context to weave a tapestry of defamation. Interestingly, if Jay thought that the colonization society should be ignored, that same body had attempted to take the high ground by ignoring Garrison's scalding accusations, lest they endow them with credibility. See William Lloyd Garrison, *Thoughts on African Colonization* (New York: Arno Press and the New York Times, 1968), x–xi; Staudenraus, *African Colonization Movement*, 200–201.

23. *The Emancipator,* June 22, 1833, 1. The letter also appeared in *The Emancipator* on May 1 and June 29, 1833.

24. *The Emancipator,* March 10, 1835, 3. This is just one example. John Jay's name was invoked more as the violence directed at antislavery forces increased.

25. *The Emancipator,* June 22, 1833.

26. Kerber, "Abolitionists and Amalgamators," 37; Tuckerman, *William Jay,* 57.

27. Sean Wilentz, *Chants Democratic: New York City and the Rise of the American Working Class, 1788–1850* (New York: Oxford University Press, 1984), 264–265; Richards, *Gentlemen of Property,* 54–62.

28. William Jay to John Jay, June 25, 1835, JJC.

29. Carroll Smith-Rosenberg, "Sex as Symbol in Victorian Purity: An Ethnohistorical Analysis of Jacksonian America," *American Journal of Sociology* 84, Supplement (1984), S212–S247; John d'Emilio and Estelle B. Freedman, *Intimate Matters: A History of Sexuality in America* (New York: Harper & Row, 1988), 66–69; G. J. Barker-Benfield, *The Horrors of the Half-Known Life: Male Attitudes Toward Women and Sexuality in Nineteenth Century America* (New York: Harper & Row, 1976), 166–167.

30. Smith-Rosenberg, "Sex as Symbol," S219–S220.

31. Wilentz, *Chants,* 264–266; Carroll Smith-Rosenberg, "Bourgeois Discourse and the Age of Jackson: An Introduction," in *Disorderly Conduct* (New York, 1985), 79–89. Smith-Rosenberg believes both sides were attempting to impose their own sense of order upon a rapidly changing America.

32. Richards, *Gentlemen of Property,* 114–115; Kerber, *Abolitionists,* 30–31.

33. William Jay, "Inquiry into the Character and Tendency of the American Colonization and American Anti-Slavery Societies," in *Miscellaneous Writings on Slavery,* 150.

34. James D. Richardson, ed., *Messages and Papers of the Presidents,* 11 vols. (Washington, D.C., 1897), IV: 175.

35. Bertram Wyatt-Brown, "The Abolitionist's Postal Campaign of 1835," *Journal of Negro History* 1 (October, 1965), 227–238.

36. *The Emancipator,* March 24, 1835, 3.

37. Jay, *Inquiry,* 78.

38. Ibid., 57.

39. Ibid., 112–121.

40. Ibid., 141, 149, 151.

41. Ibid., 163.

42. Ibid., 125.

43. Fox, *Decline of the Aristocracy,* 230–239. Fox's section on the New York Constitutional Convention of 1821 shows that such Federalist prejudices had a verifiable political purpose.

44. Jay, *Inquiry,* 147.

45. Ibid., 195.

46. Ibid., 179, 181, 199.

47. Ibid., 140, 166.

48. Louis Filler, *The Campaign Against Slavery, 1830–1860* (New York: Harper & Brothers, 1960), 62.

49. Tappan to Clay, March 24, 1835, in *The Papers of Henry Clay,* Robert Seager III, ed., 10 vols. (Lexington: University Press of Kentucky, 1984), VIII: 768.

50. Lydia Maria Child to Francis Shaw, August 17, 1838, *The Collected Correspondence of Lydia Maria Child, 1817–1880* (Millwood, N.Y.: KTO Microform, 1979).

51. David M. Reese, *Observations on the Epidemic of 1819, As It Prevailed in a Part of the City of Baltimore* (Baltimore: John D. Toy, 1819); David M. Reese, *Letters to the Hon. William Jay, Being a Reply to His Inquiry into the American Colonization and American Anti-Slavery Societies* (New York: Leavitt and Lord, 1835), VII: 66–73, 80–81; William Jay to Peter A. Jay, Bedford, June 11, 1835, JJC.

52. *The Emancipator,* June 9, 1835.

53. *African Repository* (September, 1835), 284–285.

54. Leon Litwack, "The Abolitionist Dilemma: The Antislavery Movement and the Northern Negro," *New England Quarterly* 34 (1961), 682–691.

55. Douglass, *Papers,* 443, 476–477; Frederick Douglass, *My Bondage and My Freedom* (New York: Classics of Liberty Library, 1994), 406.

56. William H. Pease and Jane H. Pease, "Antislavery Ambivalence: Immediatism, Expediency, and Race," *American Quarterly* (Winter, 1965), 682–691.

57. Wyatt-Brown, *Lewis Tappan,* 179.

58. David H. Donald, *Charles Sumner* (New York: Da Capo Press, 1996), 298; Hugh Davis, *Joshua Leavitt: Evangelical Abolitionist* (Baton Rouge: Louisiana State University Press, 1990), 109.

59. Lewis Tappan, March 9, 1836, April 6, 1836, *Diaries and Letters of Lewis Tappan* (DLT), Library of Congress, Washington, D.C.; Wyatt-Brown, *Lewis Tappan,* 179.

60. Kerber, "Abolitionists and Amalgamators," 28–39.

61. Theodore Dwight Weld and John Montieth to James Birney, October 30, 1835, *The Letters of James Gillespie Birney, 1831–1857,* Dwight L. Dumond, ed., 2 vols. (New York: D. Appleton–Century, 1938), I: 251–254.

62. *The Emancipator,* December, 1835, 2.

63. Freidman, *Gregarious Saints,* 43, 68.

64. Whittier to the *Pennsylvania Freeman,* May 6, 1838, *The Letters of John Greenleaf Whittier,* John B. Pickard, ed., 3 vols. (Cambridge: Harvard University Press, 1975) 1: 292–293, Garrison, *Thoughts,* II: 349.

65. William Jay to Lewis Tappan, March 28, 1838, JJC.

66. Ibid.

67. *The Emancipator,* May 17, 1838, 9. Throughout the initial stages of this debate, Garrison's *Liberator* was strangely silent. The paper noted the New York convention and recorded Stewart's motion; it then concentrated upon more sensational riots in Philadelphia. *The Liberator,* May 18, 1838.

68. William M. Wiecek, *The Sources of Antislavery Constitutionalism in America, 1760–1848* (Ithaca: Cornell University Press, 1977), 265–266.

69. Ibid., 266; *The Emancipator,* May 17, 1838.

70. Wiecek, *Sources,* 266–267.

71. *The Emancipator,* May 31, 1838, 17.

72. Ibid.

73. Davis, *Joshua Leavitt,* 147.

74. *The Emancipator,* May 17, 1838, 11.

75. Theodore Dwight Weld, *Letters of Theodore Dwight Weld, Angela Grimke Weld, and Sarah Grimke, 1822–1844,* 2 vols. (Gloucester, Mass.: P. Smith, 1965), II: 670.

76. William Jay and Gerrit Smith, *Letter to the New York Candidates,* October, 1839, JJC.

77. David Brion Davis, *The Slave Power Conspiracy and the Paranoid Style* (Baton Rouge: Louisiana State University Press, 1969), 7–13; Richard Hofstadter, *The Paranoid Style in American Politics and Other Essays* (Chicago: University of Chicago Press, 1979). Hofstadter is mentioned because he provided the inspiration for Davis's examination. It is Hofstadter's contention that American politics has been an almost seamless transition from one conspiracy theory to the next.

78. Will Durant, *The Story of Philosophy: The Lives and Opinions of the Greater Philosophers* (New York: Simon and Schuster, 1953), 103.

79. William Jay, *A View of the Action of the Federal Government in Behalf of Slavery* (New York, 1839), 217.

80. Ibid., 218–219.

81. Ibid., 219–328.

82. Finkelman, "Problem of Slavery," 135–157; Banner, *To the Hartford Convention,* 327.

83. Jay, *View,* 229.

84. Ibid., 232–233.

85. Ibid., 235.

86. The law was based upon Article IV, Section 2 of the Constitution, which states: "No person held to service or labor in one state under the laws thereof, escaping into another, shall, in consequence of any law or regulation therein, be discharged from such service or labor, but shall be delivered up on a claim of the party to which such service or labor may be due."

87. Jay, *View.*, 247–248; David S. and Jeanne T. Heidler, *Old Hickory's War: Andrew Jackson and the Quest for Empire* (Mechanicsburg, Pa.: Stackpole Books, 1996), 62–74.

88. Jay, *View,* 290.

89. Ibid., 292–293. The work that Jay referred to was Buxton's *The African Slave Trade,* published in 1839.

90. Jay, *View,* 326–331.

91. Ibid., 332–337.

92. Ibid., 347.

93. Ibid., 347–351.

94. Ibid., 354.

95. Ibid., 361.

96. Ibid., 357–363.

97. Ibid., 355.

98. Ibid., 356–361.

99. Sidney Fine, *Laissez-Faire and the General Welfare State: A Study of Conflict in American Thought, 1865–1901* (Ann Arbor: University of Michigan Press, 1956), 3.

100. James Bryce, *The American Commonwealth,* 2 vols. (London: Macmillan, 1889), II: 404–406. It must be noted that Bryce believed such principles were overrated, and that all men would happily resort to governmental action when it suited their interests.

101. Please note that Jay author is not referring to the Transcendentalist doctrines of Emerson.

102. Bryce, *Commonwealth,* 409.

103. Ibid., 376.

104. Ibid., 378–386.

105. Ibid., 372–373.

106. Davis, "Emergence of Immediatism," 209–230.

CHAPTER 3

1. Filler, *Campaign Against Slavery,* 132–136.

2. DuBois, "Women's Rights and Abolition," 241.

3. Dorothy Sterling, "Abby Kelley," in *The American Radical,* Mari Jo Buhle, Paul Buhle, and Harvey J. Kaye, eds. (New York: Routledge, 1994), 44; Kraditor, *Means and Ends,* 41–43. Kraditor suggests that the threat, or confrontation, of crumbling spheres derived from the fact that, at this time, women were the most interesting antislavery speakers available.

4. Filler, *Campaign Against Slavery*, 133.

5. Ibid., 135–136.

6. Wyatt-Brown, *Lewis Tappan*, 188–191, 197–198; Sterling, "Abby Kelley," 44. Sterling states that, upon Kelley's election, the conservatives walked out taking most of the society's assets with them. In fact, there were few assets, and squabbling over the poor financial condition of the national society had added yet another iron to the fire of controversy.

7. John Jay to William Jay, May 14, 1840, JJC.

8. *The Liberator*, June 7, 1839, 1.

9. Wyatt-Brown, *Lewis Tappan*, 194–196. Although Jay did not attend the May meeting, he did keep abreast of the efforts to form a new society. A letter to jay from Joshua Leavitt in London was written on the back of a copy of the American and Foreign Anti-Slavery Society constitution, and describes the meeting. Joshua Leavitt to William Jay, July 2, 1840, JJC.

10. William Jay to American Anti-Slavery Society Committee of Arrangements, April 17, 1840, JJC.

11. William Jay to Lewis Tappan, August 23, 1839, JJC.

12. William Jay to Lewis Tappan, September 12, 1840, JJC.

13. William Lee Miller, *Arguing About Slavery: John Quincy Adams and the Great Battle in the United States Congress* (New York: Vintage Books, 1998), 79; David Turley, *The Culture of English Anti-Slavery, 1780–1860* (London: Routledge, 1991). Any number of works, including Miller's, confirm American conservatism in this period. Turley's book is of interest because it shows how English abolitionists, like their American counterparts later, had to tailor their appeal to the lower classes as a practical matter of gaining support.

14. Kraditor, *Means and Ends*, 41–42, 60.

15. Richard J. Carwardine, *Evangelicals and Politics in Antebellum America* (New Haven: Yale University Press, 1993), 3–13.

16. Ibid., 22–25.

17. William A. Wiecek, *The Sources of Antislavery Constitutionalism in America, 1760–1848* (Ithaca: Cornell University Press, 1977), 228–233; Mayer, *All On Fire*, 414–415. The precepts of nonresistance were later defined more famously by Henry David Thoreau as "civil disobedience."

18. William Jay to Joshua Leavitt, March 13, 1838, JJC; William Jay to Elizur Wright, April 13, 1838, JJC.

19. Although he did not refer to them specifically, Jay clearly invoked Article IV, Section C, which stated that the AASS's only weapons were "appeals to the consciences, hearts, and interests of the people" to arouse public sentiment; and Article VI, which confirmed the sovereignty of each state to legislate in its own interest regarding slavery.

20. William Jay to Elizur Wright, New York, November 13, 1838, JJC.

21. *The Liberator*, July 5, 1839, 2.

22. Luther Rawson Marsh, ed., *Writings and Speeches of Alvan Stewart on Slavery* (New York: Negro Universities Press, 1969), 1–17, 251–254.

23. Walter M. Merrill and Louis Ruchames, eds., *The Letters of William Lloyd Garrison,* 6 vols. (Cambridge: Belknap Press of Harvard University Press, 1971–1981), II: 566.

24. Wyatt-Brown, *Lewis Tappan,* 199; Margaret Plunkett, *A History of the Liberty Party with Emphasis upon Its Activities in the Northeastern States* (unpublished PhD diss., Cornell University, 1930), 99.

25. William Jay to Gerrit Smith, July 25, 1840, JJC. Smith appears to have been the happy warrior, or at least a consummate politician, remaining on good terms with both Garrison and the Tappanites.

26. *The Liberator,* July 5, 1839, 2.

27. Ibid.

28. Ibid.

29. Ibid.

30. Ibid.

31. Ibid.

32. Hugh Davis, *Joshua Leavitt* (Baton Rouge: Louisiana State University Press, 1990), 159–160; Lewis Tappan to William Jay, September 11, 1840, JJC; Lewis Tappan to William Jay, October 1, 1840, JJC.

33. William Jay to Lewis Tappan, September 13, 1840, JJC.

34. Howard Jones, *Mutiny on the Amistad: The Saga of a Slave Revolt and Its Impact on American Abolition, Law, and Diplomacy* (New York: Oxford University Press, 1987), 23; Filler, *Campaign Against Slavery,* 167–168; Wyatt-Brown, *Lewis Tappan,* 205–209.

35. Jay to Tappan, October 7, 1840, JJC. A review of *The Emancipator* at the time of Jay's letter does not bear out his complaint, with the Amistad case being admirably covered.

36. John Niven, *Martin Van Buren: The Romantic Age of American Politics* (New York: Oxford University Press, 1983).

37. Charles Francis Adams, ed., *Memoirs of John Quincy Adams: Containing Portions from His Diary, 1795–1848,* 12 vols. (Philadelphia: J. B. Lippincott, 1876), X: 379.

38. Filler, *Campaign Against Slavery,* 169.

39. Edward D. Jervey and C. Harold Huber, "The Creole Affair," *Journal of Negro History* 50 (October, 1965), 196–204.

40. *Congressional Globe,* 2nd Session, 27th Congress (City of Washington: Globe Office, 1842), 115, 205.

41. Robert Remini, *Daniel Webster: The Man and His Time* (New York: W. W. Norton, 1997), 538–540; Wilbur Devereux Jones, "The Influence of Slavery on the Webster-Ashburton Negotiations," *Journal of Southern History* 22 (February, 1956), 48–58.

42. *Congressional Globe,* 205.

43. Ibid., 206.

44. Remini, *Webster,* 535–542; William Jay, *The Creole Case and Mr. Webster's Despatch* (New York: Office of the New York American, 1842), 5–11.

45. Jervey and Huber, *Creole Affair*, 206.

46. William Ellery Channing, *The Duty of the Free States* (Boston: S. N. Dickinson, 1842), 2, 27–29.

47. Jay, *Creole Case*, 12.

48. Ibid., 11–18.

49. Ibid., 21–22.

50. Paul Finkelman, *An Imperfect Union: Slavery, Federalism, and Comity* (Chapel Hill: University of North Carolina Press, 1981), 11–14.

51. Stanley Harrold, *Gamaliel Bailey and Antislavery Union* (Kent, Ohio: Kent State University Press, 1986), 42–43.

52. Ibid., 43; Richards, *Gentlemen*, 42–43.

53. *The Liberator*, November 26, 1841.

54. David Lee Child to Lydia Maria Child, November 10, 1841, *Collected Correspondence*. This letter was reprinted in the *National Anti-Slavery Standard* on November 25, 1841.

55. Plunkett, *History of the Liberty Party*, 100–101.

56. Ronald G. Walters, *The Antislavery Appeal: American Abolitionism After 1830* (Baltimore: Johns Hopkins University Press, 1976), 15–16; Carwadine, *Evangelicals and Politics*, 135–137.

57. Steven Mintz, *Moralists and Modernizers: America's Pre–Civil War Reformers* (Baltimore: Johns Hopkins University Press, 1995), 132; William Jay to Lewis Tappan, September 12, 1840, JJC.

58. Mintz, 116–118; Wyatt-Brown, *Lewis Tappan*, 274–276.

59. Theodore Clarke Smith, *The Liberty and Free Soil Parties in the Northwest* (New York: Russell and Russell, 1967), 66–67; Wyatt-Brown, *Lewis Tappan*, 273–274; Harrold, *Gamaliel Bailey*, 33–34.

60. John Niven, ed., *The Salmon P. Chase Papers, 1829–1872* (Kent, Ohio: Kent State University Press, 1993), I: 147; Smith, *Liberty and Free Soil Party*, 60–61; Plunkett, *History of the Liberty Party*, 117–119; Harrold, *Bailey*, 62–63.

61. Lewis Tappan to William Jay, March 13, 1842, TLD.

62. Gamliel Bailey to James Birney, March 31, 1843, *Letters of James Gillespie Birney*, II: 725–728.

63. Ibid., 727.

64. Davis, *Joshua Leavitt*, 209; Joshua Leavitt to James Birney, February 28, 1843, *Letters of James Gillespie Birney*, 719–720; Plunkett, *History of the Liberty Party*, 119. Jay's support of Birney should not be interpreted as an enthusiastic endorsement of the candidate or his party. The word "hatchet" in Leavitt's letter is illegible. Other historians have interpreted it as "satchel."

65. Wyatt-Brown, *Lewis Tappan*, 275. Wyatt-Brown touches upon Tappan's belief in a return to disinterested government.

66. Lewis Tappan to Gamaliel Bailey, March 6, 1843, JJC; James G. Birney to William Jay, July 20, 1836, JJC.

67. James G. Birney to Charles H. Stewart and Joshua Leavitt, August 17, 1843, *Letters of James Gillespie Birney*, 754–757.

68. DeAlva Stanwood Alexander, *A Political History of the State of New York,* 2 vols. (New York: Henry Holt, 1906), II: 82; Plunkett, *History of the Liberty Party,* 119; Davis, *Joshua Leavitt,* 208–211.

69. Robert Remini, *Henry Clay: Statesman for the Union* (New York: W. W. Norton, 1991), 645.

70. William Jay, *Letter to the Hon. Theodore Frelinghuysen* (New York, 1844), 1.

71. William Jay, *Address to the Non-Slaveholders of the Slave States* (New York: William Harned, 1843), 1, 18–9.

72. Ibid., 14, 53.

73. Bertram Wyatt-Brown, "Pro-Slavery and Anti-Slavery Intellectuals: Class Concepts and polemical Struggle," in Perry and Fellman, *Antislavery Reconsidered,* 308–337; Jay, *Address,* 1, 52–58.

74. Hugh C. Bailey, *Hinton Rowan Helper: Abolitionist, Racist* (Birmingham: University of Alabama, 1965); Lewis Tappan to William Jay, March 13, 1842, TLD.

75. Merton Dillon, *The Abolitionists: The Growth of a Dissenting Minority* (DeKalb: Northern Illinois University Press, 1974), 156–157; Mayer, *All On Fire,* 301–304; John R. McKivigan, *The War Against Proslavery Religion: Abolitionism and the Northern Churches, 1830–1865* (Ithaca: Cornell University Press, 1984), 93–96.

76. Ibid., 50, 203–220.

77. William Jay, "To the Reproof of the American Church Contained in the Recent 'History of the Protestant Episcopal Church in America,' by the Bishop of Oxford," in *Miscellaneous Writings,* 409–452.

78. Ibid., 448–449.

79. William Jay, "A Letter to the Right Reverend L. Sillman Ives, Bishop of the Protestant Episcopal Church in the State of North Carolina," in *Miscellaneous Writings,* 454–455.

80. Ibid., 455.

81. Ibid., 454, 466–467.

82. Ibid., 469–470.

83. Ibid., 488–489.

CHAPTER 4

1. Charles DeBenedetti, *The Peace Reform in American History* (Bloomington: University of Indiana Press, 1980), 33–37.

2. Merle Curti, *The American Peace Crusade, 1815–1860* (Durham, N.C.: Duke University Press, 1929), 42; DeBenedetti, *Peace Reform,* 38–39; *History of the American Peace Society [APS] and Its Work* (Washington, D.C.: American Peace Society, 1908), 2–3.

3. Curti, *Peace Crusade,* 43; DeBenedetti, *Peace Reform,* 36–37.

4. Mayer, *All On Fire,* 249–250.

5. Ibid., 249–250.

6. William Ladd, *An Essay on a Congress of Nations: For the Adjustment*

of International Disputes Without Resort to Arms (New York: Oxford University Press, 1916), xi, ix; Stephen P. Budney, "Peace Profile: William Jay," *Peace Review* (Winter, 1998), 655–661.

7. Ladd, *Essay*, 1, 8–11.

8. Curti, *Crusade*, 44; *History of the APS*, 3.

9. William Jay, *War and Peace: The Evils of the First and a Plan for Preserving the Last* (New York: Wiley and Putnam, 1842), 53–54.

10. Ibid., 1–5.

11. Ibid., 7–8. Moloch (or Molech) was an ancient Semitic deity associated with the Ammonites, and often mentioned in the Old Testament of the Bible. The worship of Moloch was distinguished by the burning of children offered up as sacrifice by their own parents.

12. Ibid., 8–9. In works such as *View,* Jay had used the *Congressional Record* as the source of his financial facts. In *War and Peace* the work cited was M. Adrian Balbi's, *Balance Politique du Globe.*

13. Jay, *War and Peace*, 47.

14. Ibid., 52.

15. Ibid., 23, 49–50.

16. Ibid., 52.

17. Ibid., 54.

18. Frederick Merck, *Manifest Destiny and Mission in American History* (Cambridge: Harvard University Press, 1963) 27–29; Sellers, *Market Revolution,* 423.

19. Carwadine, *Evangelicals and Politics*, 231–232.

20. Ralph Waldo Emerson, *Miscellanies* (Boston: Houghton Mifflin, 1884), 201.

21. Jay, *War and Peace,* 54–55.

22. Ibid., 62, 69, 67; Benjamin Munn Ziegler, *The International Law of John Marshall: A Study of First Principle* (Chapel Hill: University of North Carolina Press, 1984), 122.

23. Jay, *War and Peace*, 62.

24. Richard Cobden, *Speeches of Richard Cobden on Peace, Financial Reform, Colonial Reform, and Other Subjects Delivered During 1849* (London: James Gilbert, 1970), 98–99; Curti, *Peace Crusade*, 189–190. Curti claims that William Jay devoted himself to the cause of world peace in his biography of his father. I have examined three separate editions of that work and found no such evidence.

25. Samuel Flagg Bemis, *Jay's Treaty: A Study in Commerce and Diplomacy* (New Haven: Yale University Press, 1962), 348, 460–466; Robert C. Morris, *International Arbitration and Procedure* (New Haven: Yale University Press, 1911), 62–63. American ship owners received over $11 million in damage, whereas British merchants received $143,000 for damages inflicted by French privateers outfitted in American ports.

26. Remini, *Daniel Webster,* 538; Morris, *International Arbitration,* 50; Jay, *War and Peace,* 59; Donald R. Hickey, *The War of 1812: A Forgotten Conflict* (Urbana: University of Illinois Press, 1989), 238; William Jay, *A Review of*

the Causes and Consequences of the Mexican War (Boston: Benjamin B. Mussey, 1849), 66–68.

27. Jay, *War and Peace,* 56; Henry Sumner Maine, *International Law* (London: John Murray, 1894), 32–33; M. de Vattel, *The Laws of Nations, or Principles of the Laws of Nature Applied to the Conduct and affairs of Nations and Sovereigns* (Dublin: Luke and White, 1912), 2–4.

28. de Vattel, *Laws,* 2; John Locke, *Two Treatises on Government* (New York: Classics of Liberty Library, 1992), 177.

29. Jay, *War and Peace,* 29, 51.

30. Joseph Sturge and Thomas Harvey, *The West Indies in 1837* (London: Frank Cass, 1968).

31. Curti, *Peace Crusade,* 14–16; William Jay to Joseph Sturge, July 25, 1841, in *A Side Light on Anglo-American Relations, 1839–1858: Furnished by the Correspondence of Lewis Tappan and Others with the British and Foreign Anti-Slavery Society,* Anne Heloise Abel and Frank J. Klingberg, eds. (New York: Augustus N. Kelly, 1970), 81–82; Edson L. Whitney, *The American Peace Society: A Centennial History* (Washington D.C.: American Peace Society, 1928), 64.

32. Curti, *Peace Crusade,* 189.

33. Lewis Tappan to William Jay, August 9, 1843, TLD; Lewis Tappan to William Jay, September 1, 1943, TLD.

34. *New York American,* February 23, 1843, 4.

35. Beard, *Letters and Journals,* IV: 364, 397.

36. Blassingame, *Frederick Douglass Papers,* 262–263. Jay was never called upon to make the decision on whether or not to enforce the Fugitive Slave Act during his tenure as judge.

37. DeAlva Stanwood Alexander, *A Political History of the State of New York,* 2 vols. (New York: Henry Holt, 1906), II, 56–57; John Niven, *Martin Van Buren: The Romantic Age of American Politics* (New York: Oxford University Press, 1983), 513–514; *The Emancipator and Free American,* June 6, 1843, July 13, 1843.

38. *The Emancipator,* July 13, 1843.

39. Cheever, *True Christian Patriot,* 20.

40. Lewis Tappan to William Jay, October 31, 1843, TLD.

41. William Jay to John Jay, November 11, 1843, JJC.

42. David M. Pletcher, *The Diplomacy of Annexation: Texas, Oregon, and the Mexican War* (Columbia: University of Missouri Press, 1975), 72–75; Sam W. Haynes, "Anglophobia and the Annexation of Texas: The Quest for National Security," in *Manifest Destiny and Empire: American Antebellum Expansion,* Sam W. Haynes and Christopher Morris, eds. (College Station: Texas A&M Press, 1997), 114–145.

43. Pletcher, *Diplomacy of Annexation,* 43, 72–73; Lelia M. Roeckell, "Bonds over Bondage: British Opposition to the Annexation of Texas," *Journal of the Early Republic* (Summer, 1999), 257–278; E. D. Adams, *British Interests and Activities in Texas, 1838–1846* (Gloucester, Mass.: Peter Smith, 1963), 16–17.

44. Hugh Thomas, *The Slave Trade: The Story of the Atlantic Slave Trade, 1440–1870* (New York: Simon and Schuster, 1997), 572–579.

45. *National Anti-Slavery Standard,* June 6, 1842, 1. Prior to the *Creole,* the three best-known incidents (or the most notorious incidents to slaveholders) involved the vessels *Comet* (1830), *Encomium* (1831), and *Enterprise* (1835).

46. Haynes, "Anglophobia and Texas," 118–121; Adams, *British Interests,* 140–142.

47. William H. Freehling, *The Road to Disunion: Secessionists at Bay, 1776–1854* (New York: Oxford University Press, 1990), 385; Haynes, "Anglophobia," 118; Adams, *British Interests,* 140; Pletcher, *Diplomacy of Annexation,* 121.

48. Lewis Tappan to William Jay, August 9, 1843, TLD; Wyatt-Brown, *Lewis Tappan,* 250–251; Pletcher, *Diplomacy of Annexation,* 121–122.

49. Haynes, *British Interests,* 129–130.

50. Lewis Tappan to William Jay, May 15, 1844, TLD.

51. Lewis Tappan to William Jay, June 14, 1844, TLD.

52. Ibid.; Abel and Klingberg, *Side-Light,* 10, n. 11.

53. Mayer, *All On Fire,* 353; Henry I. Bowditch, *The Liberator,* April 11, 1845, 58.

54. Freehling, *Road to Disunion,* 440–449; Merck, *Manifest Destiny,* 44–45.

55. *The Liberator,* April 11, 1845.

56. Ibid.

57. Ibid.

58. Ibid.

59. Ibid.

60. Ibid.

61. Kraditor, *Means and Ends,* 204–206; *The Liberator,* April 11, 1845.

62. *The Liberator,* May 2, 1845.

63. Ibid.

64. Jay, *View,* 217.

65. Beveridge, *John Marshall,* III: 152.

66. William Jay to Lewis Tappan, July 3, 1846, TLD; *The Liberator,* April 18, 1845, 60.

67. Merk, *Manifest Destiny,* 80–86.

68. Dean B. Mahin, *Olive Branch and Sword: The United States and Mexico, 1845–1848* (Jefferson, N.C.: McFarland, 1997), 52–55, 74–75.

69. Whitney, *American Peace Society,* 83–84.

70. Jay, *A Review,* 36–52.

71. Ibid., 36–37.

72. Ibid., 29–30, 93.

73. Ibid., 325.

74. Ibid., 332–333.

75. Edward L. Pierce, ed., *Memoir and Letters of Charles Sumner,* 4 vols. (Boston: Roberts Brothers, 1893), III: 186.

76. Ibid., n. 11.

77. Beard, *Letters and Journals,* V: 408–409.

CHAPTER 5

1. Freehling, *Road to Disunion,* 507–508.

2. Ibid., 510; David M. Potter, *The Impending Crisis,* 119–120; Remini, *Henry Clay,* 742–743.

3. Freehling, *Road to Disunion,* 500–501.

4. Wiecek, *Sources of Antislavery Constitutionalism,* 280–281; Finkelman, *Imperfect Union,* 237.

5. William Jay, "Letter to the Honorable William Nelson, M.C., on Mr. Clay's Compromise," *Miscellaneous Writing,* 560–564.

6. William M. Wiecek, "Latimer: Lawyers, Abolitionists, and the Problem of Unjust Laws," in Perry and Fellman, *Antislavery Reconsidered,* 219–237.

7. William Jay, *Fugitive Slave Bill* (Birmingham, UK: R. Hadson, 1851), 1–2; *National Anti-Slavery Standard,* October 17, 1850.

8. Jay, *Fugitive Slave Bill,* 3.

9. *The Liberator,* October 4, 1850, 158; William Jay, "To the Honorable Samuel A. Eliot, Representative in Congress From the City of Boston, in Reply to His Apology for Voting for the Fugitive Slave Bill," *Miscellaneous Works,* 571–572.

10. Ibid., 573–574.

11. Ibid., 574–577.

12. Ibid., 577–579.

13. Ibid., 585–587.

14. Ibid., 619.

15. Stanley W. Campbell, *The Slave Catchers: Enforcement of the Fugitive Slave Law, 1850–1860* (Chapel Hill: University of North Carolina Press, 1970), 148–154; Thomas P. Slaughter, *The Christiana Riot and Racial Violence in the Antebellum North* (New York: Oxford University Press, 1991), 20–42; *The Liberator,* May 31, 1850, and March 14, 1851; *National Anti-Slavery Standard,* February 27, 1851.

16. William Jay, *An Address to the Antislavery Christians of the United States, Signed by a Number of Clergymen and Others* (New York: American and Foreign Anti-Slavery Society, 1852), 1.

17. Jay, *Letter to the Right Reverend L. Sillman Ives,* 488–489.

18. Ibid., 6–7; *National Anti-Slavery Standard,* October 16, 1851.

19. Jay, *Letter to the Right Reverend Sillman Ives,* 6–7, 15, 20.

20. Herbert Alan Johnson, "Magyar-Mania in New York City: Louis Kossuth and American Politics," *New York Historical Society Quarterly* 47 (July, 1964), 237–249.

21. Ibid., 242–244; John W. Oliver, "Louis Kossuth's Appeal to the Middle West, 1852," *Mississippi Valley Historical Review* 14 (March, 1928), 481–495.

22. Diary of Lewis Tappan, December 5–9, 1851, TLD.

23. Abel and Klingberg, *Side-Light*, 282–285; Cheever, *True Christian Patriot*, 16.

24. Johnson, "Magyar-Mania," 245; Remini, *Henry Clay*, 777–778.

25. Lewis Tappan to Harriet Beecher Stowe, April 5, 1852, TLD; Wyatt-Brown, *Lewis Tappan*, 330–331.

26. Lewis Tappan to Leonard W. Bacon, January 13, 1853, TLD.

27. Harriet Beecher Stowe, *Uncle Tom's Cabin, or Life Among the Lowly* (New York: Penguin Books, 1981), 626.

28. McKivigan, *War Against Proslavery Religion*, 165. The Episcopal Church remained sectionally united until the advent of the Civil War, and even then would not criticize slavery.

29. William Jay, "Letter to Sillman Ives," *Miscellaneous Writings*, 489; Lewis Tappan to William Jay, September 11, 1840, JJC; *New World*, March–April 1843.

30. McKivigan, *War Against Proslavery Religion*, 117–119.

31. William Jay to Reverend R. S. Cook, Corresponding Secretary of the American Tract Society, New York, February 14, 1853, *Miscellaneous Works*, 631–659; William Jay, *Letters Respecting the American Board of Commissioners for Foreign Missions and the American Tract Society* (New York: Lewis Bates, 1853), 2.

32. *American Tract Society Annual Report* (New York: Society's House, 1827), 57–58. On these pages, based upon donations, William Jay is listed as a member for life and Arthur Tappan as a director for life.

33. Jay, *Letters Respecting*, 3.

34. Ibid., 8.

35. Ibid., 9.

36. William Jay, *An Examination of the Mosaic Laws of Servitude* (New York: M. W. Dodd, 1854), 7.

37. McKivigan, *War Against Proslavery Religion*, 30–32; Kraditor, *Means and Ends*, 43–45. Kraditor points out that the attempt to use Biblical arguments against women's involvement in antislavery activities became uncomfortable when it was realized that they sounded like defenses of slavery.

38. Jay, *Examination*, 5.

39. Ibid., 9–12.

40. Ibid., 48–49, 55–56. The law to which Jay referred states: "And he that stealeth a man, and selleth him, or if he be found in his hand, he shall surely be put to death" (Exodus 21:16). Interestingly, while the Mosaic Laws were quite liberal with the death penalty, they failed to afford equal treatment to these same servants. Exodus (21:20) notes: "And if a man smite his servant or his maid with a rod, and he die under his hand: he shall be surely punished." Quite a difference, and one that Jay did not note.

41. Harriet Beecher Stowe, *Key to Uncle Tom's Cabin: The Original Facts and Documents upon Which the Story Is Founded* (London: Clarke, Beeton,

n.d.), 223–232; George Burrell Cheever, *The Guilt of Slavery and the Crime of Slaveholding, Demonstrated from the Greek and Hebrew Scriptures* (Boston: John P. Jewett, 1860); McKivigan, *War Against Proslavery Religion*, 30, n. 43. McKivigan cites several works in this vein, including Cheever's, all of which appeared after Jay's.

42. Abel and Klingberg, *Side-Light*, 340.

43. Interestingly, Foote was one of several Deep South politicians who had viewed the Fugitive Slave Law as potentially unworkable, and so unworthy of initial support.

44. William Jay, *Some Signs of the Times Auspicous to the Cause of Peace* (Boston: American Peace Society Annual Report, 1853), 10–18.

45. Tuckerman, *William Jay*, 150–151.

46. Phillip S. Foner, *Business and Slavery: The New York Merchants and the Irrepressible Conflict* (New York: Russell and Russell, 1968), 1–7.

47. Ibid., 15–33.

48. William Jay, *Address Before the American Peace Society* (Boston: American Peace Society, 1855), 3–4.

49. *New York Daily Times*, May 10, 1855.

50. Wyatt-Brown, *Lewis Tappan*, 179.

51. William Jay to John Jay, Liverpool, July 3, 1856, JJC.

52. William Jay to John Jay, Liverpool, June 6, 1856, JJC.

53. *New York Observer*, November 21, 1856; Lewis Tappan to William Jay, January 28, 1857, TLD.

54. Tuckerman, *William Jay*, 154–155.

55. *Report of the Special Committee Appointed at the Annual Meeting of the American Tract Society, May 7, 1857, to Inquire into and Review the Proceedings of the Society's House* (New York: Society's House, 1857), 4.

56. William Jay, *A Letter to the Committee Chosen by the American Tract Society, to Inquire into the Proceedings of its Executive Committee, in Relation to Slavery*, 1857 (Daniel A.P. Murray Collection: Library of Congress), 3–5.

57. Ibid., 14–15.

58. Nehemiah Adams, *A South-Side View of Slavery, or Three Months at the South in 1854* (New York: Negro Universities Press, 1969), 64–65, 116–119, 158–161.

59. William Jay to John Jay, January, 2, 1857, JJC.

60. Diary of Lewis Tappan, April 10, 1858, TLD.

61. William Jay to Lewis Tappan, September 6, 1858, TLD; *New York Tribune*, October 19, 1858.

62. Blassingame, *Frederick Douglass Papers*, 269.

63. Ibid.

64. Ibid., 270–271.

65. Cheever, *True Christian Patriot*, 15; *New York Times*, May 9, 1859, 5.

Bibliography

PRIMARY SOURCES

Abel, Annie Heloise, and Klingberg, Frank J., eds. *A Side-Light on Anglo-American Relations 1839–1858: Furnished by the Correspondence of Lewis Tappan and Others with the British and Foreign Anti-Slavery Society.* New York: Augustus M. Kelley, 1970.

Adams, Charles Francis, ed. *Memoirs of John Quincy Adams.* Philadelphia: J. B. Lippincott, 1876.

Adams, Henry. *The Education of Henry Adams.* New York: Modern Library, 1918.

American Bible Society Annual Reports. New York: American Bible Society, 1816– .

American Tract Society Annual Reports. New York: Society's House, 1827–1857.

Bailyn, Bernard, ed. *The Debate on the Constitution.* 2 vols. New York: Gryphon, 1993.

Beard, James Franklin, ed. *The Letters and Journals of James Fenimore Cooper.* 6 vols. Cambridge: Harvard University Press, 1960.

Blassingame, John W., ed. *The Frederick Douglass Papers.* 4 vols. New Haven: Yale University Press, 1979– .

Boudinot, Elias. *A Star in the West, or A Humble Attempt to Discover the Ten Lost Tribes of Israel, Prepatory to Their Return to Their Beloved City, Jerusalem.* Trenton, N.J.: D. Fenton, S. Hutchinson, J. Dunham, and George Sherman, 1816.

Channing, William Ellery. *The Duty of the Free States.* Boston: S. N. Dickinson, 1842.

Cheever, George Barrell. *God Against Slavery, and the Freedom of the Pulpit to Rebuke it as a Sin Against God.* New York: J. H. Ladd, 1857.

———. *The Guilt of Slavery and the Crime of Slaveholding, Demonstrated from the Greek and Hebrew Scriptures.* Boston: John P. Jewett, 1860.

———.*The True Christian Patriot: A Discourse on the Virtues and Public Services of the Late William Jay.* Boston: American Peace Society, 1860.

Clay, Henry. *Life and Speeches.* 2 vols. New York, 1842.

Cobden, Richard. *Speeches of Richard Cobden on Peace, Financial Reform, and Other Subjects Delivered During 1849.* London: James Gilbert, 1970.

Congressional Globe. City of Washington: Globe Office, 1842.

Cooper, James Fenimore. *Correspondence of James Fenimore Cooper.* 2 vols. New Haven: Yale University Press, 1922.

———. *Gleanings in Europe: England.* Albany: State University of New York Press, 1982.

de Vattel, M. *The Laws of Nations, or Principles of the Laws of Nature Applied to the Conduct and Affairs of Nations and Sovereigns.* Dublin: Luke and White, 1912.

Douglass, Frederick. *My Bondage and My Freedom.* New York: Classics of Liberty Library, 1994.

Dumond, Dwight L., ed. *Letters of James Gillespie Birney, 1831–1857.* 2 vols. New York: D. Appleton–Century, 1938.

Emerson, Ralph Waldo. *Miscellanies.* Boston: Houghton Mifflin, 1884.

Gales and Seaton's Register of Debates in Congress. Washington, D.C.: Gales and Seaton, 1826.

Garrison, William Lloyd. *Thoughts on African Colonization.* New York: Arno Press and the New York Times, 1968.

Heads of Families at the First Census of the United States Taken in the Year 1790: New York. Baltimore: Genealogical Publishing, 1966.

Hobart, John Henry. *A Reply to a Letter to the Right Reverend Bishop Hobart, Occasioned by the Strictures on Bible Societies, Contained in His Address to the Convention of New York, by a Churchman of the Diocese of New York, in a Letter to that Gentleman by Corrector.* New York, 1823.

Issac, Robert, and Wilberforce, Samuel, eds. *The Correspondence of William Wilberforce.* 2 vols. Philadelphia: H. Perkins, 1841.

Jay, John. *Memorials of Peter A. Jay Compiled for His Decendents.* Holland: G. J. Thieme, 1929.

Jay, William. *Address to the American Peace Society.* Boston: American Peace Society, 1845.

———. *Address to the Non-Slaveholders of the Slave States.* New York: William Harned, 1843.

———. *The Creole Case and Mr. Webster's Despatch.* New York: Office of the New York American, 1842.

———. *An Essay on Duelling.* Savannah, Ga.: Savannah Anti-Duelling Association, 1829.

———. *An Examination of the Mosaic Laws of Servitude.* New York: W. W. Dodd, 1854.

———. *Letter to the Hon. Theodore Frelinghuysen.* New York, 1844.

———. *A Letter to the Right Reverend Bishop Hobart, Occasioned by the Strictures on Bible Societies, Contained in His Late Charge to the Convention of New York.* New York, 1823.

———. *Letters Respecting the American Board of Commissioners for Foreign Missions and the American Tract Society.* New York: Lewis J. Bates, 1853.

———. *The Life of John Jay, with Selections from His Correspondence and Miscellaneous Papers.* New York: J. J. Harper, 1833.

———. *Miscellaneous Writings on Slavery.* Freeport, N.Y.: Books for Libraries Press, 1970.

———. *A Review of the Causes and Consequences of the Mexican War.* Boston: Benjamin B. Mussey, 1849.

———. *War and Peace: The Evils of the First and a Plan for Preserving the Last.* New York: Wiley & Putnam, 1842.

Ladd, William. *An Essay on a Congress of Nations for the Adjustment of International Disputes Without Resort to Arms.* New York: Oxford University Press, 1916.

Locke, John. *Two Treatises on Government.* New York: Classics of Liberty Library, 1992.

Marsh, Luther Rawson, ed. *Writings and Speeches of Alvan Stewart on Slavery.* New York: Negro Universities Press, 1969.

Mason, John M. *Essays of Episcopacy and the Apology for Apostolic Order and Its Advocates Reviewed, Edited by Reverend Ebeneezer Mason.* New York: Robert Carter, 1844.

Merrill, Walter M., and Ruchames, Louis, eds. *The Letters of William Lloyd Garrison.* 6 vols. Cambridge: Belknap Press of Harvard University Press, 1971–1981.

Montesquieu. *The Spirit of Laws.* 2 vols. New York: Gryphon, 1994.

Morris, Richard B., ed. *John Jay: The Making of a Revolutionary: Unpublished Papers, 1745–1780.* New York: Harper & Row, 1975.

———, ed. *John Jay: The Winning of the Peace—Unpublished Letters, 1780–1784.* New York: Harper & Row, 1980.

Niven, John. *The Salmon P. Chase Papers, 1829–1872.* Kent, Ohio: Kent State University Press, 1993.

Pickard, John B., ed. *The Letters of John Greenleaf Whittier.* 3 Vols. Cambridge: Harvard University Press, 1975.

Pierce, Edward L., ed. *Memoir and Letters of Charles Sumner.* 4 vols. Boston: Roberts Brothers, 1893.

Reese, David M. *Letters to the Hon. William Jay, Being a Reply to His Inquiry into the American Colonization and American Anti-Slavery Societies.* New York: Leavitt and Lord, 1835.

———. *Observations on the Epidemic of 1819, As It Prevailed in a Part of the City of Baltimore.* Baltimore: John D. Toy, 1819.

Report of the Special Committee Appointed at the Annual Meeting of the American Tract Society, May 7, 1857, to Inquire into and Review the Proceedings of the Society's Executive Committee. New York: Society's House, 1857.

Richardson, James D., ed. *Messages and Papers of the Presidents.* 11 vols. Washington, D.C., 1897.

Ripley, C. Peter, ed. *The Black Abolitionist Papers.* 4 vols. Chapel Hill: University of North Carolina Press, 1991.

Simpson, Lewis P., ed. *The Federalist Literary Mind: Selections from the Monthly Anthology and Boston Review, 1803–1811.* Baton Rouge: Louisiana State University Press, 1962.

Stanlis, Peter J., ed. *Selected Writings and Speeches of Edmund Burke.* Chicago: Regnery Gateway, 1963.

Taylor, Robert J., ed. *The Adams Papers: The Diary of John Quincy Adams.* 12 vols. Cambridge: Belknap Press, 1981.

Seager, Robert III, ed. *The Papers of Henry Clay.* 10 vols. Lexington: University Press of Kentucky, 1984.

Sturge, Joseph. *A Visit to the United States in 1841.* New York: A. M. Kelly, 1969.

Sturge, Joseph, and Harvey, Thomas. *The West Indies in 1837.* London: Frank Cass, 1968.

Weld, Theodore Dwight. *Letters of Theodore Dwight Weld, Angelina Grimke Weld, and Sarah Grimke, 1822–1844.* 2 vols. Gloucester, Mass.: P. Smith, 1965.

Primary Sources on Microfilm

Adams Family Papers. Boston, Massachusetts Historical Society, 1954–.

Child, Lydia Maria Francis. *The Collected Correspondence of Lydia Maria Child, 1817–1880.* Millwood, N.Y.: KTO Microform, 1979.

Lewis Tappan Letters and Journals. Washington, D.C.: Library of Congress.

Manuscript Collections

American Peace Society Collection. Swarthmore, PA: Swarthmore College.

DeWitt Clinton Papers. New York: Columbia University.

John Jay Collection. New York: Columbia University.

Newspapers and Journals

African Repository and Colonizer
The Emancipator
The Liberator
National Anti-Slavery Standard
New York Daily Times
New York Evening Post for the Country
New York Times

SECONDARY SOURCES

Abbott, Carl. "The Neighborhoods of New York City, 1760–1775." *New York History* 55 (April, 1976), 35–53.

Adams, E. D. *British Interests and Activities in Texas, 1838–1846.* Gloucester, Mass.: Peter Smith, 1963.

Alexander, Arthur J. "Federal Officeholders in New York State as Slaveholders, 1789–1805." *Journal of Negro History* 28 (July, 1943), 326–350.

Alexander, DeAlva Stanwood. *A Political History of the State of New York.* 2 vols. New York: Henry Holt, 1906.

Anbinder, Tyler. *Five Points.* New York: Free Press, 2001.

Bailey, Hugh C. *Hinton Rowan Helper: Abolitionist-Racist.* Birmingham: University of Alabama, 1965.

Bancker, Evert Jr. "List of Farms on New York Island, 1780." *New York Historical Society Quarterly* 1 (April, 1917), 8–11.

Barker-Benfield, G. J. *The Horrors of the Half-Known Life.* New York: Harper & Row, 1976.

Barnes, Gilbert Hobbs. *The Anti-Slavery Impulse, 1830–1844.* New York: D. Appleton–Century, 1933.

Bemis, Samuel Flagg. *Jay's Treaty: A Study in Commerce and Diplomacy.* New Haven: Yale University Press, 1962.

Ben-Atar, Doron, and Oberg, Barbara B., eds. *Federalists Reconsidered.* Charlottesville: University of Virginia Press, 1998.

Benson, Lee. *The Concept of Jacksonian Democracy: New York as a Test Case.* Princeton: Princeton University Press, 1961.

Beveridge, Albert J. *The Life of John Marshall.* 4 vols. Boston: Houghton Mifflin, 1916.

Blackmar, Elizabeth. *Manhattan for Rent, 1785–1850.* Ithaca: Cornell University Press, 1989.

———. "Rewalking the 'Walking City': Housing and Property Relations in New York City, 1780–1840." In *Material Life in America, 1600–1860.* Robert Blair St. George, ed. Boston: Northeastern University Press, 1988.

Bolton, Robert Jr. *History of the County of Westchester: From Its First Settlement to the Present Time.* 2 vols. New York: Alexander S. Gould, 1848.

Bowers, Claude G. *Jefferson and Hamilton: The Struggle for Democracy in America.* Boston: Houghton Mifflin, 1926.

Boyd, George Adams. *Elias Boudinot, Patriot and Statesman, 1740–1821.* Princeton: Princeton University Press, 1952.

Brown, Richard H. "The Missouri Crisis, Slavery, and the Politics of Jacksonianism." *South Atlantic Quarterly* (Winter, 1966), 55–72.

Bryce, James. *The American Commonwealth.* 2 vols. London: Macmillan, 1889.

Budney, Stephen P. "Peace Profile: William Jay." *Peace Review* (Winter, 1998), 655–661.

Buhle, Mari Jo, Buhle, Paul, and Kaye, Harvey J., eds. *The American Radical.* New York: Routledge, 1994.

Burrows, Edwin G., and Wallace, Mike. *Gotham: A History of New York City to 1898.* New York: Oxford University Press, 1998.

Carson, David A. "The Louisiana Purchase Debates." *The Historian* (Spring, 1992), 477–491.

Carwardine, Richard J. *Evangelicals and Politics in Antebellum America.* New Haven: Yale University Press, 1993.

Clark, Barbara Louise. E.B., *The Story of Elias Boudinot IV, His Family, His Friends, and His Country.* Philadelphia: Dorrance, 1977.

Conforti, Joseph A. *Jonathan Edwards, Religious Tradition, and American Culture.* Chapel Hill: University of North Carolina Press, 1995.

Curti, Merle. *The American Peace Crusade, 1850–1860.* New York: Octagon Books, 1965.

Davis, David B. "The Emergence of Immediatism in British and American Antislavery Thought." *Mississippi Valley Historical Review* 49 (1962–1963), 209–230.

———. *The Slave Power Conspiracy and the Paranoid Style.* Baton Rouge: Louisiana State University Press, 1969.

Davis, Hugh. *Joshua Leavitt, Evangelical Abolitionist.* Baton Rouge: Louisiana State University Press, 1990.

Dawson, William Harbutt. *Richard Cobden and Foreign Policy: A Critical Exposition, with Special Reference to Our Day and Its Problems.* London: George Allen and Unwin, 1926.

DeBenedetti, Charles. *The Peace Reform in American History.* Bloomington: University of Indiana Press, 1980.

d'Emilio, John, and Freeman, Estelle B. *Intimate Matters: A History of Sexuality in America.* New York: Harper & Row, 1976.

Dexter, Franklin Bowditch. *Biographical Sketches of the Graduates of Yale College: With Annals of the College History.* New York: Holt, 1885–1912.

Dillon, Merton. *The Abolitionists: The Growth of a Dissenting Minority.* DeKalb: Northern Illinois University Press, 1974.

Donald, David. *Charles Sumner.* New York: Da Capo Press, 1996.

Drescher, Seymour. *Econocide: British Slavery in the Era of Abolition.* Ithaca: Cornell University Press, 1975.

Duberman, Martin, ed. *The Antislavery Vanguard: New Essays on the Abolitionists.* Princeton: Princeton University Press, 1965.

Durant, Will. *The Story of Philosophy: The Lives and Opinions of the Greater Philosophers.* New York: Simon and Schuster, 1953.

Elkins, Stanley, and McKitrick, Eric. *The Age of Federalism.* New York: Oxford University Press, 1993.

Fehrenbacher, Don E. *Slavery, Law, and Politics: The Dred Scott Case in Historical Perspective.* New York: Oxford University Press, 1981.

Filler, Louis. *The Crusade Against Slavery, 1830–1860.* New York: Harper & Brothers, 1960.

Fine, Sidney. *Laissez-Faire and the General Welfare State: A Study of Conflict in American Thought, 1865–1901.* Ann Arbor: University of Michigan Press, 1956.

Finkelman, Paul. *An Imperfect Union: Slavery, Federalism, and Comity.* Chapel Hill: University of North Carolina Press, 1981.

Fischer, David Hackett. *The Revolution of American Conservatism: The Federalist Party in the Era of Jeffersonian Democracy.* New York: Harper & Row, 1965.

Flick, Alexander C., ed. *History of the State of New York.* 11 vols. New York: Columbia University Press, 1934.

Foner, Eric. "Politics and Predjudice: The Free Soil Party and the Negro, 1848–1852." *Journal of Negro History* 50 (October 1965), 239–256.

———. "Racial Attitudes of the New York Free Soilers." *New York History* 46 (October, 1965), 311–329.

Foner, Phillip S. *Business and Slavery: The New York Merchants and the Irrepressible Conflict.* New York: Russell and Russell, 1968.

Fox, Dixon Ryan. *The Decline of Aristocracy in the Politics of New York.* New York: Columbia University Press, 1919.

Freehling, William H. *The Road to Disunion: Secessionists at Bay, 1776–1854.* New York: Oxford University Press, 1990.

Friedman, Lawrence J. *Gregarious Saints: Self and Community in American Abolitionism, 1830–1870.* New York: Cambridge University Press, 1982.

Griffin, Clifford Stephen. "The Abolitionists and the Benevolent Societies, 1831–1861." *Journal of Negro History* 44 (July, 1959), 195–216.

———. *Their Brothers Keepers: Moral Stewardship in the United States, 1800–1865.* New Brunswick, N.J.: Rutgers University Press, 1960.

Hanyan, Craig, and Hayan, Mary L. *DeWitt Clinton and the Rise of the People's Men.* Montreal: McGill-Queen's University Press, 1996.

Hardman, Keith J. *Charles Grandison Finney, 1792–1875: Revivalist and Reformer.* Syracuse: Syracuse University Press, 1987.

Harrold, Stanley. *Gamaliel Bailey and Antislavery Union.* Kent, Ohio: Kent State University Press, 1986.

Haskell, Thomas L. "Capitalism and the Origins of Humanitarian Sensibility." *American Historical Review* 90 (April–June, 1985), 339–351, 547–566.

Haynes, Sam W., and Morris, Christopher, eds. *Manifest Destiny and Empire: American Antebellum Expansion.* College Station: Texas A&M Press, 1997.

Heidler, David S., and Heidler, Jeanne T. *Old Hickory's War: Andrew Jackson and the Quest for Empire.* Mechanicsburg, Pa.: Stackpole Books, 1996.

Hickey, Donald R. *The War of 1812: A Forgotten Conflict.* Urbana: University of Illinois Press, 1989.

History of the American Peace Society and Its Work. Washington, D.C.: American Peace Society, 1908.

Hofstadter, Richard. *The Paranoid Style in American Politics and Other Essays.* Chicago: University of Chicago Press, 1979.

Howarth, Stephen. *To Shining Sea: A History of the United States Navy, 1775–1991.* New York: Random House, 1991.

Isaac, Rhys. *The Transformation of Virginia, 1740–1790*. New York: W. W. Norton, 1982.

Jervey, Edward D., and Huber, C. Harold. "The Creole Affair." *Journal of Negro History* 65 (Summer, 1980), 196–211.

Johnson, Herbert Alan. "Magyar-Mania in New York City: Louis Kossuth and American Politics." *New York Historical Society Quarterly* 47 (July, 1964), 237–249.

Jones, Devereux. "The Influence of Slavery on the Webster-Ashburton Negotiations." *Journal of Southern History* 22 (February, 1956), 48–58.

Jones, Howard. *Mutiny on the Amistad: The Saga of a Slave Revolt and Its Impact on American Abolition, Law, and Diplomacy*. New York: Oxford University Press, 1987.

Kass, Alvin. *Politics in New York State, 1800–1830*. Syracuse: Syracuse University Press, 1965.

Kerber, Linda K. "Abolitionists and Amalgamators: The New York City Race Riots of 1834." *New York History* 48 (January, 1967), 28–40.

Kraditor, Aileen S. *Means and Ends in American Abolitionism: Garrison and His Critics on Strategy and Tactics, 1834–1850*. New York: Pantheon Books, 1967.

Lacy, Creighton. *The Word Carrying Giant: The Growth of the American Bible Society, 1816–1966*. South Pasadena, Calif.: William Carey Library, 1977.

Litwack, Leon. "The Abolitionist Dilemma: The Antislavery Movement and the Northern Negro." *New England Quarterly* 34 (1961), 50–73.

Lowenthal, David. *Possessed by the Past: The Heritage Crusade and the Spoils of History*. New York: Free Press, 1996.

Mahin, Dean B. *Olive Branch and Sword: The United States and Mexico, 1845–1848*. Jefferson, N.C.: McFarland, 1997.

Maine, Henry Sumner. *International Law*. London: John Murray, 1894.

Mayer, Henry. *All On Fire: William Lloyd Garrison and the Abolition of Slavery*. New York: St. Martin's Press, 1998.

McKivigan, John R. *The War Against Proslavery Religion: Abolitionism and the Northern Churches, 1830–1865*. Ithaca: Cornell University Press, 1984.

Merck, Frederick. *Manifest Destiny and Mission in American History*. Cambridge: Harvard University Press, 1963.

Miller, Wiliam Lee. *Arguing About Slavery: John Quincy Adams and the Great Battle in the United States Congress*. New York: Vintage Books, 1998.

Mintz, Steven. *Moralists and Modernizers: America's Pre–Civil War Reformers*. Baltimore: Johns Hopkins University Press, 1995.

Monaghan, Frank. *John Jay, Defender of Liberty Against Kings and Peoples, Author of the Constitution and Governor of New York, President of the Continental Congress, Co-Author of the Federalist, Negotiator of the Peace of 1783, and the Jay Treaty of 1794, First Chief Justice of the United States*. New York: Bobbs Merrill, 1935.

Morris, Robert C. *International Arbitration and Procedure.* New Haven: Yale University Press, 1911.

Niven, John. *Martin Van Buren: The Romantic Age of American Politics.* New York: Oxford University Press, 1983.

Ogg, Frederic Austin. "Jay's Treaty and the Slavery Interests of the United States." *Annual Report of the American Historical Association* 1 (1901), 275–298.

Oliver, John W. "Louis Kossuth's Appeal to the Middle West, 1852." *Mississippi Valley Historical Review* 14 (March, 1928), 481–495.

Pease, William H., and Pease, Jane H. "Antislavery Ambivalence: Immediatism, Expediency, and Race." *American Quarterly* (Winter, 1965), 682–695.

Pellew, George. *John Jay.* Boston: Houghton Mifflin, 1899.

Perry, Lewis. *Radical Abolitionism: Anarchy and the Government of God in Antislavery Thought.* Ithaca: Cornell University Press, 1973.

Perry, Lewis, and Fellman, Michael, eds. *Antislavery Reconsidered: New Perspectives on the Abolitionists.* Baton Rouge: Louisiana State University Press, 1979.

Pletcher, David M. *The Diplomacy of Annexation: Texas, Oregon, and the Mexican War.* Columbia: University of Missouri Press, 1975.

Plunkett, Margaret L. *A History of the Liberty Party with Emphasis upon Its Activities in the Northeastern States.* Cornell University, unpublished PhD diss., 1930.

Pocock, J.G.A. "Machiavelli, Harrington, and English Political Ideologies in the Eighteenth Century." *William and Mary Quarterly* 22 (October, 1965), 549–583.

———. "Virtue and Commerce in the Eighteenth Century." *Journal of Interdisciplinary History* 3 (1972), 119–134.

Potter, David M. *The Impending Crisis, 1848–1861.* New York: Harper & Row, 1976.

Remini, Robert V. *Daniel Webster: The Man and His Time.* New York: W. W. Norton, 1997.

———. *Henry Clay, Statesman for the Union.* New York: W. W. Norton, 1991.

Richards, Leonard L. *Gentlemen of Property and Standing: Anti-Abolition Mobs in Jacksonian America.* New York: Oxford University Press, 1970.

Roeckell, Lelia M. "Bonds over Bondage: British Opposition to the Annexation of Texas." *Journal of the Early Republic* (Summer, 1999), 257–278.

Rosenberg, Carroll-Smith. *Disorderly Conduct: Visions of Gender in Victorian America.* New York: A. A. Knopf, 1985.

———. "Sex as Symbol in Victorian Purity: An Ethnohistorical Analysis of Jacksonian America." *American Journal of Sociology* 84, Supplement (1984), S212–S247.

Rotundo, E. Anthony. *American Manhood: Transformations in Masculinity from the Revolution to the Modern Era.* New York: Basic Books, 1993.

Sellers, Charles. *The Market Revolution: Jacksonian America, 1815–1846.* London: Oxford University Press, 1991.

Smith, Theodore Clarke. *The Liberty and Free Soil Parties in the Northwest.* New York: Russell and Russell, 1967.

Sorin, Gerald. *The New York Abolitionists: A Case Study in Political Radicalism.* Westport: Greenwood, 1971.

Staudenraus, P. J. *The African Colonization Movement, 1816–1865.* New York: Columbia University Press, 1961.

Stokes, I. N. Phelps. *New York: Past and Present, 1524–1939.* Printed for the 1939 World's Fair.

Taylor, Alan. *William Cooper's Town: Power and Persuasion on the Frontier of the Early American Republic.* New York: Random House, 1995.

Thomas, Hugh. *The Slave Trade: The Story of the Atlantic Slave Trade, 1440–1870.* New York: Simon and Schuster, 1997.

Tuckerman, Bayard. *William Jay and the Constitutional Movement for the Abolition of Slavery.* New York: Dodd, Mead, 1893.

Turley, David. *The Culture of English Anti-Slavery, 1780–1860.* London: Routledge, 1991.

Walters, Ronald G. *The Antislavery Appeal: American Abolitionism After 1830.* Baltimore: Johns Hopkins University Press, 1976.

Walvin, James. *Slavery and British Society, 1776–1866.* Baton Rouge: Louisiana State University Press, 1982.

Weddle, David L. *The Law as Gospel: Revival and Reform in the Theology of Charles G. Finney.* Metuchen, N.J.: Scarecrow Press, 1985.

Whitney, Edson L. *The American Peace Society: A Centennial History.* Washington, D.C.: American Peace Society, 1928.

Wiecek, William M. *The Sources of Antislavery Constitutionalism in America, 1760–1848.* Ithaca: Cornell University Press, 1977.

Wilentz, Sean. *Chants Democratic: New York City and the Rise of the Working Class, 1788–1850.* New York: Oxford University Press, 1984.

Williams, T. Harry. *Lincoln and the Radicals.* Madison, Wis., 1941.

Wosh, Peter J. *Spreading the Word: The Bible Business in Nineteenth Century America.* Ithaca: Cornell University Press, 1994.

Wyatt-Brown, Bertram. "The Abolitionist's Postal Campaign of 1835." *Journal of Negro History* 50 (October, 1965), 227–238.

———. *Lewis Tappan and the Evangelical War Against Slavery.* Cleveland, Ohio: Case Western Reserve University Press, 1969.

Ziegler, Benjamin Munn. *The International Law of John Marshall: A Study in First Principles.* Chapel Hill: University of North Carolina Press, 1939.

Index

Abolitionists, 32–35; Fugitive Slave Law, 115; political action, 62–64

Adams, John, 14, 46

Adams, John Quincy, 8, 22, 26, 28, 66, 72, 87; Texas annexation, 107

Adams, Nehemiah, 130–31

American and Foreign Anti-Slavery Society (AFASS), 57, 65, 110–11, 121

American Anti-Slavery Society Convention of 1840, 56–58

American Bible Society, 16–17

American Colonization Society, 31–32, 33

American Peace Society, 85

American Tract Society, 29, 124–25, 129–30

Amistad, 65–66, 68, 100

Andrews, Stephen Pearl, 100–101

Articles of Confederation, 8, 104

Bailey, Gamaliel, 70, 72, 74

Bedford, New York, 16, 18, 27, 28; citizens and Jay, 70–71, 116–17; Jay's funeral, 132–33; remoteness of, 14–15

Birney, James, 3, 62; 1842 election, 71–76

Boudinot, Elias, 16, 20, 21

Bowditch, Henry Ingersoll, 103–7

British and Foreign Bible Society, 16

Calhoun, John C., 13, 66, 114; Pakenham Letter, 101–2; role in annexation of Texas, 104

Channing, William E., 68, 85, 86

Chase, Salmon, 72–76

Cheever, George Burrell, 31, 124, 133–34

Child, David Lee, 71

Cincinnati, 70

Clay, Henry, 46, 102, 113–14, 115

Clinton, DeWitt, 21
Cobden, Richard, 93
"Come-outerism," 79–83
Comity, 67–70
Compromise of 1850, 113–16, 120
Congress of Nations, 87–88, 96
Cooper, James Fenimore, 12, 29, 111
Creole, 67–69, 90, 100, 117
Cuba and the slave trade, 48

District of Columbia, 22–23, 47, 51
Dodge, David Low, 86
Douglass, Frederick, 39, 120, 133
Dueling, 28–29

Eliot, Samuel A., 117–19
Ellison, Thomas, 12
The Emancipator, 32, 35, 65
Emerson, Ralph Waldo, 91–92
Episcopalian Church, 5, 17, 25, 80–82, 124
Everett, Edward, 67

Federalists, 9, 21, 28, 46, 63; Louisiana Territory, 107–8; as slave owners, 24
Finney, Charles Grandison, 31, 34
Forsyth, John, 47, 66
Frelinghuysen, Theodore, 39, 76–77, 131–32
Fugitive Slave Act (1793), 47, 116
Fugitive Slave Law, 114–15, 116, 126; northern reaction to passage, 119

Garrison, William Lloyd, 32, 36, 56–57, 106, 120; involvement in peace movement, 86–87; meets Jay, 41; political involvement, 60
Great Britain, 9; and the slave trade, 99–100
Green, Duff, 100
Grotius, Hugo, 94–95
Grundy, Felix, 46

Haiti, 24, 48–49
Hamilton, Alexander, 4, 9, 11, 19, 24; and manumission, 33
Helper, Hinton Rowan, 79
Hobart, John Henry, 17–18
Horton, Gilbert, 22–24, 25

Ives, L. Sillman, 81–83

Jackson, Andrew, 24, 35, 47, 51
Jay, Augusta McVickar, 15, 129, 132
Jay, John, 8–11, 13, 15, 16, 18, 25; biography, 27; Jay Treaty, 93; and slavery, 19–20, 33, 38; withdraws from public life, 14
Jay, John (son), 34, 57–58, 132
Jay, Maria (Banyer), 11, 13, 15, 111, 129
Jay, Peter Augustus, 12, 15, 16, 20, 25; correspondence with James Fenimore Cooper, 29; death of, 97; and John Jay's documents, 28
Jay, Sarah Van Brugh Livingston, 11, 15
Jay Treaty, 10–11, 26, 27; stipulated arbitration and the Jay Treaty, 92–94
Jay, William, *Address to the Non-Slaveholders of the South*, 77–79; attitude toward blacks, 39–40, 52, 58, 80–81, 128; defends American Antislavery Society, 35; disunion sentiment, 105–6, 110, 129; examines Mosaic Law, 125–26; and Federalist ideology, 21, 63–64; *Inquiry into the Character and Tendencies of the American Colonization and American Anti-Slavery Societies*, 35–38; involvement in the American Peace Society, 88, 109; Liberty Party, 72–76; and nullification crisis, 29–30; *A Review of the Causes and Conse-*

quences of the Mexican War, 109–
10; *A View of the Action of the
Federal Government in Behalf of
Slavery*, 44–51; *War and Peace*, 88–
96; and westward expansion 21
Jefferson, Thomas, 8, 10, 51
Johnson, Richard M., 46

Kansas-Nebraska Territory, 127
Kelley, Abby, 56–57
King, Rufus, 24
Kossuth, Louis, 121–23

Ladd, William, 86–88, 92
Leavitt, Joshua, 44, 61, 65, 74
Leopold I (King of Belgium), 96–97
The Liberator, 32, 57, 62, 70, 106
Liberia, 31, 66
Liberty Party, 3, 63, 71, 102
Livingston, Robert, 24
Locke, John, 95
London, 94, 98

Madison, James, 10
Magna Carta, 42
Maryland slave laws, 22
Mason, James, 114
Mexico, 94, 99, 108–9
Missouri Compromise, 5, 6, 20, 47
Moral stewardship, 31
Moral suasion, 3, 33, 53, 59, 69

New York (state), 7–8; politics 23–
24, 25; state constitutional
conventions 20
New York City, 8, 14, 15; arrival of
Louis Kossuth, 121–23; commerce with the south; 127–28;
race riots, 1–2, 33, 40
New York Peace Society, 86

O'Sullivan, John, 91

Phelps, Amos, 30
Polk, James K., 102, 103–4, 108–9

Quincy, Josiah, 85, 86

Randolph, Edmund, 10
Rees, David M., 38–39

Second Great Awakening, 5
Seward, William, 72
Slidell, James, 108
Smith, Gerrit, 3, 41, 44, 62–63, 70,
85
Spain, 10, 19
Sparks, Jared, 28
Stewart, Alvan, 41–44, 59–61, 62,
74
Story, Joseph, 42, 43, 69
Stowe, Harriet Beecher, 123–24,
126
Sturge, Joseph, 57, 96
Sumner, Charles, 85, 110, 128

Tappan, Arthur, 30, 34
Tappan, Lewis, 30–32, 34, 39, 40,
56, 70; American Peace Society,
85, 96, 100–103; *Amistad*, 65;
friendship with Jay, 75, 98, 102–
3, 122, 126, 132; involvement in
Liberty Party, 72–76
Taylor, Zachary, 109
Texas, 49, 98, 99–104, 108
Three-fifths Compromise, 45–46,
107, 118
Treaty of Ghent, 48, 94
Tyler, John, 98

United States Constitution, 23, 30;
legality of slavery, 41–42, 45, 60;
violation, 104–5
Upshur, Abel, 100, 101

Van Buren, Martin, 20, 46, 66, 97
Vattel, Emmerich de, 94–95

Washington, George, 10
Webster, Daniel, 67–68, 87, 114,
115, 127
Weld, Theodore Dwight, 31, 44

Westchester County, 14, 18, 22, 23;
    Bible Society, 16–17; Westchester
    Resolutions; 22
Whigs, 63, 72, 76
Whipple, George, 31
Whittier, John Greenleaf, 41, 70, 85

Wilberforce, Reverend Samuel, 80
Wilberforce, William, 19, 38
Wright, Elizur, 3, 61, 72, 74
Wright, Theodore S., 40

Yale, 12–13

About the Author

STEPHEN P. BUDNEY is Professor of History at Pikeville College. Born in Connecticut, he studied history at the University of Maine and the University of Mississippi.